LINCOLN BIBLE INSTITUTE

W9-BQX-254

JUDAISM
IN THEORY AND PRACTICE

Other Books by Beryl D. Cohon

INTRODUCTION TO JUDAISM

THE PROPHETS:
THEIR PERSONALITIES AND TEACHINGS

FROM GENERATION
TO GENERATION

JUDAISM
IN THEORY AND PRACTICE

BY

BERYL D. COHON

REVISED

NEW YORK

BLOCH PUBLISHING COMPANY

"The Jewish Book Concern"

1954

Copyright, 1948, by
BLOCH PUBLISHING COMPANY, INC.

Copyright, 1954, by
BERYL D. COHON

Printed in the United States of America

R96
C67

PREFACE

The present volume issues from the conviction that the time has come when we Jews must clarify our minds, teach our children, and declare to the world what we consider sacred and why, what we mean to be in the world. Judaism has been profoundly disturbed and cruelly tried in the seething cauldron of history from the days when it came upon the Great Divide created by the French and American Revolutions. It has been on the rolling prairies of eighteenth-nineteenth century liberalism, its eyes on the far-off, sun-lit hills of enlightenment and emancipation, and it has been deep in the valley of the shadows of Nazi concentration camps and gas chambers. Jewry has known exalted dreams and bitter frustrations. The secular story has been told and will be retold more amply as the century advances. The present volume is concerned with the searching of heart in religious Israel by those who would be faithful to the vision of the Eternal. It is therefore concerned with the mind of the synagogue, particularly with those convictions that have taken on a reasonably clear pattern in the Jew's adjustment to the modern world.

The effort made in these pages is to present objectively the several schools of thought and practice in contemporary Judaism, against historic backgrounds and present-day realities. In the chapter "Basic Questions" the author permits himself a critical appraisal of the pattern of contemporary Judaism. His concern in the critical paragraphs, as in the entire work, is the integrity of Judaism as a living, rational faith. The Supplement is motivated by the question repeatedly put to the author by Christian students and laymen, and frequently by Jews, "Why did the Jews reject Jesus?" The question merits a forthright answer. 12108

The material presented here was debated in popular discussion meetings over a number of years and in college class room. To the men and women of Temple Sinai, Brookline, and to the students of Tufts College, whose questionings were uninhibited, I extend my grateful appreciation. To my brother and teacher, Professor Samuel S. Cohon of Hebrew Union College, I am indebted for his patient reading of the manuscript and for a number of suggestions which helped guard the integrity of fact.

BERYL D. COHON

Brookline, Massachusetts
1948

PREFACE TO REVISED EDITION

Since the appearance of the present book in 1948, historic developments have clarified certain aspects of Jewish religious thought and confused others. The terms "Israel" and "Diaspora" need new definitions.

The chapters on Israel and Conservative Judaism have therefore been revised. On the basis of class room experience, the chapter on Why the Jews Rejected Jesus has been expanded. New titles have been added to the bibliography, as an aid to the student.

The author's approach to living Judaism remains constant. He has not deviated from his determined aim of avoiding the partisan and presenting a student's description of contemporary Jewish religious thought and practice on the American scene.

BERYL D. COHON

Brookline, Massachusetts
1954

CONTENTS

PREFACE   v

INTRODUCTORY

I.   SOURCES   3
The Landscape and the Creative Process – The
Bible, Divine and Human – Talmud – Halakah –
Midrash – Haggadah – Codes – Exegesis – Prayer-
book – Extra-Literary.

THE SYNAGOGUE

II.   ORIGIN AND HISTORIC CHARACTERISTICS OF THE SYN-
AGOGUE   13

III.   DIVISIONS OF THE CONTEMPORARY SYNAGOGUE   18
Eighteenth-Nineteenth Century.

IV.   ORTHODOX JUDAISM   20
Foundations of Faith: Divine Law, Written and
Oral – The Mitzwoth – The Essence of the Mitz-
woth – Dogmas – Israel and the Nations: Jewish
Separatism.

V.   REFORM JUDAISM   29
The Spirit of the Age: Central Issue – Israel Jacobson – Abraham Geiger – Specific Reforms – American Development – Guiding Principles – "Guiding
Principles" and "I Believe with Perfect Faith" – Impulses of Reform.

VI.   CONSERVATIVE JUDAISM   43
Positive-Historic Judaism – Zechariah Frankel –
The Authority of Tradition – Within the Law –
Nationalism.

VII.   BASIC UNITY   52

THEOLOGIC FOUNDATIONS: GOD, TORAH, ISRAEL

VIII. God—the Holy One of Israel   57
Words and Realities – Ethical Monotheism – Faith
and Reason – The Doctrine of God in Rabbinic
Teaching – Testimony of the Mystics – Affirmation
and Negation.

IX. Torah—His Testimony   71
Meaning of Torah – Torah in the Experience of the
Jewish People.

X. Israel—His Witness   77
Israel the Religious Community – Peoplehood,
Not Race – The Chosen People – Basis of Adjust-
ment – The People of the Covenant.

THE ETHICS OF JUDAISM

XI. Man and His Capacities   93
The Human Personality – Body and Soul – Spirit-
ual Endowment – Moral Endowments – Instinct –
Conscience – Freedom of the Will – Immortality –
Destiny.

XII. The Ethics of Judaism   101
The Nature of Jewish Ethics – Basic Principles.

XIII. Social Ideals   109
Truth – Justice – Peace – Charity – Labor – Love –
Friendship.

XIV. Personal Virtues   120

INSTITUTIONS AND RITUALS

XV. Jewish Prayer Books   127
Folk – Creation – *Siddur* – *Mahzor* – Union Prayer-
book – *Haggadah* – *Selihot* – *Kinot* – *Zemirot* –
Hymnal – Psalter.

XVI. What Is Prayer—and Why Pray?   133
Nature of Prayer – Types of Prayer – Conditions of
Prayer – The Values of Prayer.

CONTENTS

XVII.   CUSTOMS, CEREMONIES, INSTITUTIONS   146
The Jewish Home – *Mezuzah* – *Tzitzith* – *Tallith* – *Tefillin* – Dietary Laws – The Covering of the Head – In the Synagogue.

XVIII.   FROM CRADLE TO GRAVE   156
Naming of Child, Circumcision, Redemption, *Bar Mitzvah*, Confirmation, Marriage and Divorce, Marriage Laws, Rites and Customs, Burial and Mourning.

HOLY DAYS

XIX.   INTRODUCTORY   169
Nature of Jewish Holy Days.

XX.   THE SABBATH   173

XXI.   DAYS OF AWE   177
New Year – Day of Atonement.

XXII.   THE THREE FESTIVALS   188
Characteristics of the Festivals – Passover – Shabuoth – Feast of Weeks – Tabernacles.

XXIII.   FASTS AND MINOR FESTIVALS   201
Fasts – Purim – Hanukkah.

XXIV.   BASIC QUESTIONS   208
Questions Facing Orthodoxy – Question Facing Reform – Questions Facing Conservative Judaism.

SUPPLEMENT   215
Why the Jews Rejected Jesus – Three Considerations – The Answer from Theology – The Answer from History – Why Do Not Jews Accept Jesus To-Day?

ABBREVIATIONS   227

NOTES   229

SELECTED ENGLISH BIBLIOGRAPHY   240

INDEX   247

INTRODUCTORY

I. SOURCES

The Landscape and the Creative Process

Judaism is the religion of the Jewish people. It is both the deed and the creed, the life of Jewry and the faith that motivates this life and gives it distinction. It represents the aspirations and the conduct of Israel as a community and of every soul in Israel as a free, morally responsible personality. Judaism is at once theory and practice, personal and social, ancient and contemporary. Issuing from the heights of Sinai several thousand years ago, meandering 'round the world and across the centuries, contracting and broadening with the nature of the cultural topography it traverses, whipped by all the winds of intellectual unrest that sweep the earth, absorbing the joys and the sorrows, hopes and frustrations of its children, forever lured by a vision of God the Eternal and His Kingdom, Judaism expresses itself in a vast literature, a comprehensive theology, a functioning ethic, a varied sociology, historic institutions, colorful customs, ceremonies, and sacred days. These are the basic sources in the study of Judaism. We cite them to unroll the literary landscape and reveal the creative process in Judaism.

The primary source is the Bible. It is the basis of everything in Judaism. In present-day Judaism the Bible is read from two standpoints. This it is that gives rise to the divisions in contemporary Judaism. *First,* the Bible, particularly the Pentateuch, is read as a supernaturally revealed body of divine truth, every word of the Five Books of Moses is God's own dictation made to His chosen servants; *second,* as a body of sacred literature, the result of more than a thousand years of evolution, reflecting various levels of truth and beauty, subject to critical appraisal. The first of these approaches to the

3

Bible is the basis of Orthodox Judaism; the second is the groundwork of liberal, or "Reform" Judaism. But supernatural revelation or historic evolution, the Bible is the word of God, or the search for the word of God, in all branches of Judaism and as such is the chief well of inspiration. Judaism is the interpretation and application of the word of God as understood in historic Jewry.

The word of God must be integrated in the life of the individual and the community. The abstract word must become the rule of conduct. Hence we gain the second source, the *Talmud.*[1]

Judaism is intensely practical. It is not satisfied with abstract faith or disembodied sentiment. "Study is not the most important thing but deed," say the talmudic sages,[2] who extolled study to a form of worship. It seeks to guide the conduct of its followers in every sphere of life. Hence the abstract word of God must be implemented in law, covering every situation in the life of the individual and his community. Life means change. Constant adjustment of the officially immutable word of God to an ever-changing scene had to be effected. The Talmud is the result of this endeavor. It grew out of more than seven hundred years of Jewish experience in bringing life and Torah together.

The base of the Talmud is the *Mishnah,* a body of laws compiled by Judah ha-Nasi about the year 220. But this code too had to be applied to a constantly changing scene. This effort resulted in the second part of the Talmud, the *Gemara,* literally, "completion." There are two *Gemaras,* the Palestinian, completed in the academies of Palestine about the end of the fourth century, and the Babylonian, compiled by the school-men of Babylon toward the end of the fifth century. Thus there are two Talmuds, the Palestinian and the Babylonian. The Mishnah is the same in both; the Gemaras differ. The Mishnah is a consistent legal code; the Gemaras hold a great deal of non-juridic material: discussions, legends, folklore, Bible exposition, snatches of biography. The Mishnah is in Hebrew, the Gemara is in Aramaic and Hebrew.

Though organized into six "Orders" and sixty-three "Tractates," each under specific headings, the Talmud is not systematic. It includes much more than the application of the word of God to the life of the Jew.

The contents of the Talmud fall into two major categories; Halakah, the law, and Agada,[3] the non-juridic material. Halakah includes every branch of law: civil, religions, criminal, etc. Agada includes everything discussed by the schoolmen and the masses over a period of more than seven hundred years: Bible exposition, legend, superstition, medicine, astronomy, snatches of biography, homiletics, dissenting opinions of all sorts touching a large variety of subjects, even bits of humor. Halakah is the authoritative opinions of the recognized scholars; agada represents the opinions of the individual teacher or preacher.

Between the Bible and the Talmud, chronologically, is a large body of literature: the Apocrypha, the Pseudepigrapha, the writings of Philo and Josephus. Historically, this material played little part in Jewish thought. With the rise of the historic approach in the study of Judaism, in the nineteenth century, this material has been reclaimed as an important branch of Jewish literature.

The word of God has to be preached to the masses as well as implemented in law. This gives us the Midrash, or Haggadah.[4]

The Torah should not be taught at all unless it is taught attractively, say the rabbinic masters. The love and understanding of the Torah—that is, the authoritative written and oral traditions of Jewry—had to be conveyed to the hearts and minds of the Jewish people. Hence the resort to parables, metaphors, legends, similes, homilies. These utterances may be based on a Bible verse, on a Bible incident, on some experience in the life of a biblical or rabbinic character, on a detail of Jewish tradition, or it may be an independent observation. It is material in the hands of popular preachers. There was, as there still is, good-natured rivalry between stern halakah and fanciful haggadah. One spoke to the trained jurist in formal terms; the other spoke to the heart of the average person. Several instances from rabbinic lore may be cited by way of example, and by way of tasting the flavor of haggadah.[5]

> Two masters held discourses in one building. Rabbi Hiya bar Abba expounded the law; Rabbi Abbahu expounded the haggadah. The people deserted Rabbi Hiya bar Abba and crowded around Rabbi Abbahu. Hiya bar Abba was despondent. His colleague comforted him. He said to him, 'I will tell you a parable. To what may this situation be compared? To two men who enter a city. One sells precious stones—large, costly jewels; the other, bits of imitation and tinsel. Around whom do the crowds gather? Of course, around him who sells the tinsel.'

Preached Rabbi Samuel, the son of Rabbi Yose:

> "The rich man is wise in his own eyes; but the poor that hath understanding searcheth him through." (Prov. 28:11)

The rich man is wise in his own eyes. That is the scholar of the *Gemara* (or *Halakah*). *But the poor that hath understanding searcheth him through.* That is the man of the *Haggadah.*

> Rabbi Ami and Rabbi Asi sat at the feet of Rabbi Isaac Nafha. One said, 'Expound the law;' the other said, 'Narrate a parable.' He began expounding the law but was stopped by the one who wanted to hear a parable (or *midrash*). He began narrating a midrash, but was stopped by the one who wanted an exposition of the law. Rabbi Isaac Nafha said to them, 'To what may this be compared? To a man who has two wives, one young, one old. The young wife plucks the gray hair out of his head; the other plucks out the black hair. Between the two he is left bald!'

The Royal Highway is *halakah*. It is the authoritative word. Midrash is the humble path. It is not authoritative; it represents only the word of the preacher. But the masses loved these winding paths. "Let not the parable be a trivial matter in your sight," say the masters of the haggadah, "for it is by means of a parable that one can understand the word of

God." "If thou wishest to know Him at whose word the world
came into being, then learn the Haggadah, for through it thou
shalt know the Holy One, praised be He, and follow His
ways." It is like unto a king who lost a precious stone or pearl.
Does he not recover it by means of a two-cent candle? Even
so it is with a parable. "The delights of the sons of man," reads
a verse in the Bible. The *delights* refers to the parables, say
the popular preachers; for they are the choice morsels of the
Torah.

But no conflict must be supposed as existing between the
two. The rabbinic masters expressed it in their own way. "My
doctrine shall drop as the rain." Just as the same rain falls on
all the trees of the forest, giving each its fruit according to
its own nature—grapes to the vine, olives to the olive tree, figs
to the fig tree—so are the words of the Torah one. Some are
Bible and others are Mishnah, some are *halakah* and some
haggadah.

Rabbinic law grew to enormous proportions as century followed century. The major concern of the rabbis to make the
Law coextensive with life compelled them to engage in a perpetual effort to stretch the law to cover every new situation
in the unceasing river of life. Thus commentary followed
commentary. In the course of time these commentaries and
decisions and amendments became bewildering and sys-
tematization and codification became necessary. Many codes
were thus produced. The most popular of these is the *Shulhan
Aruk,* a digest of Jewish law meant for ready use, made by
Joseph Caro (1488–1575). This is still the most popular code
in Orthodox Judaism.[6]

The word of God has to be expounded to the student. Differences of interpretation existed at all times. These, before
they might be accepted, or rejected, or harmonized, had to be
established. New schools of thought arose in the history of
Judaism. They appealed, ultimately, to biblical authority. The
Bible was subjected to close study, and this resulted in a body
of literature known as Bible *exegesis.* Some of these expositors
sought the straightforward, *rational* meaning of the text;

others resorted to the *allegoric,* or the *midrashic,* or the *kabbalistic* (or mystic) interpretation to establish their views. The Talmud and the post-talmudic literature of the synagogue, like the Bible, inspired much exegesis. These constitute an important source for a historic understanding of Judaism.[7]

The word of God had to be squared with reason, for in all ages the heart would not adore what the mind disowned. Hence issued much *philosophic* writing. To this branch of Jewish literature belong the works of such men as Philo, Saadia, Halevi, Maimonides, Gersonides, Albo, Crescas, Mendelssohn and many others.[8] Much of this literature is polemic, arising from conflicting views and values within Jewry; much of it was stimulated by the surrounding cultures: Roman, Greek, Mohammedan, Christian. Disputes arose among scholars, or in communities that did not enjoy adequate religious leadership. More prominent scholars were consulted by letter. Their replies give us the *Responsa.* This is a rich source for the understanding of Judaism as it sought to adjust itself to changing conditions.[9]

The word of God, above all, inspired prayer. From the humblest to the greatest, from the most ignorant to the most learned, came prayers of praise and thanksgiving, petition and adoration. Over King David's couch, say the rabbinic masters, hung a harp; as the breezes played upon it, making music, the monarch-poet composed psalms. The harp was ever alive in Jewry; its strings were swept by all the fears and hopes, passions and ideals known to the human heart. Hence we have in Judaism a great tradition of prayer, embodied in the *siddur,* the prayer book of the synagogue for the Sabbath and daily devotions, and the *machzor,* the prayer book for the Holy Days and Festivals. The liturgy of Judaism, like the Bible, like the Talmud, represents a long evolution, issuing from the life and faith of the Jewish people.[10]

The word of God thrilled the poet and musician and woke the tender sentiments of the pious and the sensitive. This inspired much poetry and song. The *piyyutim*—sacred poetry —became an integral part of the liturgy of the synagogue.

To this category belong such names as Kalir and Gabirol.

Two extra-literary sources for the study of Judaism must be cited. They are not easily defined but they have played an enormous part in the development of Judaism.

One is the personalities of the masters of Judaism—the patriarchs, law-givers, prophets, poets, scribes, rabbis, scholars—from the earliest days to the present. While this is true of most religions it is especially true of Judaism for the reason that Judaism is a folk religion. The individual conscience, particularly of the geniuses of religion, has been the source of the finest and noblest in Judaism. Hence we should study the lives of those men who have drawn the fire of God and brought it down to the life of their day. However, it must be noted that no one personality dominates Judaism. The synagogue has no canon of saints. No holiday commemorates the life or death of any one leader. This is a logical development in view of the historic effort of the Jewish masters to concentrate on principle rather than on person. It has been observed that the fact that Moses' grave is unknown is a positive good, for, were it known, it would have been turned into a seat of idolatry.

The second non-literary source has been the community. "Judaism derives its uniqueness from its union with the Jewish people. . . . Religion, though manifested in the individual conscience, is not a purely individual phenomenon. In its complete form religion is a social force. . . . Creeds, codes of conduct and cults evolve out of the experience of the group. They grow into full power only when they are incorporated into the life of the community." [11] Local customs and practices, in the course of time, became established as proper and authoritative. But not only from the Jewish community did Judaism draw inspiration; it has derived much nourishment from the surrounding non-Jewish culture. Assyria influenced much of prophetic utterance. The Babylonian and the Persian, the Greek and the Roman, the Christian and the Mohammedan have left their imprint on the faith of the Synagogue.*

* See Chapter III and the function of *minhag* defined in Chapter IV.

THE SYNAGOGUE

II. ORIGIN AND HISTORIC CHARACTERISTICS OF THE SYNAGOGUE

The central institution in Judaism is the synagogue. Since the collapse of the Judaean state and the destruction of the national shrine in the year 70, the synagogue has been "the heart of Jewry." It has functioned, through all these many ages, in a three-fold capacity: it has been the school, the chapel, and the social center of the Jewish people.

Its origin and early history are hidden in obscurity. The conjecture among scholars is that it originated in the informal meetings of the Hebrew exiles in Babylon. In the year 586 B.C.E., Nebuchadnezzar conquered Judah, reduced the Temple to a heap of ashes and carried a large number of the population to Babylon as war captives. There they were granted a fair measure of freedom to organize their own communal and religious life.

Uprooted from the sacred soil, where alone they might practice their religion in keeping with established standards, their central shrine in ruins, the priests could not function at the altar, the Levites could not chant the hymns and the people could not worship. Quite naturally, the homesick exiles would meet, especially on the holy days, for mutual consolation and to talk old times. Thus they kept alive the memories of Zion and the traditions of the Temple. As the years advanced, these meetings became a habit and finally a fixed institution. Thus the synagogue was born in Babylon. It is the oldest functioning institution in the Western World; some two thousand five hundred years old.[1] Moreover, a new mode of worship had to be found. The heavy-laden heart must find expression. The unhappy exiles would supplicate their God, beseeching His mercy for their restoration to their native land and holy places. They recalled their past and

13

prayed fervently for the return of God's presence to Zion. Fearful of losing their sacred wisdom and the loyalty of their children, who were under the spell of the Babylonian gods and goddesses, they committed much of their lore to writing. Thus the liturgy and the curriculum of the synagogue were born. By the time of the beginning of the Christian era, the synagogue was already an institution of long standing, possessed of a definite ritual and curriculum, meeting in special buildings devoted to the housing of its activities. When the Temple fell in the year 70, the synagogue took its place as the central shrine of the Jewish people.

Ever since those ancient days the synagogue has carried on as the school, the house of worship, and the communal center of the Jewish people. Its program of study and worship underwent much change in the course of the ages, but these changes have not swerved its moorings. It has disciplined the mind, refined the emotions, whetted the conscience, cultivated the loyalties, coordinated the aspirations of a people and so oriented it in the world that all the howling furies of more than two thousand terrible years could not break its will to live "and declare the glory of the Lord." The synagogue has even been the Jew's city of refuge from the cruelties of the world. "Its (Judaism's) persistent character, and, it is not too much to say, the very preservation of its existence through all the vicissitudes of its fortunes, it owes more than anything else to the synagogue," writes George Foot Moore. "Nor is it for Judaism alone that it had this importance. It determined the type of Christian worship, which in the Greek and Roman world of the day might otherwise easily have taken the form of a mere mystery; and, in part directly, in part through the church, it furnished the model for Mohammed." [2]

Several characteristics mark the synagogue from its very beginning. Four especially must be noted.

First, the synagogue is a folk creation. It is not a foreign culture imposed upon a people by a victorious civilization or a missionarizing religion; beneath it are not the vanquished cultures of conquered peoples. At this point the synagogue stands in contrast to the church. As a missionarizing religion, Christianity had to blot out the existing cults before it could establish itself. St. Augustine's confessions were written, at least in part, on a palimpsest of Cicero's *De Republica*. That is symbolic. Beneath the new Christian dispensation are the suppressed native beliefs and practices of many peoples. In times of major social crises the old gods emerge from their graves and shake the church to its very foundations.

No such resurgence is possible in the synagogue; beneath it are no vanquished cultures of foreign peoples. It is the creation of the Jewish masses. It came into being in direct response to the needs of the Jewish people. This folk character it has retained throughout the ages. Human needs, therefore, human passions, human perplexities, the deep, elemental yearnings of the human breast, tempered or accentuated by the storm and stress of the age, have shaped its character.

Second, the synagogue has ever been a democratic institution. Being the continuous creation of the Jewish masses it has ever remained their own. Jewish mass uprisings against the synagogue are unknown in Jewish history. Originating in the informal, obscure meetings of the people, it gradually developed into an institution in contrast to the Temple. The Temple was formal, in the hands of an hereditary aristocracy and wealthy Sadducees. Hereditary privilege, ecclesiastical hierarchies, an official priesthood, an elaborate sacrificial cultus, on which the Temple rested, are entirely alien to the synagogue. Worship has ever been a matter of prayer in the mood and language of the masses. No priest is needed, nor desired. Any one may serve as rabbi who qualifies for the post by virtue of superior learning and character.

The categories of the lay and the ecclesiastic are foreign to Judaism. The rabbi is a learned layman; his ordination does not endow him with special grace. Ten Jews meeting for the purpose of public prayer form a congregation, and wherever these ten decide to hold their devotions there a synagogue comes into being, and there rests the spirit of God, the rabbinic sages tell us.

Third, the synagogue has ever been an independent institution. Even in its embryonic stages, while still in the shadows of the second Temple, it existed of its own right. It needed no charter from any hierarchial authority and owed explanations to no one but the God of Israel as it understood Him. Whatever associations of synagogues there have been, or are today, are of a voluntary character.

Fourth, the synagogue has ever defined worship in terms of learning and philanthropy as much as in prayer and meditation. The line between what is generally known as the spiritual and the secular is hazy. Being the repository of a revealed wisdom meant for all the people, and governing every aspect of the personal and social life, the synagogue made the study of the Law a religious duty on a par, if not superior, to prayer. The rabbi has been the teacher. His is not a special grace from God but information acquired by persistent study. His duty, therefore, is not to absolve from sin but to redeem from ignorance. Philanthropy is a form of worship because it is a direct application of the precepts of the synagogue. Thus religious study and philanthropy are modes of worship.

A many-sided culture developed in the synagogue in the course of the ages. Serving as a people's school, it developed a tremendous literature. Until yesterday Jewish literature was written in the shadows of the house of worship. It is a search for those things by which a people might live and realize its destiny. The literature written within the synagogue walls is essentially scripture. At its core is the search for the Word of God, as we have seen in the previous chapter.

In the course of its history the synagogue has heard mighty debates, experienced much conflict, and harbored many dissenting views; but all of them, with the exception of Karaism, remained organic parts of Judaism. In a creedal religion there would have followed a large number of independent denominations; but the synagogue, being a folk creation, responsive to the life of the masses, had to play the part of a suffering mother, admit these troublesome children, care for them and win them over, rather than disown them. The heretics of one age may be the orthodox of the next. The result is that in Judaism we have divisions, rather than creedal denominations, determined by sociologic and cultural factors fully as much as by theologic principles.[3]

III. DIVISIONS OF THE CONTEMPORARY SYNA-GOGUE

Present-day Judaism, particularly on the American scene, falls into three major categories: *Orthodox, Reform,* and *Conservative.* These three issue from the same trunk and the same roots. They are three expressions of the same faith. A pronouncement by rabbinic masters characterizing the opposing schools of Judaism in the early talmudic period applies to the present-day divisions: all are equally the words of the living God.

Judaism acquired its present three-fold alignment from its reaction to the enlightenment and the liberalistic movements that came in the wake of the French Revolution. The Renaissance was late in penetrating the ghetto walls, and when it finally did break through, carried by the fury of the age, it wrought a major crisis in the spiritual life of the Jewish people. A people excluded from European culture for centuries found itself catapulted into the blaze of a revolutionary day. All spiritual moorings were loosed; ancient landmarks were swept away. The synagogue was compelled to make a rapid and radical adjustment. The attack came from without and within Jewry; from without, European culture, science, literature, philosophy, art, education came with violent impact and dazzled the restless Jewish minds, diverting a generation from the synagogue; from within came an unsettling and a prying loose of the theologic foundations and the consequent disturbance in the practices of the synagogue and the home. The critical—or historic—approach to Jewish tradition—the *Wissenschaft* school—initiated by faithful scholars, disrupted the very foundations of the established Judaism, and produced new patterns of thought and conduct.

In the main, three paths opened before Jewry in the latter

part of the eighteenth century. One was the extreme right, the ancient path of complete separation, rejection of the enlightenment and distrust, if not complete repudiation, of the promises of civil emancipation; for the new order, it was feared, meant jeopardizing the established beliefs and *mores* of the synagogue. Emancipation was the kiss of death. This sternly pious choice, softened and modified despite itself, is represented today by Orthodox Judaism. Another choice to the extreme left, was complete assimilation, Israel losing his identity and ceasing to be. The synagogue, to many intoxicated with the new wine of the enlightenment and tantalized by political emancipation, had lost its reason for being. It belonged to the dark days that were giving way to the new. Many sought salvation in assimilation or in the baptismal fount. An epidemic of baptism swept German Jewry. Those that took this course disappeared from Jewish life. Between the two extremes was a large group that sought to meet the new world, accept what was good in European enlightenment, accept emancipation as a coveted prize, rethink their Judaism, reject what was no longer tenable, and interpret the valid in more esthetic terms. This course evolved into the Reform and the Conservative synagogues of our time.

IV. ORTHODOX JUDAISM

Foundations of Faith: Divine Law, Written and Oral

The Torah is a divine document miraculously transmitted by God to Moses on Mount Sinai who, in turn, transmitted it to the subsequent authoritative sages. Upon this premise Orthodox Judaism is founded.[1] The *Torah* is a revelation from God, *torah min hashamayim*. The talmudic masters express their minds in this matter in words that have become classic in the lore of the synagogue: "Moses received the Torah at Sinai and transmitted it to Joshua, Joshua to the elders, the elders to the prophets, and the prophets to the men of the Great Synagogue." [2] Thus there is a continuous succession of authoritative interpreters of the Torah. Their interpretations constitute the Oral Law, which, in the course of the ages, became established in the Talmud and post-talmudic synagogue lore.

The Written Law is that which today constitutes the Scriptures, particularly the Pentateuch; the Oral Law is the traditional interpretation of the Scriptures. Both the Written and the Oral Law are a direct revelation from God. By means of the Oral the Written is implemented in life. Both are binding. "God gave the Israelites two Laws, the Written Law and the Oral Law," state the rabbinic masters.[3]

Said R. Levi b. Hama, in the name of Simeon b. Lakish:

> What is meant by the passage, 'And I will give thee the tables of stone, with the Law and the commandments, which I have written, that thou mayest teach them?' (Exod. 24:12) *The tables of stone* refers to the Ten Commandments; *the Law* refers to the Bible; *the commandments* refers to the Mishnah; *which I have written* refers

20

to the prophets and the Hagiographa; *to teach them*
refers to the Gemara. Hence we infer that all were given to
Moses on Mount Sinai.[4]

Maimonides agrees with this rabbinic interpretation. "All
the precepts which Moses received on Sinai were given together with their interpretation," he states. "Although the
Oral Law was not committed to writing, Moses taught the
whole of it, in his court, to the seventy elders. . . . To Joshua,
his disciple, Moses, our teacher, delivered the Oral Law and
charged him concerning it." [5]

A day came when direct revelation ceased in Israel. Thenceforth God's word was to be found in the pages of the sacred
text and its authoritative interpretations—the primary authority of the synagogue.

Two corollaries issue from this central proposition. *First,*
the divine wisdom vouchsafed to Israel at Mount Sinai is *complete*. Nothing might be added and nothing substracted. "Ye
shall not add to the word which I command you, neither shall
ye diminish from it, that ye may keep the commandments of
the Lord thy God which I command you." [6] In actual practice
the Torah was not nearly so rigid as it might appear. The Oral
Law and its practical character gave it release and growth.
Consciously or unconsciously the school-men stretched the
law to conform to new situations by exercising the method of
interpretation and reinterpretation. The prophetic impulse
stretched new horizons and gave it progressive expansion. In
days of crisis revolutionary reforms were instituted; these un-
orthodox innovations became established usage and thus,
eventually, part of the Law itself.[7] Moreover, the rabbinic
authorities developed a healthy respect for popular usage as
it developed in the life of the community. "The custom (*minhag*) of our fathers is law." "No custom should be abolished or
mocked at, for it is not for nothing that the customs were
established in days gone by." [8] From the standpoint of official
Orthodoxy, however, all the efforts to make the Law cover
every new circumstance in the constantly shifting stream of
life was only application, not modification, of the original

revelation. The word of God revealed from the smouldering heights of Sinai is complete. No second Moses would ever arise to fetch a new edition of the Law from heaven. Hence Maimonides confesses his faith, "I believe with perfect faith that this Law will not be changed, and that there will never be any other Law from the Creator, blessed be His name." [9]

Second, the Law being divine and complete is true, final, and binding. More than that, it is eternally binding. There is no superior authority to the Law, for the Law—the Torah—is the eternal word of the Eternal God. The principle of gradual change wrought by natural laws, the entire concept of evolution in religious thought and practice, is alien to Orthodox Judaism. There is no room for gradual change in a system of thought that rests on supernatural revelation at one grand moment of revelation. "Orthodox Judaism holds to one principle doctrine, the doctrine of revelation, which means that the Torah contains absolute truth, that it is not the work of Moses but the word of God." "Judaism stands or falls with its belief in the historic actuality of the Revelation on Sinai." [10]

The same applies to talmudic law. "No man should say, 'I will not observe the precepts of the elders since they are not contained in Scripture,' for God hath said, 'Nay, my son, but whatever they decree thee, do thou perform.'" [11] The individual conscience must find its peace and its freedom within, not without, the Law. No one is beyond the Law. "According to the word which they (the authoritative spokesmen) shall teach thee, and according to the judgement which they shall tell thee, thou shalt do; thou shalt not turn aside from the sentence which they shall declare unto thee, to the right hand or to the left." [12] Here—the divine word as interpreted by the authoritative teachers—is the central seat of authority for Orthodox Judaism.

A divine revelation miraculously made to the chosen teachers—supernatural, complete, binding, final—in Written and Oral form, is the foundation of Orthodox Judaism. Upon this foundation the entire system of Orthodoxy rests. Tampering with it endangers the whole edifice.

The Mitzwot

Resting on the foundations of a revealed legislation, Orthodox Judaism is built in terms of *mitzwot*. The Orthodox Jew walks the sure road of *halakah*—law.[13]

Not merely a system of beliefs but a pattern of *mitzwot*—sacred commandments, precepts, practical religious duties, the performance of ethical and ceremonial law—are the girders of the Orthodox synagogue. Judaism is a way of life, and this way of life is clearly prescribed. Orthodoxy looks askance at vague sentiment in religious matters. It decrees and commands in terms of authoritative forms. It expresses the abstract faith in terms of specific duties. It speaks with an authoritative voice: "Thou shalt!" and "Thou shalt not!" The recurrent formula in rabbinic law is, "Blessed be Thou, Lord our God, King of the universe, who has commanded us to. . . ." observe this or that precept, fulfill this or that commandment; never does it say, "Blessed be Thou, Lord our God, King of the universe, who hast commanded us to believe" this or that dogma. The synagogue, therefore, developed an elaborate system of commandments—six hundred thirteen *mitzwot;* three hundred positive, two hundred forty-eight negative, govern the every day life of the pious Jew." *

But all these commandments never fettered the spirit nor cramped the life of the Jew. The reverse is true. These commandments have been liberating bonds; they have been the pearls of a necklace, the gift of the Holy One of Israel to His beloved. In counting, recounting, multiplying them—and smiling in his beard at the bit of romanticism involved in this system—the pious Jew communed with his Father in Heaven. "He who loves the commandments is never satiated with them," say the rabbinic teachers. "When the Law came into the world, freedom came into the world," they assert.[14] They spoke of "the joy of the commandments," and considered

---

* Mystics and casuists, in their love of the *mitzwot*, interpreted these numbers to equal the supposed number of bones in the human body and the number of days in the year—that is, with every bone in his body, every day of the year, the pious Jew observes the Law.

themselves especially blessed of God in that He had enriched
them with His gift of Law. "Beloved are Israel," Rabbi Akiba
declares, "for unto them was given a precious instrument." [15]
With the Psalmist the observant Jew has prayed for centuries:

> "Blessed art Thou, O Lord;
> Teach me Thy statutes.
>
> .   .   .   .
>
> I have rejoiced in the way of Thy testimonies,
> As much as in all riches,
> I will meditate in Thy precepts,
> And have respect unto Thy ways.
> I will delight myself in Thy statutes;
> I will not forget Thy word." [16]

These *mitzwot* covered every aspect of life. No practice,
however personal, was outside the Law. The mystic and the
philosophic avenues run through Judaism; many saintly souls
have traversed them and follow them today. A great deal of
the beauty and depths of Judaism has come from these non-
legal aspects of the faith of Israel. But the Highway and the
Way is Law. The masters of rabbinic Judaism are not the philosophers, not the poets, but the legislators; the philosophers
and poets revered in Jewish tradition lived and taught within
the Law. Their gifts were used to vitalize the Law. The logic
of the philosophers must not contradict the Law; but "must be
rectified by the teaching of the Torah," [17] for the Torah is the
supreme source of truth. The authoritative literature is not
the poetic, not the philosophic, but the juristic—the Talmud
and the later codes.

While the commandments were many and minute, basically
they were not more than eleven, or six, or three, or only one
—the love of God! The rabbinic sages state this in a passage
classic in Judaism:

> Rabbi Simlai taught, saying, 'Moses gave to the Israelites
> six hundred thirteen commandments to be obeyed.' Then
> came David and embraced them all in eleven, for it is said
> (Ps. 15): 'Lord, who shall abide in Thy tabernacle? Who
> shall dwell in Thy holy hill? He that walketh uprightly,

and worketh righteousness, and speaketh the truth in his
heart. He that backbiteth not with his tongue, nor doeth
evil to his neighbor, nor taketh up a reproach against his
neighbor. In whose eyes a vile person is condemned; but
he honoreth them that fear the Lord. He that sweareth to
his own hurt and changeth not. He that putteth not out
his money to usury, nor taketh reward against the inno-
cent. He that doeth these things shall never be moved.'
Then came Isaiah and reduced them to six, for it is said
(Is. 33:15–16): 'He that walketh righteously and speaketh
uprightly; he that despiseth the gain of oppressions, that
shaketh his hands from holding of bribes, that stoppeth
his ears from hearing of blood, and shutteth his eyes
from seeing evil; he shall dwell on high; his place of de-
fense shall be the munitions of rocks; bread shall be given
him; his waters shall be sure.' Then came Micah and reduced them to three (Micah 6:8): 'He hath showed thee,
O man, what is good, what doth the Lord require of thee,
but to do justly, and to love mercy, and to walk humbly
with thy God.' At last came Habakkuk who included them
all in one word (Hab. 2:4): *Faith*—The righteous shall
live by his Faith.[18]

DOGMAS IN JUDAISM

What is the creed of the synagogue?

Scholars have debated the question. Being essentially a religion of laws, traditions, customs, the masses were concerned
with abstract theology but little. It was only the advanced
intellectuals of a speculative turn of mind who ventured into
this aspect of Judaism, and these differed widely in their formulations of the basic principles implied in the life and aspiration of the synagogue.[19]

Dogmas are basic in the life of the synagogue. Some of them
have been stated explicitly; some are implicit in the life of the
institution and control its behavior. This is particularly true
of the Orthodox synagogue. It repeats a specific, and what has
come to be, an official creed, the Thirteen Principles formulated by Maimonides in the twelfth century.

Before turning to this formulation of the creed, we must
grasp the fact that in the thinking of the synagogue there are

specific dogmas controlling its life and thought. The Jew repeats them in his prayers; countless martyrs have sanctified them with their lives. Maimonides, in the Introduction to his code of Jewish Law, states, "The basic principle of all basic principles and the pillar of all sciences is to realize that there is a First Being who brought every existing thing into being." [20] Joseph Caro similarly prefaces his code, the *Shulhan Aruk*, with a plea for belief in God and glad obedience of His will.

But while dogmas are basic to Judaism, they do not have other-worldly redeeming power in themselves. Belief alone does not bring salvation. Dogmas are essentially basic premises and must lead to action. They must be obeyed in the living world. The synagogue requires not beliefs alone but conduct; but conduct is meaningless without a clear understanding of standards and values. If a choice must be made between creed and deed, the talmudic masters would prefer deed, for deed implies creed. "We will do and we will hearken." Deed comes first. Obeying the word of God leads ultimately to belief in it.

In the prayer book of the Orthodox synagogue is embodied the formulation of the creed made by Maimonides. "The Thirteen Principles," long the subject of debate, rejected as incomplete in various quarters of Jewry, have, in the course of time, become part of the very liturgy and hymnology of the synagogue. Today they may be considered as the authoritative formulation of the creed of the Orthodox synagogue.[21]

1. Belief in the existence of a Creator.
2. . . . in His unity.
3. . . . in His spirituality.
4. . . . in His eternity.
5. . . . that all worship and adoration belong to Him alone.
6. . . . in Prophecy.
7. . . . that Moses was the greatest of all the prophets.
8. . . . in the revelation of the Torah to Moses on Mount Sinai.

9. . . . in the immutability of the Torah.
10. . . . that God knows the acts of men.
11. . . . in reward and punishments.
12. . . . in the coming of the Messiah.
13. . . . in the resurrection of the dead.

ISRAEL AND THE NATIONS: JEWISH SEPARATISM

Belief in a divinely revealed Torah with its emphasis upon conduct, according to specific rules given by the authoritative teachers, made for *separatism* as a principle in itself. Seeking to live "and declare the glory of the Lord" as a distinctive, Jewish group in a non-Jewish world, Orthodox Judaism found itself in need of protective safeguards against the disintegrating forces issuing from the gentile environment. The rabbinic teachers built "a fence around the Torah," and a fence around the people of the Torah.

Israel is a priest-people, separated from the rest of the peoples as the priest is separated from the laity. Israel is to the rest of mankind what the Sabbath is to the rest of the week —a sanctified people, dedicated to His word. In every avenue of life the Jew must integrate himself as a responsible member of society; in civil matters he must obey the civil laws of the land, whatever the laws be: *Dina d'malchuta dina*—"the law of the land is the law!" [22] In religious matters, however, he must obey God, not Caesar. In religious matters the Jew remains distinctive and apart. *Hukat-Hagoim*—the practice, or custom, of the gentiles—became a principle of negation in rabbinic thinking. Originally this principle was aimed against the idolatrous practices of the heathen; popularly, however, it remained as a principle of separation.[23]

Jewish separatism, as fostered in Orthodoxy, issues from the will to live as a religious Jewish community in an over-whelmingly non-Jewish and seductive environment. The hostility of the non-Jewish world, harassing the Jew in every age, demanding his demise, intensified the desire for separatism. The whole object of the ceremonial law thus came to be interpreted as a means of separating and sanctifying Israel. From the days of Ezra the nerve center of Jewish piety has been religious isolation from the heathen world.

"Zangwill once said," writes one distinguished scholar,

'History, which is largely a record of the melting of minorities in the majorities, records no instance of the survival of a group not segregated in space or not protected by a burning faith as by a frontier of fire.' This lesson of history had evidently been discerned by Ezra. He understood that the Jews could not be utterly segregated in space. Not only were there branches of the national tree in Egypt, Babylon, and Persia to be taken into consideration; but contact between the Jews in Judea and their neighbours could not be avoided. If, then, the Jewish nation was to be preserved, it must be ringed round 'by a burning faith as by a frontier of fire'—a most apposite metaphor, since the Bible itself speaks of a 'fiery law.' The Jew must have a religion which would not only continually distinguish him from the heathen, but would likewise be a constant reminder to him that he was a member of the Jewish race and faith. The Jew was to be demarcated from his neighbours not merely by a creed, but by a mode of living. His manner of worship would be different; his home would be different; even in the common acts of daily life there would be distinguishing features which would constantly recall his Jewishness. His life, in every detail, was to be controlled by Torah—by the written enactments of the Mosaic code and their development in the corporate life of the people, as the altered conditions demanded change.[24]

Behind these ramparts of faith the Orthodox Jew lives and worships, and "sanctifies His Name."

V. REFORM JUDAISM

THE SPIRIT OF THE AGE: CENTRAL ISSUE

Reform Judaism issues from the high resolve made by faithful sons of the synagogue when, in the crisis that confronted religious Israel in the latter part of the eighteenth and the beginning of the nineteenth centuries, they dedicated themselves to the rethinking and reformulating the religion of their fathers in the hope of making it the faith of their children. They sought to build more stately mansions for the soul; they would rear anew and rededicate the altar of the Lord which had collapsed to the impact of the forces—creative and destructive—released by the tantalizing promises of the cultural enlightenment and civic emancipation of Jewry. A wave of apostacy was sweeping German Jewry. Thousands of Jews— particularly the young, the gifted, the daring—found in Judaism a cruel burden hampering their way in the world. Emancipation and assimilation to them meant baptism. Reform came to build dykes against the waves of assimilation.

The Reform movement did not seek to parallel in Judaism what the Protestant Reformation accomplished in Christianity; it was not an attempt to return to a pristine and pure deposit of the faith made to the fathers, despite the initial passion of the early Reform zealots. It was not a return to an original Mosaism, though a number of extremists did speak of a return to "the Mosaic persuasion." Rather, it sought to lift the anchors and allow the ship of faith to brave the new world, lured by the same morning star that had guided the noblest spirits in Israel all through the ages. It would consciously encourage and guide the historic process in Judaism. It was not a repudiation of rabbinic Judaism, as some said, but a continuation of it. The founders of Reform Judaism would do in their

29

day what the talmudic masters did in theirs: make the word of God the motivating force in the life and faith of Jewry. Spurred by the new learning and daring spirit of the age, Reform sought to divest Judaism of its unlovely garb acquired in the ghettos of the Dark Ages and release all that was ethical and beautiful in Jewish tradition, thus rendering it fit for the unfolding ages.

The key to the differences between Orthodox and Reform Judaism is their respective attitudes toward Torah and tradition. Orthodoxy, as we have seen, rests on the central dogma that the core of its faith is a divine deposit made by God Himself to Moses on Mount Sinai; Reform, assuming the historic attitude, views Judaism as the accumulated lore of many centuries, the result of the Jew's search for the sacred as he sought to live and realize himself from the beginnings of his history. Thus Judaism is not merely a supernatural revelation embodied in the Pentateuch but a slow development of religious thought and practice, which must be understood in terms of the shifting centuries that produced it. That requires free investigation, free and critical search for the truth.

Israel Jacobson

This central issue was at the bottom of the earliest attempts at Reform, though some of its protagonists were unaware of it. It started with attempts to reform the externals of the faith only. Israel Jacobson (1763–1828),[1] pioneer in the Reform movement, was a devout Jew and, at the same time, strongly attracted to the exciting promises of the Enlightenment and Emancipation of his time. He sought what were, apparently, only minor changes, convinced that he was not tampering with the mainsprings of Judaism. An abridged ritual, instrumental music in the synagogue, a sermon and selected portions of the prayer book in the vernacular, more consideration to women as members of the congregation, elimination of obsolete customs, and, especially, a more progressive school—in which he had abundant faith—were his ultimate aims. A disciple of Moses Mendelssohn, he sought to remain true to the ancestral faith, and, at the same time, true to the liberalistic aspirations of his age. He was enthralled by the vision of a free Jewry in a free, enlightened state, enjoying equality of rights and obligations. His aim, therefore, was to reform Jewish practice, rendering Judaism a harmonious element in its new environment. Only the externals of Judaism, he thought, needed revision.

But these details, bitterly contested, started a drift which caused the dislocation of the very foundations of established Judaism. A generation of scholars arose who started disentangling the complicated bundle of Jewish lore. At first, they were investigating the rabbinic, the ritualistic, the institutional, tracing the various threads to their sources. The ultimate source, it was discovered, was not the revelation to Moses on Mount Sinai, but Israel's experience in every age. Thus these scholars, introducing the critical method of investigation, developed a new science and shifted Judaism to a new basis. "The Science of Judaism" arose. It demolished the theology of the fathers, and disrupted the seat of authority.

More than that, the world at large was in the grip of a new science and philosophy. Darwin's theory of evolution was the storm center of the age. Jewry, along with the rest of enlightened humanity, was buffeted about by winds of strange doctrines. A new mind was in the making. The old faiths were at bay. A new vision enthralled the spiritually daring. It struck the synagogue with a double impact, for the reason that the Enlightenment had been long withheld from the Jewish masses. The Copernican revolution had missed Jewish life. With the exception of a daring few, the Jews had remained in a static little universe, unaware that a vast intellectual upheaval had taken place in the early part of the sixteenth century. New paths of destiny lay before man. The Enlightenment came with the explosive force of the suppressed heresies of many centuries.

Jewish scholarship was transformed. The traditional erudition, now disciplined by the critical method, produced a new Golden Age in Jewish learning. The *Wissenschaft des Judentum* recreated the Jewish heritage. Brave minds tilled anew the ancient fields and produced a rich harvest—and a mighty heresy.

God and His will might no longer be ascertained in "the four ells of the Halakah." "Blessed be the Lord from His place," Israel prayed again, as he once did in despair by the waters of Babylon. *From His place!* The ancient process of transplantation was at work once more, intellectually as well as physically. His place was everywhere, in every land and in every age, even in the eighteenth century, with all its upsetting sciences and philosophies, if only men sought Him in truth. God was speaking still. His will must be read not only in the canonized Scriptures but in every area of the universe and the life upon our planet. Every age is a Bible through which God speaks to man. Mankind is in a living, growing world; His will is revealed in the process of the suns and the planets. Judaism is not a sealed dispensation, fixed and final, but an ever expanding spiritual force. Ancient phrases assumed new significance. "The Lord of all worlds," "He who called the generations into being," "He who renews daily the works of creation," "All the world shall come to serve Thee," became enthralling realities.

ABRAHAM GEIGER

Its anchors dragging in the storm of heresy, early Reform veered to extreme positions. Conferences of rabbinic and lay leaders devoted to the reformulation of the faith were storm centers. Gradually Reform acquired a coherent pattern and balance. The mind of Abraham Geiger may be taken as the best expression of the Reform of this early period.

Geiger (1810–1874) was the pathfinder of the second generation of Reform rabbis in Germany. Profound scholar and religious personality, carried by a high sense of responsibility, reverent of the past yet zealous in behalf of the new liberalistic aspirations of his time, seeking peace and ready for battle, a dominant spirit in the conferences called to redefine Judaism, he gave early Reform its characteristic forms.

Releasing and giving direction to his thinking were two principles: *First,* Judaism represents an evolution, not something transmitted in one miraculous moment of revelation. Revealed it is, but in a spiritual sense; this revelation came slowly, haltingly, in the course of many ages, suffering setbacks and experiencing defeats. *Second,* this spiritual development must be studied critically. Free investigation, objective search for truth, must characterize the learning of the synagogue.

Two corollaries followed, in direct contradiction to the two corollaries issuing from the major dogma of Orthodoxy. *First,* not everything in Scripture is necessarily true. Truth is not something static but a progressive power. What was considered divinely true might be invalidated by the advances of the mind. New ages catch new visions and teach new duties. These are not a break with the past but a continuation. *Second,* not everything in the Pentateuch is binding. Some of its teaching remained authoritative; some turned obsolescent. The striving for truth and the sacred had shifted to other battlefields.

Thus the spirit of the age and its own basic logic drove Reform into a radical position. It came to challenge the authority of the Talmud and the later Codes and more: it challenged the authority of Bible text. Geiger, like his fellow Reformers, was bent upon reformulating Judaism in such a manner as to make it a fit instrument in the new age—fit intellectually and socially. Accordingly, he sought to mimimize the national and ceremonial character of Judaism and to bring to the fore the universal and ethical. Emphasis had to be shifted from the group to the individual, from the particular to the universal, from the legal to the inspirational. The inner spirit had to be liberated from formalism and legalism; the eternal from the temporary. Free investigation would accomplish this transformation. Far from breaking with the past it would release the living waters that had been dammed up by sanctified legalism.

Thus Reform was viewed as a historic continuity. Geiger's motto was, "To search in the past, to live in the present, to build for the future." "Every reform," he declared, "is a transition from the past into a regenerated future; such reform does not break with the past but rather preserves carefully the bond that connects the present with the past; it not only continues the once living spirit in new vital forms, thereby strengthening the spirit anew, but it retains all the charming attachments to that which has grown precious and dear to religious life. Such reform proceeds not with inexorable logic; it follows the laws of historical development." Again, "Let us honor worthily the great names that have become historical, let us honor their memory; but then courageously forward, new aims before us! Let not the mouldy smell of the past as it arises from graves benumb us, but let the energizing breath of the atmosphere of the future be wafted toward us." [2]

In one of the major controversies of his career as Reformer, the opposing, Orthodox, point of view was clearly stated and brought to a sharp contrast: talmudic legislation is "binding for all time upon the Jews and not one of these commandments or prohibitions, be the character what it may, can ever be abolished or modified by any human authority." [3]

SPECIFIC REFORMS

Free inquiry and the consequent shift in authority from a divine Law, supernaturally revealed, embodied in a sacred text, defined in authoritative codes by authorized masters versus a divine spirit imperfectly but progressively grasped by free and searching minds—ever growing and expanding with the advancing ages—meant a radical revision of Judaism at specific practices, sanctified by many ages of piety and martyrdom. Geiger sought practical reforms at the following points; he was heading the onward march and directing the procession.

Language of prayer. Ancient authorities permitted prayers in any language. "When you pray," declared the talmudic masters, "do not make your prayer mere routine, but a plea before God for mercy and grace." [4] That meant that the worshipper must understand the prayers he was speaking. However, Hebrew was vital to Jewish worship. "The significance of the prayers consists not alone in their content but also in their traditional forms, in the verbiage in which they have been bequeathed to us." [5] Hebrew prayers are freighted with historic sentiment, and Geiger was too much of a scholar to sacrifice that for rationalistic modernity. Hence he pleaded for the vernacular *and* Hebrew in Jewish worship.

The *contents* of the prayer book had to be appraised anew and choices made. The traditional prayer book was too long and too repetitious. Anthropomorphism and angelology had to be eliminated; belief in immortality had to be rephrased to embrace only spiritual survival, rejecting flatly the belief in the physical resurrection of the dead. The nationalistic had to be either eliminated or radically reinterpreted; Jewry's world mission extolled as one of the dominant ideals of Israel. In place of the prayers for the restoration of the Judean state, the ancient Temple, the sacrificial cult were substituted prayers for the brotherhood of man. The "Chosen People" idea was given prophetic meaning; election imposes responsibility, not privilege. Israel is not the pet darling of the Almighty but His suffering servant. The prayers for a personal messiah gave way to a prayer for the coming of the messianic age, "the realization on earth of the ideals of universal peace and good will." [6]

Ceremonies were retained in modified form and sparingly. Ceremonies must be vital and significant, not mere survivals of a dead past; they must be reverent modes of the sacred, not mere perfunctory rites.

The Sabbath presented special problems and meant deep searching of heart for Geiger and his colleagues. It was the profoundest institution in Judaism, freighted with sacred sentiment and ethical import; but it had fallen into disuse and

36   JUDAISM IN THEORY AND PRACTICE

swamped in obscurantism. The essential idea of the day, Geiger argued, was consecration, rather than mere abstention from work. He sought its primary significance and brushed aside the negative legalism that had slowly strangled the spirit of the sacred day. "The significance of the Sabbath lies in the composure of the spirit and of our whole nature." [7]

Circumcision, to Geiger, was "a barbarous and bloody act." However, he did not displace it. Seeking a substitute but finding none, he retained it.

The Status of Women cried to high heaven for reconsideration. Religious emancipation of woman was long overdue. In 1837 Geiger published one of his profound essays pleading for woman's religious equality with men. This meant a revision of the marriage laws and the marriage service, placing man and woman on a footing of equality, as two free moral agents. The partition in synagogues segregating women from the male congregation was removed.

Confirmation, marking the religious coming of age of girls as well as boys, replaced *Bar Mitzvah,* which was for boys only; the age of confirmation was not necessarily thirteen, as practiced in Orthodoxy, but the confirmand's completion of the religious school curriculum.

AMERICAN DEVELOPMENT

Originating in Germany, Reform developed to its full stature in America. The liberalistic dreams of German Jewry were rudely shattered. Political and social reaction engulfed Germany with the recession of French liberalism. Stalwart teachers of Reform, like the Pilgrim Fathers, migrated to America in search of freedom and opportunity to live and build the faith of their fathers in keeping with their hearts' desires. On the free shores of America they found their opportunity. From America it spread throughout the English-speaking world.

Among these pioneers of Reform was Isaac Mayer Wise, Bohemian-trained rabbi.[8] Teacher, preacher, zealot, indefatigable worker with a genius for organization, he reared the institutions that have fostered Reform Judaism in the new world. He organized the Union of American Hebrew Congregations, the federation of Reform congregations to encourage and steady the young congregations throughout the land; founded the Hebrew Union College, for the training of Reform rabbis for the upsurging movement, and established the Central Conference of American Rabbis, to deal corporately with the various issues in American Judaism. From these three sources Reform Judaism has drawn its organized strength and cohesion.

GUIDING PRINCIPLES

What is the specific platform of Reform Judaism? We are avoiding the words, "dogmas," "creeds," for Reform is suspicious of the authority accredited to them. It would not close the system that is Judaism; it seeks to keep its channels open. It distrusts external authority. However, if Reform constitutes a distinct branch of the synagogue, we have the right to ask just what it is that gives it its distinctive character.

Several attempts were made by the leaders of Reform Judaism in America to formulate its distinctive tenets. In 1869, meeting in Philadelphia, a group of Reform rabbis announced a statement of beliefs. In 1885, meeting in Pittsburgh, this statement was revised and reissued as "The Pittsburgh Platform." [9] In 1937, meeting in Columbus, Ohio, the Central Conference of American Rabbis, after several years of debate, adopted officially a new formulation under the heading, "Guiding Principles of Reform Judaism." [10]

The title is significant. It is not a creed to which members of the Conference must subscribe; it is not a confession of faith. It is a platform—that is, a set of principles upon which the Reform Temple rests. It is open to revision at all times. It does not outlaw dissenting opinion. It lays no claim to finality, nor does it require complete acceptance. It seeks to coordinate and guide the movement on the basis of glad acceptance of basic principles, thus saving it from individualistic extremes.

The principles are grouped under three major headings:

1. Judaism and its Foundations
2. Ethics
3. Religious Practice

Judaism is viewed in all-inclusive terms. Theologic and sociologic differences are absorbed into one whole. Care is taken to avoid a partisan view of Judaism. Thus Judaism is defined as "the historical religious experience of the Jewish people." This historical religious experience is a functioning process, not a closed system. It is assuming new forms today, and will attain to new patterns of faith in the ages yet unborn, even as it has in ages past. Hence Judaism welcomes all truth, "whether written in the pages of scripture or deciphered from the records of nature."

The foundations of Judaism are belief in God, belief in Man as the child of God, belief in Torah, and in Israel as the servant of the Lord.

"God. The heart of Judaism and its chief contribution to religion is the doctrine of the One, living God, who rules the world through law and love. In Him all existence has its creative source and mankind its ideal of conduct. Though transcending time and space, He is the indwelling Presence of the world. We worship Him as the Lord of the universe and as our merciful Father.

"Man. Judaism affirms that man is created in the Divine image. His spirit is immortal. He is an active co-worker with God. As a child of God, he is endowed with moral freedom and is charged with the responsibility of overcoming evil and striving after ideal ends.

"Torah. God reveals Himself not only in the majesty, beauty and orderliness of nature, but also in the vision and moral striving of the human spirit. Revelation is a continuous process, confined to no one age. Yet the people of Israel, through its prophets and sages, achieved unique insight in the realm of religious truth. The Torah, both written and oral, enshrines Israel's ever-growing consciousness of God and of the moral law. . . . Each age has the obligation to adapt the teachings of the Torah to its basic needs in consonance with the genius of Judaism. "Israel. Judaism is the soul of which Israel is the body. Living in all parts of the world, Israel has been held together by the ties of a common history, and above all, by the heritage of faith.

The ethics of Judaism issues from the relationship believed to exist between God and man. "Seeking God means to strive after holiness, righteousness and justice." Justice to all is "the inalienable right and inescapable obligation of all." The state exists to enable man to live as an ethical, morally-responsible being. Social justice is the attainment of a just society—economically, socially, nationally, and internationally. Peace is the great ideal. Judaism "abhors all violence and relies upon moral education, love and sympathy to secure human progress." The condition for peace and social stability is justice.

The religious practices are the tangible expressions of Jewish ideals in the home, the synagogue, and the community. Home and synagogue have been the strongholds of Judaism. Education is the breath of Jewish life, uniting the generations in Israel. Prayer is the voice of religion and the communion with God. The Jewish way of life, in addition to its moral and spiritual demands, requires "the preservation of the Sabbath, festivals,

> "and Holy Days, the retention and development of such customs, symbols and ceremonies as possess inspirational value, the cultivation of distinctive forms of religious art and music and the use of Hebrew together with the vernacular, in our worship and instruction."

"Guiding Principles" and "I Believe with Perfect Faith"

The principles of Judaism as formulated by American rabbis in 1937, expressive of contemporary Reform, and the Thirteen Principles as formulated by Maimonides in 1168, expressive of Orthodoxy, agree and differ at basic points. Maimonides' formulation is entirely theological; the Guiding

Principles take into full consideration the social scene of the twentieth century as well as the theologic. The Thirteen Principles are creedal in form; the Guiding Principles are a summary and a synthesis of many tendencies of Jewish thought.

On the subject of God the two formulations present no differences whatever. Maimonides is more specific. The view of man as a spiritual agent is, no doubt, assumed by Maimonides. There was no thought on his part of stating it explicitly; the liberal rabbis had to meet the materialistic arguments from biology and certain schools of psychology. Israel as the people of God and Torah is assumed by Maimonides; there was no need to stress the conviction. The twentieth century interpreters of Judaism had to meet the secularistic and nationalistic interpretations of Israel, which were unknown in the twelfth century. In the sphere of social ethics, and the home and the synagogue as indispensable nurseries of Judaism, Maimonides is silent, again no doubt, for the reason that in his age they were realities which no one doubted. Maimonides makes no reference to Palestine in the life and destiny of Israel; the American rabbis speak of it as "a Jewish homeland" which all Jewry is asked to help build anew in the hope of creating there "a center of Jewish culture and spiritual life."

Major differences between Maimonides and the modern rabbis are in the character of Torah, the authority of Moses, the nature of divine retribution, and the belief in resurrection. The modernists, as we have seen, repudiate the divine authority of Torah, substituting a man-made, though sacred, literature; deny the Mosaic authorship of the Pentateuch and classify Moses among the great lawgivers of mankind but make no dogma of his being chief of the prophets. The beliefs in personal resurrection and in a personal Messiah are completely ignored by the framers of the Guiding Principles for the reason, no doubt, that these beliefs, so basic in the twelfth century, are of no consequence to the modern mind. Instead, the belief in the immortality of the soul is affirmed.

Impulses of Reform

Viewing the work of the fathers of Reform Judaism from the standpoint of the historian, beyond the smoke of battle and the passion of the conflict, three impulses may be identified as the impelling forces of the movement.

First, intransigent Orthodoxy was no longer possible for the Jewish men and women touched by the wings of the Enlightenment. A new spirit brooded over the Jewish community; it penetrated the homes and challenged the synagogues. Jewish values were being transmuted. The new generation of rabbis, trained in the universities, initiated into the social and physical sciences, brought a new mentality to Jewish life. They had the choice of quitting Judaism altogether, for the reason that they could not observe it honestly in its existing forms, or of transforming it in keeping with their own thinking. Some chose the former and thus wrote their own epitaphs of oblivion in the book of Jewish remembrance; some chose the latter and created a new epoch in Judaism.

A *Second* set of factors made Reform inevitable; they issued from the social and political life of the age.

The dominant passion of German Jewry—at least of that portion that had embraced the Enlightenment—was emancipation and enfranchisement. They sought the rights, liberties and responsibilities of citizens on equal terms with all other citizens. They no longer considered themselves aliens on German soil; they had lived, labored, produced over many generations. They had enriched their land and merged their fondest dreams with the striving liberalism of the age. Their Judaism was outlandish. It was a cruel yoke. It held no inspiration. The fires had died upon the altar. Only ashes were left to vast numbers of young Jews. If they could only remove the external trappings and obsolete dogmatism and release the inner beauty—still there to the faithful lover—it would enable them to be free German citizens *and* Jews. They rejected separatism as an ideal and sought integration. Hence the particularistic and temporary, the ceremonial and nationalistic, had to be removed and the ethical and universal cultivated.

A *Third* principle sustained the fathers of Reform; the desire to save Judaism from total disintegration.

The masters of Reform were loyal to the faith of their fathers, as they understood it. They saw it scorned and repudiated by hosts of Jewish young men and women.[11] They could not stand idly by. They would restore the faith to its own best self, and restore Jews to their faith.

This reformation and restoration of Judaism was made by men who were driven by the logic and the circumstances of the age as they sought to make the faith of the fathers the living religion of their children. In the history of Judaism they found ample warrant for their new standards.

Kaufmann Kohler—scholar, preacher, teacher, zealot—invokes the rabbinic sages to justify the course of Reform:

> When Moses stood on Mount Sinai, wrapped up in the smoke which hid the majesty of God from his sight, he beheld the future generations of Israel's teachers along the vista of time, hosts of pupils sitting at the feet of each. With wonder and amazement he listened to their discussions, and there, lo! his ear caught the words of Rabbi Eliezer and Rabbi Joshua, the one asserting emphatically: 'This is what our great teacher Moses said'; the other contradictingly said, 'No, Moses our teacher spoke differently.' Moses felt quite bewildered, as he overheard the strange controversy, and exclaimed, 'O Lord, I fail to recognize my teaching in what they claim on my authority'. But God rejoined, 'Forsooth, it is thy teaching, nevertheless. It is the same truth, the same underlying idea, only applied to another age and other conditions.' [12]

Impelled by the principle of progressive revelation, negating separatism as a principle, Reform Judaism braves the depths of the world's thought and humanity's aspirations for the sacred and the just—for all that heals, unites and sanctifies mankind. Its morning star is the prophet's vision and the rabbi's prayer: to bring mankind "under the sovereignty of the Almighty, when all flesh shall call upon His name." "On that day the Lord shall be One and His Name one." [13]

VI. CONSERVATIVE JUDAISM

Positive–Historic Judaism

Conservative Judaism, like Reform, issues from the storm and stress released in Jewry by the liberalistic movements of the eighteenth-nineteenth centuries, and, like Reform and Orthodox Judaism, derives its distinctive character from its peculiar attitude toward tradition.

The fall of the ghetto, the tantalizing vision of liberty, equality, and fraternity, the lure of European science and philosophy, arts and letters, commerce and industry—the vision of an emancipated Jewry among the nations, as we have seen, forced open the ancient gates and compelled Jewry to seek a new orientation in the world. A portion of the Jewish community preferred religious isolation and spurned the flesh pots of the Enlightenment. This school evolved, as we have noted, into the Orthodoxy of our time. A large portion of Jewry, however, yearned for the fruits of the tree of the new knowledge. They saw in the dawn of the new era the answer to their ancient prayer when "the Lord shall be One and His name One." They dreamed of a time when they and their children might walk the earth in dignity and worship the God of their fathers. They did want—desperately, for themselves and for their children—the spiritual and material opportunities of European culture. But they would remain Jews in all that was basic and eternal. They wanted emancipation *and* Judaism, not emancipation at the expense of what was basic in Judaism. A formula had to be found for this adjustment. A portion of this community found the formula in Reform. Many, however, were dissatisfied with Reform. They could not conscientiously follow the movement to its logical conclusion. To them the Reform fathers were too radical in ap-

43

proach, too lacking in historic sentiment, too much given to the shibboleths of the day; their efforts, it was feared, would render Judaism too anaemic to function as a vigorous and creative religion worthy of historic Judaism. They sought a positive, historic Judaism that would ring true to the noblest teachings of the biblical and rabbinic masters and which would, at the same time, enable the Jew to live honorably in the modern world.

ZECHARIAH FRANKEL

The first to direct the stream of Jewish aspirations into the channel that came to be Conservative Judaism was Zechariah Frankel (1801–1875), historian of the Halakah, staunch traditionalist, and, at the same time, zealous champion of the Jew's rights and liberties in the new age.[1] He had followed the debates of the day at the conferences of the Reform leaders with deep interest. But as the issues assumed form and the views of the Reform fathers acquired consistency and clarity, he found that he could not in conscience follow the movement. It was too violent a break with the past.

Frankel, giving the reasons for withdrawing from the Reform movement, coined the phrase "positive-historic Judaism." This slogan has been the battle cry of the Conservative school ever since. His position may be stated as follows: in the sphere of scholarship, freedom of research must obtain; in the realm of belief and observance, however, the authority of tradition must be upheld. He was too romantic and too zealous a lover of Jewish tradition to bring himself to break with it. Changes he did permit; but reluctantly and sparingly, and only when approved by the true representatives of Jewish consciousness. But who may be taken as the authoritative spokesmen for Jewry? "Frankel could only make the reply that only those '. . . who accepted the distinctiveness of Judaism in the Law could decide.'"[2] The pious, competent scholar, not the rebel reformer, must be recognized as the authority. But who is the pious scholar and who the rebel?

The answer is, presumably, that the pious scholar is the one who conforms closest and disturbs least the tradition as it is established.

THE AUTHORITY OF TRADITION

When pressed for an explanation as to what he meant by "positive-historic Judaism," Frankel's answer was, "Judaism is the religion of the Jewish people." Hence, whatever the Jewish people have created is Jewish and binding; hence, too, only the Jewish people through its duly recognized authorities may abrogate or modify any tradition. It is not the origin of any usage or institution that is of primary significance but the meaning the usage or institution acquired in the life of Israel. Hebrew as an integral part of Jewish worship, the Jewish Sabbath with all its historic forms of observance, the wearing of the hat, the traditional prayers, circumcision, the separation of the sexes in the synagogue, the dietary laws, law as the peculiarly Jewish channel of religious sentiment— all these and the many other historic forms of Jewish belief and ceremonial are binding, whatever their origins be. Frankel's disciples have clarified his view and project it as the groundwork of Conservative Judaism. "The dietary laws are not incumbent upon us because they conduce to moderation, nor the family laws because they further chastity and purity of morals. The law as a whole is not the means to an end, but the end in itself; the law is active religiousness, and in active religion must lie what is specifically Jewish. . . . For an adherent of this school the sanctity of the Sabbath reposes not upon the fact that it was proclaimed at Sinai, but on the fact that the Sabbath idea found for thousands of years its expression in Jewish souls. It is the task of the historian to examine into the beginnings and developments of the numerous customs and observances of the Jews; practical Judaism, on the other hand, is not concerned with origins, but regards the institutions as they have come to be." The controlling principle is that "whatever observance is spread throughout the whole community must not be abrogated by any authority . . . That which the whole community has adopted and recognized may not be repealed; to do so would be to dissolve Judaism, which is nothing else than the sum of the sentiments and views which dominate Jewish consciousness." [3]

Thus the Conservative synagogue is dedicated to the conservation of tradition. "There is no other Jewish religion but that taught by the Torah and confirmed by history and tradition, and sunk into the consciousness of Catholic Israel," Solomon Schechter averred.[4] "All that the (historic, or Conservative) school maintains is that usages and customs receive a certain sanction and holiness by having been observed by Israel for many generations. They become identified with Israel, and unless there are serious moral objections to their continuation, they have still to be observed." [5]

Judaism is thus viewed not as an organic system of thought but as a historic process. It has its own distinctive standards and its own logic. They are the standards and logic of Jewish tradition. To appraise Judaism properly, one must think in terms of Jewish tradition; to observe Judaism faithfully, one must accept the authority of tradition. Logic as it obtains elsewhere—in the natural sciences, for instance, which have revolutionized the mind of Western man and compelled a radical revision of his theology—is not entirely valid when applied to the thinking of the synagogue. The Conservative synagogue would escape the impact of the scientific approach to the Bible and religious traditions by shifting the center of gravity from the Bible as such to the Bible as interpreted in Jewish tradition. Granted that the Bible represents an evolution of thought and idealism that must be read critically against the environments that produced it, and is not a supernaturally revealed divine dictation to Moses on Mount Sinai, in Jewish practice it functioned as a divine code. Hence, in the life and practice of the Jew it must be maintained as a divine code, whatever the findings of the scientific scholars

be. The authority of the Bible issues not from its Sinaitic
origin but from what it has come to mean in Judaism. What it
has come to mean it must continue to mean. Freedom of
research is thus granted; but the authority of tradition is retained. The root of the matter is that the primary consideration is not the Bible as such but the Bible as it has been
interpreted in Jewish tradition, and Jewish tradition has its
own code of interpretation.

Judaism is not a fixed system; rather, it is a living, ongoing
process. In the literature of the Conservative synagogue we
have no distinctive presentation of the totality of Jewish
religious thought and conviction, as is the case in Orthodoxy
and its codes, or in Reform with its *Guiding Principles*.
System and scientific method are for the specialists in their
scholarly work in the various branches of Jewish lore; in the
sphere of belief and practice consistent systems are treated
lightly. Thus, in the realm of scholarship Conservative Judaism breaks with the dogma of supernatural revelation and its
corollaries upon which Orthodoxy rests; in the sphere of religious belief and practice it maintains the dogma, and breaks
with the corollaries of free inquiry as expounded in Reform.
Solomon Schechter, in the formative period of the Conservative synagogue in America—if it is permitted to speak of a
formative period in a movement that is averse to creating new
forms—defined the central characteristic of the movement:
"On the whole, its attitude towards religion may be defined
as an enlightened Scepticism combined with a staunch conservatism which is not even wholly devoid of a certain mysti-
cal touch. . . . Its theological position may perhaps be thus
defined: It is not the mere revealed Bible that is of first importance to the Jew, but the Bible as it repeats itself in
history, in other words, as it is interpreted by Tradition." 6
The Conservative synagogue is devoted to the preservation
of the pattern wrought by history, with all its apparent inconsistencies. The "inconsistencies" are the results of an alien
logic.

WITHIN THE LAW

Flexibility and adaptation to the needs of the new age are not only permitted but earnestly sought; however, all reforms must be within the authoritative channel of law, in keeping with the established canons of law. "There are those who think that we have but two alternatives, to reject or to accept the law, but in either case to treat it as a dead letter. Both of these alternatives are repugnant to the whole tradition of Judaism. . . ." Jewish law must be preserved, "but it is subject to interpretation by those who have mastered it . . . the interpretation placed upon it by duly authorized masters in every generation must be accepted with as much reverence as those which were given in previous generations."

Thus speaks Louis Finkelstein, the official head of the Jewish Theological Seminary of America, the cradle of the Conservative synagogue in America.[7] His predecessors in office, colleagues, and disciples emphasize the same principle as the groundwork of their interpretation of Judaism. Whatever differences obtain among them, and they are considerable, are on the periphery. At the core of the movement is the insistence on the authority of tradition and change within the law. "Let it become known once and for all," declared Israel H. Levinthal as one-time President of the Rabbinical Assembly of America, "that we stand firmly on the rock of Jewish tradition and Jewish law; but let it also become known . . . that we seek the lenient view, the liberal view . . . and not the severe view in Jewish tradition. There is a difference between the abrogation of law and the liberal interpretation of the law. Law itself is flexible. . . . Perhaps it is the genius of the Jewish soul that it created a word for law—unlike any other language—*halakah*—"to go," "to walk," "to move." The very word *halakah* is opposed to stagnancy. Halakah represents a living process, in keeping with life itself."[8]

A lay leader of the Conservative movement wrote, "Judaism rests upon God-inspired laws and teachings. Coeval with the transmission of the Law by Moses, there began the tradi-

tion of its interpretation, continued in the writings of the
great men of Israel through all the ages. That tradition is to
be studied and maintained without break, lest the whims of
passing generations—introduced by one to be discarded by
the other—be permitted to impair the fundamentals of the
faith." [9]

The seat of authority thus remains where it was, only
reached by a new road. From the charter of the Jewish Theological Seminary of America, a faithful son infers "that historical Judaism sponsors the principle that Scripture and the
Talmud are final authorities in all matters pertaining to belief
and observance." Even the Shulhan Aruk retains its validity.
"It is my deepest conviction that traditional Jewish law as
codified in the Shulhan Aruk can best be brought into harmony with contemporary conditions by interpretation, and
not by innovation or abrogation." [10] Infallible it is not; final
it is not. Valid it is.

Authority thus remains where it was, despite the heretical
studies in which the very same exponents of Judaism may
engage. In his study the rabbi may operate with a non-Mosaic
Pentateuch, as established by the scientific scholarship; in his
pulpit he upholds the traditions of the Pentateuch as revealed
to Moses on Mt. Sinai. There is no inconsistency in that for
him for the reason that the study is dedicated to free investigation, while the pulpit is committed to the traditional values.
"One of the most fundamental principles in our approach to
Jewish law must be the preservation of the continuity of Jewish tradition which was maintained in unbroken succession
from remote antiquity." [11]

But a time comes when old laws are rendered obsolete, and
new interpretations are imperative. How shall Conservative
Judaism proceed at such turns in the road? Professor Finkelstein replies, "If the shifting of values and the introduction of
new devices will actually bring Jews back to God, to the
Torah, and to the synagogue, they will doubtless be accepted.
. . . But pending such proof of the value of these changes,
and pending their acceptance by all Israel, some of us prefer

to stand aside and watch like Eliezer at the well 'steadfastly, holding our peace, to know whether the Lord had made their way successful or not.' " [12]

The Committee on Law of the Rabbinical Assembly states clearly: "We should take proper note of the fact that certain laws are obsolete, e.g. the laws against shaving, because they do not meet with the approval of the people; yet we may not declare them null and void, as they are scriptural commands." [13]

It is characteristic of Conservative Judaism that there is discrepancy between the official views and the actual procedure on the part of many of the synagogues. The legal pronouncements made by the official Committee on Law are not enforced. There is neither the desire nor the means for enforcement. They are mandatory only to that extent to which the constituent synagogues accept them. Rabbis who do not subordinate themselves to the decisions remain in good standing, and may even serve as members of the committee whose decisions they violate.

NATIONALISM

Next to its emphasis on tradition, Conservative Judaism stresses the importance of Jewish nationalism. The nationhood and the religion of the Jewish people are one and inseparable. Nationhood and Palestine, like God and Torah, are organic to "positive, historic Judaism." "For Frankel, it is true, nationalism does not belong to the essence of Judaism, but it is nevertheless necessary to its existence. Breath is not a part of man, it comes to man from without, yet no one can live without breathing. So nationalism is the very air in which Judaism breathes." [14] Frankel's disciples consider Jewish Nationalism the very breath of life for Judaism.*

This nationhood assumes a racial *volk*, common descent, a

* This was stressed before the State of Israel was established in 1948. The Conservative Synagogue was the citadel of Jewish religious nationalism. Since 1948 there has been an easing of this emphasis. In theory, however, no official revision has been made. [15]

common language, common traditions, customs, folk ways. The Conservative synagogue, shifting the center of gravity from the revealed word of God to the will of "catholic Israel," extolls the people, and the nation that gives it corporate being. The racial and nationalistic aspects of Jewish tradition are therefore given a new emphasis. Hebrew, Palestine, folk ways are of the essence of the faith.

The authority of tradition and the binding power of Jewish nationhood are the two strands that dominate the pattern of Conservative Judaism. Both are broad and deep and allow a wide diversity of interpretation. Moreover, Conservative Judaism, as we have noted, is instinctively averse to a fixed system of faith, insisting on viewing Judaism rather as a historic process. This gives the individual the opportunity to find himself within the household of Conservative Judaism, whatever be the bent of his mind or the general bias of his personality.[16]

The dictum of ancient rabbinic masters stands true:

"Even though these sages declare a thing impure while others declare it pure, these say it is prohibited and others say it is permissible, and you may be tempted to say, 'Whom shall I heed?' know then that they all have one source, they all derive their common inspiration from the one shepherd." [17]

Solomon Schechter, who impressed his powerful personality on the movement, and whose genius rests like a benediction on the Conservative synagogue, taught his disciples:

"The Torah gave spiritual accommodation for thousands of years to all sorts and conditions of men, sages, philosophers, scholars, mystics, casuists, school men and skeptics; and it should also prove broad enough to harbor the different minds of the present century. Any attempt to place the center of gravity outside the Torah must end in disaster." [18]

VII. BASIC UNITY

We have examined the three major divisions in Jewish religious life on the American scene. Within each division are found various finer distinctions. In Jewish life generally are many further differences, some issuing from radically different philosophies of Jewish life and destiny, some from the exigencies of the day. But these differences are within a larger unity; they are like the differences of thought and taste that may obtain within a family. Israel is one. However wide the theologic differences may be, however varied the standards of culture or levels of sentiment may be among the scattered millions of Jews the world over, Israel is one. What makes for this basic unity?

The answer is to be found in the primary fact in Jewish life and faith, namely, the *peoplehood of Israel.* Judaism is not only a body of theologic doctrine and a system of practices; basically it is the historic religious experience of the Jewish people functioning today. "History ranks as a vital part of faith." [1] The various turns in Jewish history assumed religious significance. Much of what is considered divine precept in Orthodoxy, or religious tradition in Reform or Conservative Judaism, is only folk custom in origin; much is borrowed from the non-Jewish environment and transformed into distinctive religious values. Some of the holy days are national in origin. They commemorate events in the life of the people as a people or as a nation; but they have been invested with religious significance for all Jewry of all time, and for the larger world beyond Jewry. The source of this experience and teaching is religious Israel. The literary sources of Judaism, as we have noted, issued from the application of the Word of God to the expanding Jewish life. The authors of Judaism are innumerable sages, law-givers, prophets, psalmists, rabbis. No one personality stands central in Jewish life. Practically all the prayers of the synagogue are in the plural form, and by "us" and "we" is meant the people of Israel. When the Psalmist chants, "In my distress I called upon the Lord," or "The Lord is with me, I shall not fear," he becomes the symbol of a whole people.

The destiny of every soul in Jewry is bound up in the destiny of the whole people, and the fate of the whole people is thus in the hands of each Jew. Thus Judaism may harbor every orthodoxy and heterodoxy; essentially it is one. The peoplehood of Israel makes it one. He who is born to Jewish parents remains a Jew though he deny every theologic principle and ignore every ceremonial. He is a bad Jew, but a Jew he is. No one has the power to declare him a non-Jew. Excommunication even in Medieval Judaism was only a legal device. It quarantined a person; it did not erase him from Jewry.[2] Only when he deliberately removes himself from the Jewish people does he cease to be a Jew. This makes not only for a basic unity, but, also, for a profound liberalism.

THEOLOGIC FOUNDATIONS:
GOD, TORAH, AND ISRAEL

In Judaism, God, Torah and Israel are one and indivisible. God is the flame; Torah is the oil; Israel is the wick. This formula, given by rabbinic mystics, has come to be the accepted demarcation of the faith of Israel.[1] For an adequate understanding of the mind of the synagogue we must explore these three areas in Jewish thought and aspiration.

VIII. GOD—THE HOLY ONE OF ISRAEL

Entering on his sacred duty as scholar and teacher, the pious Jew speaks a prayer, asking for God's grace, so that he may not err nor cause others to err. It is a prayer of thanksgiving and petition: thanksgiving for the privilege of contemplating and expounding his *Torah,* and petition for integrity. Such a prayer we speak now upon undertaking an exposition of the nature of God as understood in Jewry.

Two basic considerations must be borne in mind by way of introduction.

First, God and our ideas of God may not be the same. One is the reality; the other is our fumbling attempts to grasp the reality in words. What we know is little, and that little is subject to radical revision; what we do not know is infinite, the supreme Mystery. "The hidden things belong to the Lord our God; but (or, *only*) the revealed things are for us and our children." [1] The insights of our masters—in every sphere of knowledge: the religions, the sciences, the philosophies—add up to little in view of the vast Unknown. But the Unknown must be chartered. God has placed eternity in our hearts, and "deep calls unto deep." [2] The Unknown rouses, challenges, beats with powerful wings on the imaginations of men. Man is not at peace with himself as long as he considers himself chaff blown by the winds of futility; he would be an arrow from the quiver of the Almighty shot at a mark. He must achieve harmony within himself and between himself and the universe. He therefore storms the gates of heaven, like a moth fluttering around a lamp. He returns from the adventure with rumors of the eternal, having caught, at best, whispers of the music of the spheres, and of God beyond.

Despair and disillusionment have beset him in his quest; many have counselled against entering the *pardes* altogether.

Zophar, addressing himself to suffering Job, seeking to calm his friend's tempestuous spirit, spoke for many, the submissive saint and rebellious skeptic alike:

> Canst thou find out the deep things of God?
> Canst thou attain to the purpose of the Almighty?
> It is high as heaven; what canst thou do?
> Deeper than the nether world; what canst thou know?
> The measure thereof is longer than the earth,
> And broader than the sea.[3]

Nevertheless, man must seek, learn, understand, harmonize. That is in the nature of the sensitive mind, and that is the will of God. We are haunted by a promise and by a faith: If with all your hearts ye really seek Him, ye shall ever truly find Him.

Words and realities must not be confused. What botany is to plants, geology to the earth, astronomy to the heavenly bodies, theology is to God and religion. One is the discipline, the other is the object of study. Our knowledge changes with deeper insight. With our growing knowledge may come the still, small voice of wisdom. God remains constant, the Mystery. When men reject any of the ideas of God they do not necessarily repudiate the reality of God. All we can do in this chapter is concern ourselves with the ideas of God basic in Jewish teaching.

Second, language is an inadequate instrument for the complete expression of the Infinite. In sounding the depths of the Eternal, words assume a varied function: they turn into symbols, allegories, usually without warning. They intimate rather than describe. Like the spirit of God in the story of Creation, they only hover over the Reality. They are not like plaster pigeons on a stone wall—sure, solid, immovable, lifeless; rather, they are like seagulls following a ship in a storm and trying to alight on its mast. Here is the line between religion and superstition. In superstition words are brute facts; if not ultimate reality in themselves they hold the supreme reality as a vise holds a nut. They are solid, final, unchangeable; they are accepted without question and spoken without imagination. The sensitively religious person knows that words are intimations, and he uses them as the poet uses metaphors, or the musician sounds. The conscious reason of the rationalist as well as the intuition, apprehension, surmise of the mystic resorts to symbolism. Words are thus pressed into a service for which they were not intended. The reality is beyond the words.

In the names for God found in Bible text we see the efforts of the ancients to grasp in words the meaning of God. Names are attributes.

God is *El*, a word for the deity found in most Semitic languages and means, it would seem, Mighty One, The Ruler. He is called, also, *Shaddai*, or *El Shaddai*, the Almighty God, and *El Elyon*, God Most High. *Elohim*, the common Hebrew word for God is, probably, the plural. It is used, also, to designate the polytheism of the heathen word. *Adonai*, used especially by the Hebrew prophets, means Lord, thus expressing dependence. The particular God of Israel is known by four letters, YHWH (יהוה). The origin and etymological meaning of the Tetragrammaton are lost in obscurity. The earliest Bible authors and scribes were badly confused. In time YHWH became the God of Israel and Israel became wedded to YHWH; a covenant bound the two. The Tetragrammaton became too sacred for common utterance. During the Second Temple, only the High Priest, on the Day of Atonement, in the Holy of Holies, might pronounce the Ineffable Name. The pronunciation of the four consonants was forgotten. The vowels of *Adonai*, Lord, was given to them, and thus YHWH came to mean "the Lord," the Ever-Present One, or the Self-Existent One. "He Who is wont to be," "He who will be." It denotes Existence, active and self-manifesting Existence.

Often in Bible text YHWH is joined with *Tsebaoth*, "hosts." In its primitive stages the hosts referred to were the armies of Israel; in time, as the idea of God matured, the name referred to the hosts of heavenly bodies and the powers of nature.

Jahweh (YHWH) is the Lord of nature, Ruler of the Universe, and He is the God of Israel:

The voice of יהוה (YHWH) is upon the waters;
The אל (El) of glory thundereth,
Even YHWH upon many waters,
The voice of YHWH is powerful;
The voice of YHWH is full of majesty.
The voice of YHWH breaketh the cedars;
Yea, YHWH breaketh in pieces the cedars of Lebanon.
He maketh them also to skip like a calf;
Lebanon and Syria like a young wild ox.
The voice of YHWH heweth out flames of fire.
The voice of YHWH shaketh the wilderness;
YHWH shaketh the wilderness of Kadesh.
The voice of YHWH maketh the hinds to calve,
And strippeth the forest bare;
And in His temple all say: "Glory."
YHWH sat enthroned at the flood;
Yea, YHWH sitteth as King forever.

Universal Lord, He is at the same time the particular God of Israel. The psalm thus concludes:

YHWH will give strength to His people;
He will bless His people with peace.[4]

YHWH, in the life of Israel, became the Supreme Lord; He who delivered Israel from bondage, gave them a Moral Law by lawgiver and prophet, and consecrated Israel as His peculiar people.

These are the technical, proper names for God in the Bible. We see in them, despite the fact that scholars have much difficulty ascertaining their true etymologies, what the ancients sought to say. They thought of God as the Creator, Sustainer, Guardian of life and the world, of the forces within man and of the vast universe. In the non-technical metaphors for God in Bible literature we see the strain of the persistent reaching out for the primary meaning of God.

God is the *Rock of Ages*, standing fast amidst the swirls of time and change, *the Shadow of a great rock in a weary land.* He is the *Eternal* in the shifting sands of mortal life, the *Holy One* in a secular, often crass and cruel world; *Father, our Father in Heaven, Merciful Father* who sustains, disciplines, shields lonely man in a vast world that would crush him; He is the *Shepherd* who guides man in the valley of the Shadow and in the valley of decision, when crises come into his life; He is the *Righteous Judge* of all the earth, who created the world out of the attributes of justice and mercy and sustains it by these attributes; He is *Sovereign*, the *King of Kings* (or, *King of the King of Kings* where men arrogated to themselves the title King of Kings) in a world where men are exploiting and crushing their fellows. Above all, He is the *Saviour, Redeemer*, who refines mortal man, purging him at times in the cauldron of adversity, as gold is refined, freeing him from all that cramps, thwarts, and vulgarizes life.

These appellations seek to express an illusive, a complex reality. The attempt is to reach down to the *Fountain of Life* for its living waters.

In the language of modern rationalists as well appellations for God become symbols: First Cause, Creative Power, World Reason, Cosmic God. They are intimations of something seen from afar and seen by the eyes of faith.

Anthropomorphism is thus inevitable. Human, we must express ourselves in human terms; but God is not man and our human terms do not fit His nature. Mortal, finite, we inevitably express ourselves in mortal, finite terms; mortal, finite terms do not describe the nature of the immortal and the infinite. Disturbed by moral aspirations and seeking integrity, we see in God the source of the moral imperative, and express ourselves in concepts peculiarly human. The rabbinic teachers warn us: Anthropomorphic terms are used "to sink it into the ear," and resort freely to anthropomorphic expressions. "The Torah," they aver, "speaks in human terms." Does the Holy One have eyes, ears, tongue that He sees, hears, speaks? These are human ways of saying that He sees, hears, communicates. Words are symbols, and should be used with imagination. These words are intimations of the supreme Fact at the heart of all things. They are only the tremblings of the needle in the compass.

ETHICAL MONOTHEISM

Ethical Monotheism is the master-term in the Jewish conception of God. It represents the idea of God in Judaism at its highest point of development. It is the brilliant flowering of centuries of growth.

Bible pages hold preserved the stages of this development. As among all primitive peoples so in Israel did the God concept pass through the lowly stages of animism, spiritism, polytheism, henotheism; the gods and spirits were local, tribal, national before they attained the exalted development of the universal Lord who commands the Hebrew Jonah to rouse the pagan Ninevites to repentance and salvation. A unique power infused the Hebrew conception of God even in early Bible days: He was a moral God, demanding justice, love, compassion. A covenant obtained between Jahweh and Israel. He ceased being a deification of a power in nature and became the Creator and Ruler of nature and human nature. He was no longer to be coerced with the rites of the magician, propitiated with the sacrifices of humans or animals, but served in just human relationships. The tribal and national was a passing phase. He became the universal Lord, summoning to Himself all of his children of whatever race.[5]

Primary is the fact that the Hebrew people discovered the unity of the world, the unity of human life, the unity of the human family, the unity of human destiny, through the conscience, not through abstract speculations. Beyond all, having created and sustaining all, harmonizing chaos into cosmos, enduing man with the eternal, thus making him a combination of finite matter and infinite spirit, is a universal Intelligence, a supreme moral dynamic. Creative impulse of all, this Power guides, sustains, regenerates all—throughout time, throughout space; Lord of all worlds, "He is, He was, He shall remain."

There lives a God! God is. He is One—unique, incomparable, absolute. The historic battle-cry of Israel has been: *Sh'ma Yisroel Adonoy Elohenu Adonoy Echod:* "Hear O Israel, The Lord our God, the Lord is One."[6] The word *echod*, usually

translated as *One*, means more than a number. The *Sh'ma*
should be translated to express the conception that God is not
only one, but a *unity, unique, only*. Thus Ibn Ezra renders the
verse, "Hear O Israel: the Lord is our God, the Lord alone." [7]

Unrestricted in space, unlimited in time, He is the First and
Last, the Lord of all generations. Spiritual—and no attempt
must be made to envisage him physically— He is, nevertheless, immanent.

In the literature of Judaism we have magnificent expressions of the conviction that a supreme and conscious moral
intelligence permeates the universe and seeks to realize itself
in the life of man. Lawgiver, prophet, psalmist, sage; rabbi,
mystic, philosopher in post-biblical Judaism have given inspired expression to the conviction that a beneficent Supreme
Power rules the universe and human destiny; the universe
and human life are expressions of His mind. In the *Adon
Olam,* one of the great hymns of the synagogue, we have, perhaps, the classic expression of ethical monotheism as understood in Judaism:

> The Lord of all did reign supreme
> Ere yet this world was made and formed
> When all was finished by His will,
> Then was His name as King proclaimed.

> And should these forms no more exist,
> He still will rule in majesty.
> He was, He is, He shall remain;
> His glory never shall decrease.

> And one is He, and none there is
> To be compared or joined to Him.
> He ne'er began, and ne'er will end,
> To Him belongs dominion's power.

> He is my God, my living God;
> To Him I flee when tried in grief;
> My banner high, my refuge strong,
> Who hears and answers when I call.

> My spirit I commit to Him,
> My body, too, and all I prize,
> Both when I sleep and when I wake;
> He is with me, I shall not fear. [8]

FAITH AND REASON

The philosophers of Judaism have sought to square belief in God with speculative reason. Their speculations issue from and are controlled by their theory of knowledge. Differing though they do, the Jewish scholastics accept, in one form or another, four sources of knowledge: sense-perception, self-evident truths, logical inference, or necessitated truths, and tradition, revelation being the fountain head of tradition. For the most part, their speculations were carried on, consciously or unconsciously, under the pressure of Christian and Moslem scholasticism. For the most part they stressed the central argument in theism: the *cosmological,* supplemented with the *teleological.* To this they added the argument from *tradition,* which includes *revelation.* The *ontological* and the arguments from *assent* and *innateness* of the idea of God do not figure in their reasoning.[9]

The cosmological argument, based as it is on the principle of causality, was peculiarly congenial to the philosophers of the synagogue. Nature is not self-sufficient; it depends on a power beyond itself. There must be a Prime Cause—a Creator. Bible tradition is replete with this emphasis, from the story of creation in Genesis on. The prophets especially urged the thesis with much emotion and were not concerned with the weaknesses of the argument.

> Lift up your eyes on high
> And see: who hath created these?

It became the classic argument for the existence of God in Jewish philosophy. "He who believes in the creation believes in the Creator," declares the Rabbi in Judah Halevi's *Kitab Al Khazari.*[10] Rabbi Akiba voiced the same logic in folk terms when discussing the existence of God with a non-believer: just as the coat testifies to a tailor so does the universe testify to a Creator.

The teleological argument for the existence of God was employed by the Jewish scholastics as an aspect of the cosmological, or to establish God's goodness, mercy, knowledge. The order and beauty of nature cannot be an accident; implied is a conscious effort at design and purpose. The Potter is shaping his vessel in keeping with the ideal in His mind.

The ontological—the idea of God somehow guaranteeing its own truth—and the arguments from the universal assent and innateness of the idea of God were not pressed by the philosophers of the synagogue. They validate pantheism, and thus lead to embarrassment. Instead, the philosophers of the synagogue gave full validity to the argument from tradition: the integrity of the testimony as to the existence and nature of God given in the sacred Written and Oral traditions of Israel.

The primary service speculative reason rendered was not proving completely the existence of God nor establishing His nature as understood in Israel; it served as a corrective. Ultimately the belief in an ethical, conscious, personal God rests on faith. Reason disciplined the faith, refined it, held it in bounds, and directed the efforts issuing from and culminating in faith. It set man's face in the direction of "Yes,—there is a God above us. Nature is benevolent—certainly not malevolent bent on destroying us; life is good and life is sweet if man cooperates with God in doing His will."

Speculating on the nature of God, the Jewish scholastics— each in his own dialectic pattern—come to the same conclusions the practical rabbis posit as a matter of belief on the basis of biblical testimony.

The Doctrine of God in Rabbinic Teaching

The talmudic masters did not speculate on the existence or the nature of God. They accepted the testimony of the Bible and made it a practical moral dynamic in the life of the individual and society. Whatever attempts at speculative thinking we find in rabbinic literature are, for the most part, between the rabbis and non-Jews who challenged their belief. These speculations are elementary.

The *existence* of God is taken as an axiomatic truth; no proof is offered, for no proof is needed. The cosmological argument stands unquestioned. Confidently they reason back to the First Cause. Thus on witnessing lightning, or seeing falling stars, or lofty mountains, or great deserts, the pious Jew is required to speak a blessing extolling God as Creator: "Blessed art Thou, O Lord our God, King of the universe, Who hast made the creation." [11] "Nature is forever and constantly dependent upon God; creation is not a completed act, once and forever." God "renews every day the work of creation." "Every hour He makes provision for all who come into the world according to their need. In His grace He satisfies all creatures, not the good and righteous alone, but also the wicked and the idolators." [12]

The rabbinic sages were concerned with the practical rather than with the theoretic atheist. The true atheist is he who repudiates in act the moral law, not he who merely negates in theory theologic belief. The true atheist is one who affirms, "There is no judgment and no Judge." [13] Thus the center of gravity in the matter of belief in God, from the standpoint of the rabbinic teachers, is moral obligation rather than intellectual affirmation.

The rabbinic masters were strictly monotheistic. They never weary of emphasizing the *unity* of God. They oppose polytheism on moral grounds. "He who professes idolatry repudiates the Ten Commandments." "If a person is required to transgress all the ordinances of the Torah under threat of being put to death, he may do so with the exception of those relating to idolatry, immorality, and bloodshed." [14]

With the unity of God is bound up His *incorporeality*. To explain away the anthropomorphic terms in the Bible the rabbis assert: "We borrow terms from His creatures to apply to Him in order to assist the understanding." [15]

Incorporeality means that God is *omnipresent*. "His glory is over the earth and the heavens," chants the Psalmist.[16] The rabbinic preachers apply the text: "With an earthly king, when he is in his bed-chamber he can not be in the reception hall; but the Holy One, blessed be He, fills the upper regions and the lower." [17] Wherever there is life there is God. "In every place where you find the imprint of man's feet there am I." [18] Man is never beyond the presence of God; neither can man escape Him.

As there is no limitation on His presence, so is there no restriction on His might. He is *omnipotent*. On hearing thunder or seeing lightning, the rabbis suggest that the prayer be spoken: "Blessed be Thou, Lord our God, King of the Universe, Whose strength and might fill the world." [19]

He is *omniscient*. On seeing a crowd the pious Jew should speak a prayer, according to the teachings of the rabbis: "Blessed is He Who is wise in secrets." "Just as faces differ one from another, so are minds different, but God knows them all." [20]

He is *eternal*. "From eternity to eternity Thou art God." [21] "God's seal is truth," the rabbis assert. The Hebrew word for truth is *emeth*. The three consonants that spell the word are the first, last, and middle of the Hebrew alphabet. The rabbinic preachers draw the conclusion that just as truth is the beginning, end, and middle of the Hebrew alphabet, so is God the beginning, end, and middle of all time and creation.[22]

Justice and *mercy* are attributes of God. By these attributes He created the world. The word *Elohim* in rabbinic sources represents the quality of justice; *Jahweh* (YHWH) represents mercy. "Father of Mercies" is a common appellation for God in rabbinic literature and Jewish liturgy.

Above all is the *holiness* of God. He is "the Holy One, blessed be He," the source of the sacred in human experience. Justice, mercy and holiness are aspects of the same awesome reality. Jewish liturgy gives devout expression to it: "Holy art Thou, awe-inspiring is Thy Name; there is no God beside Thee, as it is written: The Lord of hosts is exalted in judgment, and the Holy God is sanctified in righteousness. Blessed art Thou, O Lord, the Holy King." [23] Isaiah's expression of the vision of the Holy One of Israel is the sanctification and highest level of worship in the synagogue:

Holy, Holy, Holy is the Lord of hosts:
The whole earth is full of His glory! [24]

Holiness means perfection—the supreme vision of the beauty irradiating human life, drawing man to itself as the magnet draws the needle.

Practical teachers, the rabbis avoided the metaphysical and concentrated on the moral dynamics and ethical patterns of life for the individual and the community. The attributes of God represent not so much attempts to prove the existence and identify the nature of the Eternal as positing a moral basis for human life in terms of the moral endowment of the universe—the sacred, just, merciful, loving. Basic to their ethical values and aspirations, as we shall see subsequently, is the imitation of God. "Be ye holy, for I, the Lord your God, am holy." [25] The noblest reaches of life culminate in the *sanctification of the Name;* degradation of life is the *profanation of the Name.* God is the supreme motive and pattern for human living. He is the sum, substance, and symbol of the meaning of life.

TESTIMONY OF THE MYSTICS

The mystics in Judaism play the same role mystics play in every developed religion: they seek direct communion with God and yearn for intimate fellowship with Him. They reach out toward Him with the non-rational elements of the human personality: apprehension, surmise, intuition, intense love. What is a stumbling block to the rationalists is a stepping stone to the mystics. The piety of intense faith is in them; they must give expression to it in prayer, song, meditation, ecstasy. Grand and exalted pronouncements have come from their lips touched by the fire of God's living presence; muddled sentimentality and wild confusion too have come from them. The Kabbalistic literature is a fantastic and miasmatic garden. It seduces the mind if too long exposed to it. But a tremendous earnestness broods over it. The waterfall seeks the eternal sea. The more obstacles in its path the more brilliant its efforts.

Something of the mystic is in every religious person, as it is in every artist, even as there is something of the rationalist in every mystic. The passion of the prophet and psalmist, and the piety of the legalist and sage issue in large measure from the mysticism within them. The world and the worldly are secondary; God and his will are primary. Disdain of the world and of life itself and concentration on the ever-beckoning, ever-receding Beyond is indigenous to their nature.

> Whom have I in heaven but Thee?
> And having Thee, I desire naught else upon earth.[26]

Life being a pilgrimage, and feeling himself estranged from his God, the mystic's prime urge is to find Him.

> As the hart panteth after the water brooks
> So panteth my soul after Thee, O God.
> My soul thirsteth for God, for the living God:
> 'When shall I come and appear before God?' [27]

From the earliest Bible authors, through the Psalmist, the prophets, the sages, the Kabbalists and Hasidim of medieval and modern Judaism, the stream of mysticism has run its course. Always it sought direct and intimate communion with God. The approach is that of the ardent lover rather than of the cautious legislator or rationalist. The prize is always one: God, and God alone.

Judah Halevi voices the mood of the mystics in haunting lines:

> Longing I sought Thy presence;
> Lord, with my whole heart did I call and pray;
> And going out toward Thee,
> I found Thee coming to me on the way [28]

AFFIRMATION AND NEGATION

Ethical monotheism is the Jew's supreme affirmation and negation. It is an affirmation of the beneficent forces of nature and the goodness of human life. The universe is not chaos but cosmos; law, order, purpose sustain it. "And God saw every-

thing that He hath made, and behold, it was very good." [29]
Nature is not a snake pit; it can be that, but need not be. It
can be a garden if man cooperates with God—in the rabbinic
phrase, "partner of the Holy One, blessed be He"—in doing
His will. Human life is not perpetual futility: it has meaning,
sanctity, purpose, issuing from and finding its culmination in
the meaning, sanctity, purpose of the Creator. Our coming in
and our going out of life, the fleeting days of our years, our
loves and our labors, our laughter and our tears, our triumphs
and our failures, like the notes of a symphony, are gathered
into a harmonious whole by the will of the Master. Nature is
malevolent only when misused; human life is evil or futile
only when it is abused. Touched by the divine, human life is
exalted and redeemed.

Also, ethical monotheism is the Jew's supreme negation:
negation of the idolatries of the world. Above the nature gods
and demons, above the greed and cruelty of the world, above
the black despairs haunting human life, above the fantastic
futility of the swiftly flying shuttle in the loom of human
destiny weaving a pattern of doom, above the greed and
tumult of nations, worshipping obscene Moloch, is He who
called the world into being, rouses us with the vision of the
eternal, consecrates us with His commandment to do justly,
love mercy and walk humbly with Him. Elijah on Mount
Carmel, challenging and defying the *baalim,* is a symbol of
Israel in history, the protagonist of "The Lord, He is God." [30]

IX. TORAH—HIS TESTIMONY

If Israel is the wick and God the flame, Torah is the oil in the sacred lamp that is Judaism.

The word *torah* has a diversity of meaning spelling one harmonious reality. Torah is the *Pentateuch,* the sacred scroll of the Law, treasured in the arks of the synagogues, from which specified portions are read on sacred and certain weekdays. Torah, further, is the entire *Bible* (O.T.), the Pentateuch plus the Prophets and plus the Wisdom Books. Torah is also the *entire Bible plus the Talmud and plus the further authoritative literature of the synagogue.*

Further, Torah is more than something written: Torah is also, and more profoundly, *teaching*—divine instruction and guidance as held sacred in Israel: Torah is *law* and *moral judgment,* and Torah, ultimately, is *revelation* as known in Israel—divine instruction and divine wisdom. Thus Torah is the mind of God as revealed to the priests, the prophets, the sages, the rabbis in Israel—Written and Oral—and accepted by the congregation of Israel as valid.

Rabbinic fancy plays upon the theme of Torah endlessly.

The mind of God, Torah is the blueprint of Creation itself: the Supreme Architect's vision of the world that was yet to be. Say the haggadic masters: "The Torah declares, 'I was the working tool of the Holy One, blessed be He.' In human practice, when a mortal king builds a palace, he builds it not with his own skill but with the skill of an architect. The architect, moreover, does not build it out of his head, but employs plans and diagrams to know how to arrange the chambers and the wicket doors. Thus God consulted the Torah and created the world." [1] Israel's acceptance of and fidelity to the Torah is what enables the world to maintain itself in law and order and divine purpose. Entrusted to Israel, by God's great love, the Torah is meant for all mankind. In fact, it was offered to many peoples, but they rejected it; it required too much self-sacrifice and self-discipline of its guardians. Only Israel accepted it—and that under divine compulsion. And the supreme revelation was made in all the languages of mankind, for it was meant for all the peoples of the earth.

Thus *Torah* has a technical, and hence, a limited meaning; and it has, also, a larger, comprehensive meaning. Technically it is the Scroll of the Law, containing the Five Books of Moses; in its comprehensive sense it means all the sacred literature of the synagogue, Bible, Talmud, and post-talmudic—i.e. the Written and the Oral traditions of Israel. Technically and comprehensively Torah is "the inheritance of the congregation of Jacob." [2]

We have delineated the two major categories of Torah— the Written and the Oral—and noted their complementary relationship.* We have defined also, the two ways of reading the Torah—as supernatural revelation and as an evolution.** We now turn to a consideration of Torah in the experience of the Jewish people.

TORAH IN THE EXPERIENCE OF THE JEWISH PEOPLE

First, Torah has been the Jew's very life. "It is thy life and the length of thy days," Moses exhorts his followers in the sunset of his life.[3] Joshua, as successor to Moses, is put under a divine mandate; this mandate was in time transferred to all the generations of Israel by the grace of God Himself: "This book of the law shall not depart out of thy mouth, but thou shalt meditate in it day and night." [4] The very world rests upon it. The study of Torah outweighs all other virtues and disciplines taught by the rabbis as heirs to the lawgivers, prophets, and sages. One's house must be a meeting place of the wise. Self-sacrifice is a privilege and privation is sweet in its behalf; martyrdom out of loyalty to the Torah is sanctify-

* See Chapter IV, Foundations of Faith.
** See Chapter V.

ing God's Name. Only eternal vigilance will keep the lamp of learning burning in Jewry and in the life of every soul in Jewry, for "he who does not increase his learning decreases it." [5] The sacred river must not be a stagnant pool. No special merit is his who acquires much Torah, "for there unto wast thou created." [6]

As the very flame of life, Torah has been the highest good in Jewry. Not by the might and pomp of empire but by Torah has the Jew lived. The cultivated Jew seeks not honor nor worldly glory; he does not hanker after the tables of kings. He is the servant of the Holy One, Blessed be He, and therefore "thy table is greater than theirs." [7] It rests like a benediction upon the Jew, for it brings the presence of God upon him who studies it faithfully.

It endows him with fine manners, grace, brings him the love of God and love of man, liberates him, and renders him immortal. Torah is the eternal life God had planted in Israel. It brings to the faithful abounding joy in this life and bliss in the world to come. Supremely happy is he "whose delight is in the Law of the Lord," for "The Law of the Lord is perfect restoring the soul." [8] Folk fancy exhausted itself in the exaltation of Torah. It wove chaplets of grace for every faithful son. Mothers rocked their babes to sleep with songs dreaming of careers of learning; the aged closed their Book in this world only to open it anew and study Torah throughout eternity at the feet of the Master.

Thus, inevitably, Torah has been the intermediary between God and man. "The heavens are the heavens of the Lord, but the earth hath He given to the sons of men." [9] God was in His high heavens, and man was on earth, very much below; between the two there was no commerce, observe the rabbinic teachers, until God entrusted the Torah to Israel. Intellectual pursuit, in the realm of the divine, performs the gracious miracle of bringing God down to man and raising man toward God.

Second, in the long sweep of Jewish history, Torah has been the Jew's portable fatherland. It was his own good earth; his

own divine landscape. In it he lived; within it he realized himself. From it he summoned his heroes, who spoke to him of
his duties, his high lineage, his patriotism, his exalted destiny.
He could always meet his adversaries with the words of the
Psalmist on his lips:

> Why are the nations in uproar?
> And why do the peoples mutter in vain?

The Lord's anointed will not be crushed by the kings of the
earth who understand only physical might.

> He that sitteth in heaven laugheth
> The Lord hath them in derision.[10]

The ramparts of Torah sustained the Jew in the teeth of every
cruelty and adversity and preserved him longer than any state
in history preserved its nationals.

Tyrants knew well that Israel was impregnable as long as
Israel remained true to its Torah. The first attacks by those
who would destroy Jewry were aimed at the schools and the
scholars. The martyrdom of Hananiah ben Teradion, in the
days of the Hadrianic persecutions, is symbolic. The imperial
command against teaching and the ordination of scholars left
Hananiah ben Teradion undismayed. He went about his sacred duties as teacher in Israel. He paid the price. Talmudic
traditions have preserved reports of his martyrdom. Wrapped
in a scroll of the law, he was burned. His pupils witnessed his
agony. "Master, what seest thou?" they are reported as asking
him. The dying man replied, "I see the parchment burning
while the letters of the Law soar upward." [11] The letters of the
Law always soared upward—a flaming, defiant vision. The
Jew's portable fatherland has been impregnable. Like David,
Israel met all the Goliaths of history with the conviction:
"Thou comest to me with a sword and with a spear and with a
javelin; but I come to thee in the Name of the Lord of hosts." [12]

Third, in the experience of Israel, Torah has been the seat
of authority.

An extra-territorial group, with no system of organization
holding the scattered communities together, with no police

power, called upon to regulate every aspect of its own life—civil as well as religious—for many centuries, with no ecclesiastic hierarchy to adjudicate, decree, and impose, Jewry, nevertheless, found in the Torah all the sanctions and precedents and principles to regulate its life, century after century.

The Pharisaic masters took the abstract word of God and made it the rule for everyday life. Juridic discussions and debates in the academies kept the law abreast of life as best it might be. The Oral Law and the process of interpretation and reinterpretation enabled them to meet the needs of the age. The sacred text, the weight of tradition, and public opinion gave them the power of enforcement. The scholar of the law became the judge by popular consent; courts were staffed by scholars and no sheriffs were on the premises to enforce the decisions. At most only minor, petty disciplines, besides excommunications, were at times invoked.

The Torah afforded the jurists the sanctions they needed. Its authority was final, for no one Jew—as a Jew—could appeal beyond the Torah. There was no higher authority. He might question the judge but not the Law.

Fourth, Torah unified Jewish life.

Interpretations always varied; every page of the Talmud is a debate. Frequently the debates are sharp. The assertion that "scholars increase the peace of the world," is only a pious wish. In practice scholars are the foci of dissension, even strife. Pious scholars—alas!—in unhappy periods of history burned the books of their opponents.

But at the core of all the debates and disputations and excommunications was always a center of unity. The Torah embraced all her faithful children and afforded every aroused mind the arguments it needed. Generations arose which reclaimed in reverence the heretics of former ages. There was no pontificating power able to freeze the word of God, for the Torah has ever been the heritage of the congregation of Jacob, not the exclusive possession of any ecclesiastic fraternity.

The Torah is Israel's beauty, its strength, its authority, its comfort, its immortality. It consecrates Israel and renders it worthy of its high destiny. Say the sages, in the words of Rabbi Hananiah, "The Holy One, blessed be He, was pleased to make Israel worthy; therefore He gave them a copious Torah and many commandments, as it is said, 'It pleased the Lord, for His righteousness' sake, to magnify the Torah and make it honorable.' " [13]

X. ISRAEL—HIS WITNESS

The appellations "Hebrew," "Israelite," "Jew" are interchangeable. The earliest designation is "Hebrew." The word is from the Hebrew *'Ibhri,* "one who is from across (the river)," referring to Abraham who had come to Canaan from across the Euphrates. The name applied to his descendants. "Hebrew" also designates the language. "Israel" is derived from the Bible story of Jacob's wrestling with the angel, as reported in Genesis 32:28: *Yisro-el, champion of God.* The name thus designates the descendants of the patriarch Jacob, the *children of Israel.* "Jew" is derived from the Hebrew *Yehudi;* originally, one belonging to the tribe or Kingdom of Judah. After the return from the Babylonian captivity under Ezra-Nehemiah, the name came to designate any member of the new state; hence it came to apply to the descendants of Abraham, Isaac and Jacob, who were known as *Hebrews,* or *Israelites.* In the course of time *Yehudi* passed through several languages: Aramaic, Greek, Old French, and was transformed to *Jew.*[1] This appellation is the preferable one for a Jewish person.

With the establishment of the State of Israel in 1948, a new need arose to clarify the meaning of *Israel.* Historically, the name applied to the Jewish people the world over; that is the significance of the name in our time. The nation is the *State of Israel,* and the two must not be confused. A citizen of the State of Israel is an *Israeli.* He may or may not be an Israelite, or a Jew. *Israeli* is a purely national term; *Israelite* or *Jew* are religious terms.[2]

ISRAEL THE RELIGIOUS COMMUNITY

In Bible and Talmud, and in all the authoritative post-talmudic literature of the synagogue, *Israel* is a religious

77

community; in the language of the talmudic masters it is a *k'neset yisroel*. The ties that bind the Jewish people into one are sacred ties; ties of faith and observance, ancestral memories, prophetic hopes, rabbinic disciplines, common responsibilities. They are historic and psychologic ties. Issuing from the smouldering heights of Sinai as the direct revelation of God to Moses, or from the aspirations of men in whose heart is His Law as a progressive revelation, Judaism is a conscious cultivation of the sacred as formulated and integrated in Jewry. The people Israel is the embodiment of this faith and discipline. Approaching Mount Sinai, where the Israelites were to enter into an everlasting covenant with their God, Moses, in the name of God, determines their faith and fate: "Now therefore, if ye will hearken unto my voice indeed, and keep my covenant, then ye shall be Mine own treasure from among all peoples; for all the earth is Mine; and ye shall be unto Me a kingdom of priests and a holy nation." [3] "Ye are My witnesses, saith the Lord," affirms the prophet; [4] or, in the language of the Psalmist,

> When Israel came forth out of Egypt,
> The house of Jacob from a people of a strange language,
> Judah became His sanctuary,
> Israel his dominion.[5]

The rabbinic masters, after the manner of Hosea, often speak of Israel as a woman betrothed to the Lord.[6]

An eternal covenant obtains between the children of Israel and God, a covenant of loyalty to the divine as revealed or developed in the course of the many ages. "I will put my law in their inward parts, and in their hearts will I write it; and I will be their God and they shall be My people." [7] Jewry is thus the living body of the faith. What the Church is to Christianity, Jewry is to Judaism. The Jewish people derives the meaning of its life, its historic purposes, its ideals and its duties from the sacred it champions. Thus does Israel stand true to its name *Yisroel*, champion of God. Priest, prophet, and psalmist, the talmudic masters and their disciples, "and all the disciples of their disciples," and martyrs in all ages, testify to the integrity of the people Israel as a religious community. This religious character of Israel it is that distinguished the Israelitish nation back in Bible times; when the theocratic state fell, Israel—largely transformed into a congregation as a result of the Babylonian exile, and particularly after the fall of the Temple and State in the year 70 of the Common Era—made religious loyalties the sole basis of its life among the nations. Thenceforth Jewry became *the adath yisroel,* the community, or the congregation, of Israel.

PEOPLEHOOD, NOT RACE, NOT NATION

Implied in the historic *religious community* conception of Israel is the *peoplehood* of Israel.

The Jews are not a race, as racists would have it, neither a primary nor secondary race. History and anthropology refute the racist claim. The Jews hold in their veins the blood of every people with whom they have come into contact in the course of their millennia of wanderings the world over.

A race is a division of mankind "the members of which, though individually varying, are characterized as a group, by a certain combination of morphological and metrical features, principally nonadaptive, which have been derived from their common descent." [8] The tests of race are physical: head and face form, color of the eyes, shape of the nose, ears, lips; color of the skin, color and character of the hair, etc. An anthropologic examination of Jewry results in the complete negation of the racist claim. [9] A glimpse into Jewish history corroborates the findings of the anthropologists.

The oldest Bible sources testify that the Hebrew stock is derived from the mixture of diverse racial strains. The diffusion has continued to the present day.

In its earliest days in Canaan the Hebrew people mixed freely with the many peoples that inhabited that tight little land. The Deuteronomist declares, "a wandering Aramean was my father." [10] The prophet Ezekiel, particularist though he was, speaks of Israel as a mixed people from its very birth.

"Thine origin and thy nativity is of the land of the Canaanites; thy father was an Amorite and thy mother was a Hittite." [11] Many of the heroes of Hebrew history took non-Hebrew wives. The mingling has continued for several thousand years. The reformation of Ezra testifies to a radical admixture of foreign blood; the book of Ruth would have us believe that King David, the most popular hero in Jewish history, was partly Moabitish. Many voluntarily embraced Judaism, in biblical, talmudic, medieval and modern times. The New Testament complains of the zeal with which the Pharisees sought converts to Judaism.[12] In the wake of the Maccabaean war the Asmonean dynasty compelled conversion to Judaism. The talmudic masters prescribe the conditions and ritual for conversion. Some of the leading Jewish masters were proselytes, or descendants of proselytes. Josephus reports conversions to Judaism among the ruling aristocracy of his day. In the eighth century the Chazars, a people of Turkish or Finnish ancestry, embraced Judaism. The Jews, like all peoples that have lived along the highways of history, are a mixed people.

The crucial evil in the claims of the racists is the assertion that physical characteristics carry spiritual corrolates. Anthropology repudiates this notion. The claims of the racists anywhere rest on political romanticism with a will to superiority.

The only basis in history Jewish racists have is that there were always some Jews, as there were some non-Jews, who thought and taught in terms of racial purity. Ezra and his emphasis on the "holy seed" is a historic fact which has had a particularistic influence in Judaism. Two facts must be noted in this connection: *First,* there was violent opposition to Ezra, not only among the prophetic spirits in Israel, who gave us the books of Ruth and Jonah in protest, but among the masses. There is no evidence whatever that Ezra's decree requiring Jewish men to divorce their non-Jewish wives was enforced. *Second,* even Ezra subordinated the so-called race to God and the Moral Law. The highest good for Israel is not Israel the race, but God and His will. Thus the Pentateuch legislates in behalf of the alien. "And the stranger (alien) shall ye not oppress. . . . And ye shall love the stranger. . . . The stranger shall be unto you as the home-born (native). As for the Congregation, there shall be one statute both for you, and for the stranger that sojourneth with you, a statute forever throughout your generations; as ye are, so shall the stranger be before the Lord." [13] The talmudic masters, disciples of Ezra, repeatedly interpret biblical texts in terms of one humanity rather than separatistic races. Thus in the introductory verse to Genesis V—"This is the book of the generations of Adam" —they translate *Adam* as *Man* and see in the verse "a major premise in the Torah." [14] All men—of whatever race—ultimately issue from the same Adam and Eve, and they were made by the Lord of the Universe from the dust gathered from all parts of the earth, so that no group might say that it is made of superior stuff.

Common descent, however, is a basic fact in Israel as a religious community. Judaism is a family religion. Jews are born into Judaism, just as people are born into families, tribes, nations. A sense of kinship is a reality and a cherished ideal. It makes for communal responsibility. "Israelites are responsible for one another." [15] However, common ancestry is subordinated to the ideals of the faith and thus deflected from the racial. People of non-Jewish ancestry may embrace Judaism. "One who has become a proselyte is like a child newly born." [16] Conversion to Judaism is an ancient and honored institution. In the liturgy of the synagogue is a prayer invoking God's blessing upon the righteous gentile who identifies himself with the community of Israel.[17] And Jews can leave the faith. They do so when by word or deed they declare themselves to be no longer members of the Jewish household. When they do surrender their Judaism, or when they accept another faith, they cease being Jews. Marriage of Jews with non-Jews is opposed on religious, not racial, grounds. When the non-Jewish party accepts Judaism the prohibition is removed, and the marriage is in keeping with every standard of Jewish law and custom.

Thus the *k'neset* concept of Israel draws on the racial and transforms common ancestry and a sense of kinship into aspects of faith. Conversely, the racial concept draws on the communal by extolling ancestry and kinship into supreme values in themselves thus turning them into racism. Similarly, the *community* concept draws on the *national* and makes various factors, indigenous to modern nationalism, expressions of faith.

Neither are the Jews of the world a nation. National memories, national customs, national holidays, a historic language are the strands of which modern nationalism is woven. In Judaism they are transmuted into religion. The memory of an ancestral land, Palestine, became part of messianism; Passover, which might have been only a national holiday, became a religious festival of freedom, celebrating God's liberation of the oppressed. Shabuot, which might have become a national "Constitution Day," became a religious festival memorializing the revelation on Mount Sinai. The Maccabees were more than national liberators who expelled the invaders; they were priests who cleansed the desecrated altars and re-dedicated the sanctuary. National memories point not to empire builders but to protagonists of faith:

> "Hearken unto Me, ye that follow after righteousness,
> Ye that seek the Lord;
> Look unto the rock whence ye were hewn,
> And to the hole of the pit whence ye were digged.
> Look unto Abraham your father,
> And unto Sarah that bore you . . ." [18]

The covenant between God and Israel was made not by kings and empire builders with the command to go forth and conquer with the sword, but by the patriarch who heard the voice of God commanding him to go forth "and be a blessing," by lawgivers, prophets, psalmists. Israel is a people dedicated to the Holy One; Jewry is a covenanted community.

Not A Nation

Dispersed the world over after the fall of the Temple and the State in the year 70, Jewry considered itself in *galut*, exile.

It was an expatriated people. It led an abnormal life. It was on alien soil, in a hostile world—like Cain, a stranger and a wanderer on earth. The spiritual problem of the Diaspora was forever pressing on the conscience and consciousness of religious Jewry: "How shall we sing the Lord's song in a strange land?" And in strange, hostile, alien lands the children of Israel were compelled to live.

"Diaspora" thus designated not only a geographic condition but a spiritual depression even more.

In the geographic sense, the Diaspora was a large fact in the history of Israel long before the fall of Judah to the Romans. In Alexandria of the second-third centuries of the pre-Christian era there were a larger number of Jews than in Palestine. But it was a voluntary migration, determined by economic, social needs. With the fall of Judah, the Diaspora turned into a state of religious exile, a punishment for the sins of the people. The pious Jew supplicated his God: "Because of our sins have we been driven from our land," and prayed for righteousness and grace to merit God's redemptive restoration: ". . . lift up the ensign to gather our exiles, and gather us from the four corners of the earth. Blessed art Thou, O Lord, who gatherest the banished ones of thy people Israel." [19]

Always there was a creative relationship between Palestine and the Diaspora. The Bible landscape is Palestinian; its heroes—patriarchs, lawgivers, prophets, sages, psalmists— walked on the soil of the Holy Land. Hebrew, the sacred tongue of synagogue and academy, impregnated even the vernacular of the Jewish masses in their every-day life. Bible metaphor carried their personal feelings. The holy days— ordained in the Bible—are Palestinian in setting. Messianic dreams for restoration to the Holy Land, in God's own good time, ever stimulated Jewish thinking and aspiration.

In his daily devotions, on the Sabbath, on the Holy Days and Festivals, the Jew prayed for restoration to his land and the cradle of his heritage. "Next year in Jerusalem!"

Practical ties too united Palestine with the Diaspora. For

many generations scholars were ordained in Palestine only; from Palestinian academies the sages transmitted the tradition to "the scattered nation." A constant stream of financial aid flowed from every corner of the Diaspora to Palestinian institutions. Endless hosts of pious pilgrims journeyed to Palestine to sleep with their fathers in holy soil.

But Judaism is a Diaspora religion. Mount Sinai is not in Palestine. The Bible itself is not entirely Palestinian; large portions of it were written, and much of it edited, outside Palestine. The Babylonian Talmud has been more influential in moulding Judaism than the Palestinian. The synagogue itself is of Babylonian origin. If this be denied, and a Palestinian origin ascribed to the synagogue, as some competent scholars maintain, it can not be denied that the synagogue developed and attained its historic nature in the Diaspora. The every-day and holy day ritual of the synagogue is a Diaspora creation. The masters who shaped the mind of the synagogue were of the Diaspora. Philo, Saadia, Crescas, Maimonides, Albo, Gabirol, Halevi formulated their imposing systems of Jewish theology in response to the challenges of Hellenic, Christian and Mohammedan theologians. Many of the customs and ceremonies—observed as divine law in Orthodoxy—are borrowed from non-Jewish environments.

Rooted in Bible and the Holy Land, Judaism is, nevertheless, largely a Diaspora religion. Jerusalem beckoned Jewry like the morning star, but it has been an idealized, allegorized, Golden Jerusalem, aglow with messianic radiance.

Thus Palestine and the Diaspora have been in embrace all through the centuries, one quickening the other.

With the Emancipation of European and American Jewry in the eighteenth-nineteenth centuries, a definition of relationship between the two became an imperative necessity. The Jew in lands of freedom, where he acquired the status of a free citizen, in terms of equality with the rest of the population, his rights and liberties guaranteed by the basic laws of the lands, could no longer consider himself in exile.

When the State of Israel was established in 1948, and every Jew, citizen of a free land, could, if he wished, return to the land of Israel or remain a citizen of the land in which he lived, exile lost all meaning. Thus, politically there can be no official political ties whatever between the Jews of democratic states and the State of Israel. They are Jews, not Israelis. Their national loyalties belong exclusively to the countries of which they are citizens, in keeping with the laws of these countries. The only ties that can bind them to the State of Israel are spiritual and voluntary. The Bible, the prayers, the holy days, the language will be energizing and stimulating world Jewry; world Jewry will, in turn, bring its gifts to Zion, and these will be not merely material. World Jewry has precious spiritual gifts to bring to Israeli culture, gifts in terms of faith and freedom acquired and developed over many centuries in many lands.

THE CHOSEN PEOPLE

Jewry considers itself under the mandate of the Eternal to serve as His witness unto the nations. The purposes of God are the purposes of Jewish life. The covenant binding Israel to God and God to Israel makes Israel a dedicated people, drafted to serve as "a light unto the nations." Thus Israel is a *Chosen People*.

The word *chosen* is not an adequate translation of the Hebrew term *am segullah*, literally *a treasure people* or the *domain* of the Lord. However, the rendition *Chosen People* has come to connote Jewry as a dedicated, and hence a unique, people.

Every high calling involves a form of particularism. Israel is the particular people of the universal God. Israel is set apart by virtue of its consecration, as the priest is set apart from the laity, or the prophet is set apart from the general community. The children of Israel are to the nations what the Sabbath is to the rest of the week. Israel is a people that had heard the call and had taken vows. This doctrine of Israel's election is "the central point in Jewish theology and the key to the understanding of the nature of Judaism." [20] The zeal of separatists has at times reduced the doctrine to a narrow, exclusive force; the exalted vision of the prophets made it a powerful moral dynamic in the universal aspirations of Israel. The two tendencies have contended for supremacy in the history of Judaism.

Like all basic values in Judaism the doctrine of the *Chosen People* is the result of a long evolution. Its beginnings were primitive, originating in a primitive age. The covenant between Yahweh and Israel was a tribal one: Israel was Yahweh's own tribe; Yahweh was Israel's deity. The interests of one were the interests of the other. It differed, however, from other such tribal-deity relationships in that the covenant was voluntary and ethical, in terms of moral values, not merely in terms of blood or of tribal ethos. One might not desert the other; both were held by ties of duty. As the conception of God developed toward its awesome grandeur as the Lord of the universe—the Father of all men, He Who called the generations into being, the God of justice, mercy, holiness—the election of Israel was raised accordingly. It became a prophetic imperative in the life of Jewry.

The classic expression of the doctrine is given by the unknown prophet who is identified as Deutero-Isaiah (Isaiah 40 ff.).

God is the Lord of the universe, "the First and the Last," Whose awesome presence dominates the universe and infuses it with life and moral purpose. "Before Me there was no God formed, neither shall there be after Me." [21] Sovereign and Eternal, there can be no tribal covenants between Himself and any one branch of the human family. Universal redemption, not tribal favoritism, is His will. Israel's splendid privilege it is to serve as His servant—at times His suffering servant—to establish His justice, compassion, holiness in the life of humanity.

> Behold My servant, whom I uphold;
> Mine elect, in whom My soul delighteth;

I have put My spirit upon him,
He shall make the right to go forth to the nations.
He shall not cry, nor lift up,
Nor cause his voice to be heard in the street.
A bruised reed shall he not break,
And the dimly burning wick shall he not quench;
He shall make the right to go forth according to the truth.
He shall not fail nor be crushed,
Till he have set the right in the earth;
And the isles shall wait for his teaching.

Thus saith God the Lord,
He that created the heavens, and stretched them forth,
He that spread forth the earth and that which cometh out of it,
He that giveth breath unto the people upon it,
And spirit to them that walk therein;
I the Lord have called thee in righteousness,
And have taken hold of thy hand,
And kept these, and set thee for a covenant of the people,
For a light of the nations;
To open the blind eyes,
To bring out the prisoners from the dungeon,
And them that sit in darkness out of the prison-house.
I am the Lord, that is My name;
And my glory will I not give to another.[22]

Israel is thus consecrated as the prophetic herald of a new heaven and a new earth. His post of duty is to be a coworker with God in creating one harmonious humanity under the sovereignty of the Almighty. Not special privileges but extra obligations rest upon him. This is the prophetic interpretation of the doctrine.[23]

The rabbinic masters carried forward the doctrine, enunciating it in many ways in the voluminous literature of the synagogue; they made it part of the liturgy of every-day and holy day worship. Their central task being to fortify a harassed people and keep it faithful to its covenant, they found in the doctrine a reservoir of living waters. It fortified Jewry with the will to live and built fervent morale in the teeth of every adversity. It afforded further, a high level of idealism, lifting Jewry above the idolatries of the world.

Fear not, for I have redeemed thee,
I have called thee by thy name, thou art mine.
When thou passest through the waters, I will be with thee,
And through the rivers, they shall not overflow thee;
When thou walkest through the fire, thou shalt not be burned,
Neither shall the flame kindle thee.
For I am the Lord thy God,
The Holy One of Israel, thy Saviour.[24]

The rabbinic teachers could thus assert: "One kingdom comes and another goes; one decree against Israel follows another, but Israel abides forever. They have not been foresaken, nor shall they be consumed. . . ."[25]

The everlasting love of God has rested upon Israel by the power of this doctrine; the bitter waters of a sad earth could not quench it, for Israel had chosen God.

BASIS OF ADJUSTMENT

The people Israel has been "a people dwelling alone, not counted among the nations." The characterization spoken by a heathen seer in early Bible days became a historic reality. "The Wandering Jew" became part of the legendry of the Western World. Jewry has been *among* the peoples, not *of* the peoples. Not till the dawn of the emancipation, which came in response to the mighty poundings of the French Revolution and the cry of *Liberte, egalite, fraternite,* could Jewry seriously anticipate equality of rights and opportunities anywhere on earth.* In its long exile among the nations it had to find a footing not only politically and economically; it had to achieve a harmonious adjustment within itself and its treasured heritage in an inhospitable environment. Spiritually, Jewry had its own portable fatherland, the *Torah;* for that it reserved its supreme loyalty. As for the laws of the state, it considered them supreme in civil matters. The talmudic principle became established; the civil law is supreme in civil matters; in matters of religious belief and observance

* See Chapters III and V.

Jewry reserved the right to self-determination; *dina d'mal-chuta dina.*[26]

The adjustment was dictated by the immediate practical needs of disfranchised people and by conscience. To the exiles in Babylon, carried away by Nebuchadnezzar, the prophet Jeremiah had written his letter of advice:

> "Build ye houses, and dwell in them, and plant gardens, and eat the fruit of them; take ye wives, and beget sons and daughters; and take wives for your sons, and give your daughters to husbands, that they may bear sons and daughters; and multiply ye there, and be not diminished. And seek the peace of the city whither I have caused you to be carried away captive, and pray unto the Lord for it; for in the peace thereof shall ye have peace." [27]

The prophet's advice became the basis of Jewish adjustment to its environment among the nations: Jewry seeks its own peace and prosperity within the larger peace and prosperity, always reserving the right to worship God in keeping with the dictates of its own conscience. In the long, dark stretches of intolerance that have afflicted our earth, religious Jewry of necessity became the champion of the dissenters. It would not bow its head nor bend its knees before the tyrants and the bigots. It insisted on the right to live in peace and dignity by seeking the general well-being and observing the laws of the state, all the while it insisted on remaining true to its God in keeping with its own best understanding.

> "Let all the peoples walk each one in the name of its God,
> But we will walk in the name of the Lord our God for ever and ever" [28]

By its life as a dissenting group, Jewry has held open the gates of religious freedom, braving all the storms of tyranny. The liberalism and democracy of the Western world stands deeply indebted to religious Jewry.

THE PEOPLE OF THE COVENANT

Thoughtful men have reflected upon the Jew's immortality. They have asked: What has made the Jew immortal? Kingdoms have risen and kingdoms have passed away, but the Jews endure forever. What explains this defiant fact in history?

A number of secular reasons have been advanced. Each may be valid, within its own limited sphere of concern; none gives the complete answer. Ultimately the answer is from faith. The Jewish people have been the people of the covenant. Servants of the Eternal—by choice or by compulsion—Israel has partaken of the eternal. That is the primary answer.

In its sense of consecration Jewry has found a well of living waters. As long as faithful sons and daughters in historic Israel could say, from the depths of conviction,

> Behold, God is my salvation;
> I will trust and will not be afraid;
> For God the Lord is my strength and song;
> And He is become my salvation,[29]

the Jew found the wells of salvation and thus achieved immortality.

Religious Jewry rejoices in God and lives; may God rejoice in Jewry.

THE ETHICS OF JUDAISM

XI. MAN AND HIS CAPACITIES

BODY AND SOUL

Ultimately religion finds its embodiment in personality. Unless it does it is false religion. Neither synagogues nor churches nor mosques, neither Bible nor Koran nor Talmud embody the faith. Religion is in the lives of men and women; it is in the fiber of the human personality. "Build me a sanctuary that I may dwell among them," reads a Bible commandment.[1] The rabbis were quick to observe that the plural "in them," instead of "in it," refers to the human beings who build the sanctuary.

The primary aim of the Torah is to sanctify life. That is predicated on the spiritual potentiality of human nature. Human nature can and does respond to the call of the divine. In the human is the divine. The capacities with which Judaism endows the individual form the basis of Jewish ethics.

Man is neither angel nor brute; he is something of each. Body and soul are not in conflict; one complements the other. What lifts man above the brute is his soul; but we know no disembodied souls. Man is both: physical and spiritual. The physical and spiritual are not mutually repellent; rather, they form one harmonious whole: man endowed with the imprint of the divine. "All creatures," say the rabbinic masters, in their own allegoric way, "which are formed from heaven, both their soul and their body are from heaven; and all creatures which are formed from the earth, both their soul and their body are from earth, with the exception of man, whose soul is from heaven and his body is from earth." [2]

The human body is God's masterpiece. It is a marvelous instrument. It is the scabbard, not the prison, of the soul. Judaism and medicine are peculiarly congenial. The physi-

93

cian's calling is honored and revered. The physician is a servant of God. To care for and cultivate the body is a religious duty. "Ye shall not make yourselves abominable." [3] Physical cleanliness leads to spiritual purity.[4] "One should wash his face, and feet, and hands every day out of respect for His Maker." [5] The talmudic teachers prescribe rules of health and diet.

SPIRITUAL ENDOWMENT

But man is more than a body. Man can think brave thoughts and storm the heavens; he can delve into the mysteries of the universe, weigh the sun, split the atom; he is self-conscious and self-critical. He can think and act selflessly. He is a creator; he composes symphonies, writes poems, moulds art, rears stately mansions of mortar, brick, and steel, and stately mansions of the soul. He dreams dreams, and has capacity for martyrdom. The golden book of martyrdom, in every sphere of human endeavor, from the day when conscience dawned to our own, refutes the assertion that self-preservation is the first law of human nature. Man cherishes values and ideals and loyalties far more precious to him than his own life. He surrenders his life rather than compromise the vision.

Man is impelled by powers beyond the physical and the glandular; he has within himself powers that lift him out of the merely naturalistic. A spark of the divine is within him, disturbing the clod.

The rabbinic teachers interpret the biblical phrase, "in the image of God made He him" [6] in the spiritual sense only. Any suggestion of the physical likeness of God would be unthinkable to them. And it is to be understood, also, only in its potentiality. Man has the capacity to develop himself after the image of God. Thus developed, man is indeed, "a little lower than the angels." [7] "Beloved is man," avers Rabbi Akiba, "in that he was fashioned in the image of God." [8]

The soul, the breath of God in man, came pure from God. There is no "original sin" in Judaism. Adam was punished with mortality, not with moral depravity. The Jewish prayer book states it clearly: "The soul which Thou, O God, has given unto me came pure from Thee. Thou hast created it, Thou has formed it, Thou hast breathed it into me; Thou hast preserved it in this body and, at the appointed time, Thou wilt take it from this earth that it may enter upon life ever-lasting." [9] Man is not a fallen angel; rather, he is a risen brute reaching out for the divine.

Asceticism is therefore discouraged in Judaism. The emphases of the Essenes have not become the standard of Jewish practice. Celibacy is thwarting the divine as well as the human. Man needs a helpmeet. He finds the meaning, dignity and joy of his life in marriage and family. That is part of God's design.

MORAL ENDOWMENTS

Man has not only spiritual but, also, moral endowments. Man's moral nature, like the existence of God, is taken for granted. These moral endowments are expressed in three areas of his personality; his instincts (*yetzer*, good and bad), conscience, and the freedom of the will.

INSTINCT

In every man is the instinct for good and the instinct for evil. Whence comes one and whence the other? Is one of God and the other of the devil? Or, shall we agree that evil is non-existent altogether? Judaism accepts human nature as it is and seeks to mould it after "the image of God."

When God was about to create man, the rabbinic masters aver, the angels objected. They were panicky. Gathered about His throne of glory they pleaded with Him not to fashion so inconstant an agent as man. "What is man that Thou art mindful of him? Of what value might he be to the Almighty?" Man will desecrate His image; he will cheat and lie, covet and kill. The Holy One silenced the angelic beings. What do bloodless, angelic beings, who are eternally untempted, pure, blameless, know of life with its temptations and sins? Man with his human instincts does, and he—with all the good and evil impulses within him—can rise in the scale of human excellence to a point where he may fulfill His Law and commandments. The Moral Law is meant for human beings, not angels.[10]

What we call the evil inclination is not evil altogether. That too is part of His eternal design. Were it not for the evil *yetzer*, "man would not build a house, marry and beget children, nor would he engage in enterprise." [11] "He (the evil *yetzer*) is as necessary for the world as rain." [12] Not suppressing human instincts but refining and disciplining them by the moral law is the desire of Judaism. The righteous are the people who master their impulses; the wicked are the people who are mastered by their impulses.

CONSCIENCE

There is no Hebrew word for "conscience" in the Bible nor the Talmud; but the reality it describes is, of course, primary in the minds of the lawgivers, prophets, Psalmist, sages, rabbis. It is His Law in the heart of man. The moral compulsion of man issues from a divine endowment within him. Conscience is the voice of God, and conscience is the adviser, judge, censor. With conscience must go understanding and wisdom. The Hebrew word for the rational—*sechel*—means more than intellectuality; it means, also, wisdom and moral judgment. It is in this larger sense that the medieval Jewish philosophers, as well as the talmudic masters, use the word. Conscience, like every faculty of man, needs to be refined, cultivated, disciplined by enlightened moral judgment.

FREEDOM OF THE WILL

The freedom of the will is as axiomatic as the existence of God and the moral endowments of man. Man does have the capacity to bring himself in line with the will of God. The entire moral life rests on this premise. Ezekiel rests his case for individual responsibility on the freedom of the individual to choose the good and reject the evil.[13] In that he speaks for prophet, lawgiver, sage and rabbi. The summons to the godly life would have no meaning if man were not free to obey the summons; neither would there be any meaning to the summons if it were determined, inevitably, that man follow the good or the evil course.

> See, I have set before thee this day life and good, and death and evil, in that I command thee this day to love the Lord thy God, to walk in His ways and keep His statutes and His ordinances; then thou shalt live and multiply, and the Lord thy God shall bless thee. . . . I call heaven and earth to witness against you this day, that I have set before thee life and death, the blessing and the curse; therefore choose life, that thou mayest live, thou and thy seed.[14]

How to square human freedom with God's providence, and, further, how to square it with the contradictory experiences of life issuing from heredity and environment, occupied the minds of the Jewish philosophers as well as the minds of thinking men everywhere. They found themselves oscillating between the two horns of the dilemma—God's absoluteness and man's moral responsibility. In Judaism, however, the discomfort of this dilemma was eased considerably by the belief that God is forever active in the world, not merely as a power that has set the mechanism and released it, disowning responsibility by it. It was eased, further, by the belief that man is an active coworker with Him in evolving a world in keeping with His will. To achieve freedom the Jew need not deny God. The frustrations and defeats, and the miscarriages of justice from our human standpoint, are incidents in the ever ongoing process of creation, and ultimate fulfillment of His will.

IMMORTALITY

In man's spiritual and moral endowments, issuing as these do from the Eternal, is his immortality.

The question, "If man die shall he live again?"[15] occupied

—and even preoccupied—the minds of religious men. There
is only little of it in the Old Testament; most of the references
to life in the timeless future found in the Hebrew Bible are
concerned with the nation rather than with the individual.
The biblical emphasis is on the will of God in the life of man
and his society in the present life, and in the unfolding ages
still in the womb of time. However, a time came when the
question of immortality—continued life and just retribution
in the beyond—was raised in Israel, and was denied, as in Job,
or affirmed vaguely, as in Ecclesiastes.[16] Difficult phrases in
the Psalms have been used as evidence of the reality of the
belief in Israel.

As all major doctrines in Judaism, the belief in immortality
has undergone an evolution.

Primitive folk notions current in ancient Israel are reflected
in certain expressions in the Bible: "He was gathered to his
fathers," *Sheol, Duma;* a witch brings up the ghost of Samuel
on Saul's insistence and to his consternation. Nebuchadnezzar
is described as descending to the pit of the nether world, and
there the ghosts of the once mighty monarchs are conscious
enough to jeer his fall.[17] However, biblical Judaism is totally
indifferent to the shadowy existence after death. These mani-
festations of other-world existence were viewed, evidently, as
belonging to necromancy, sorcery, divination. Belief in immortality was not employed by the biblical masters to balance
the scales of God's justice or His apparent injustice.

The doctrine of immortality became an organic part of Judaism among the Pharisees, at the beginning of the Christian
era. It did not attain any definitely expressed form in the
Talmud. It is spoken of in a double sense: continued life and
just retribution for the individual, and judgment and ultimate
resurrection for the individual. The latter is part of the eschatology of Judaism of the early centuries of the Common Era.
Both forms of immortality are personal. The Orthodox prayerbook commits Orthodox Judaism to a belief in both these concepts of immortality. Maimonides affirms resurrection "at the

time when it shall please the Creator" to be one of the thirteen principles of Judaism.

Side by side with the belief in physical—however shadowy —immortality developed the concept of spiritual immortality. In the book of Ecclesiastes is its basic outline: "The body returns to the earth as it was; the spirit returneth unto God who gave it." [18] Reform Judaism takes its stand, officially, on this concept of spiritual immortality. The Conservative synagogue has not clarified its position in the matter.

The idea of the transmigration of souls was combated by the Jewish philosophers. The notion found its way into Jewish literature and folk belief through the kabbalists.

The Destiny of Man

Man's destiny, like his immortality, issues from his divine endowment. His ultimate goal is to realize the divine within him.

Shall he devote the days of his years to amassing material possessions? fame? power? "When man dieth, he shall carry nothing away; his glory shall not descend after him." [19] To what is the senseless acquisition of wealth comparable? "It may be likened to a fox," say the preachers of rabbinic Judaism, "which found a vineyard fenced around on all sides. There was just one hole. He wished to enter through it, but was unable to do so. What did he do? He fasted three days, until he became lean and frail, and then went through the aperture. He feasted there and grew fat again. When he wanted to go out, he was unable to go through the hole. So he fasted another three days until he had grown thin and frail, returning to his former condition, and got out. When he was outside, he turned back and, gazing upon it, cried 'O vineyard! How good are you and the fruits inside! All that is inside is beautiful and praiseworthy, but what enjoyment has one from you? As one enters so he comes out! Such is the world.'" [20]

The meaning of life and the goal of human destiny is to fulfill one's self as the child of God in the building of His Kingdom. "In the hour of a man's departure neither silver nor gold nor precious stones nor pearls accompany him, but only Torah and good works; as it is said, 'When thou walkest it shall lead thee, when thou liest down it shall watch over thee, and when thou wakest it shall talk with thee.' " [21]

1&108

XII. THE ETHICS OF JUDAISM

The Nature of Jewish Ethics

The Jew discovered the world and God, and his own mission in God's world, through the conscience, not through abstract speculation. The speculations of the philosophers in Judaism are aimed at establishing in reason the revealed Moral Law, expressed in the sacred literature of the faith, particularly in the Five Books of Moses, as expounded and integrated in life by the authoritative masters. The scaffoldings of Jewish ethics are "the commandments of the Lord."

Jewish ethics is not, therefore, an independent system within Judaism; it *is* Judaism expressing itself in conduct. Matthew Arnold was accurate in his observation that Hebraism is three-fourths conduct. The major values of Jewish ethics motivate every aspect of Judaism. To ascertain these values and identify them specifically, for the purposes of clarity, we must reflect on the nature of God, Torah, Israel, Man and his capacities, we have already delineated; and, further, observe the institutions and holy days, described in our subsequent chapters. More, the Bible is not a book of ethics; the Bible is primarily a book of religion. This religion, however, is three-fourths ethics. Reading the Bible from the critical, historic standpoint, and allowing for the various levels of aspiration —from the primitive clan henotheism to the exalted prophetic monotheism of a thousand years later—we, nevertheless, recognize basic ethical concepts, evolved and established in the course of the centuries.

Certain characteristics distinguish the nature of Jewish ethics.

First, Jewish ethics is religious and, hence, idealistic.

In our discussion of God we have observed the emphasis

101

upon the unity and holiness of God; in our discussion of man we have noted the impressive emphasis on man as the child of God, made in His image—or, with the capacity to attain His image. In our study of Israel we have noted the historic emphasis upon Israel as His priest-people. These three cardinal principles form the foundations of Jewish ethics as well as demarcate Jewish theology. The duties of life for the faithful in the household of Israel, and for Israel as a historic community, is to exemplify the holiness of God.

The *imitation of God* thus becomes the primary source of Jewish ethics. Man's duty it is to "walk in His ways." "Ye shall be holy, for I, the Lord your God, am holy." [1] The rabbinic masters are consistent with biblical doctrine: "As God is merciful and gracious, so be thou merciful and gracious. As God is called righteous, so be thou righteous. As God is holy, so do thou strive to be holy." [2] Man's duty it is to emulate God. As He "clothes the naked, nurses the sick, comforts the sorrowing, buries the dead, so should man." The attributes of God are the standards of virtue for man. God's Law is Israel's highest good.

The aim of Jewish ethics is to glorify God. Judaism, ultimately, is the sanctification of life as understood in Jewry. Always on the Jew's horizon, like the cloud by day and the pillar of fire by night, is the beckoning vision of the Kingdom of God.

Second, Jewish ethics is this-worldly and practical, since Judaism, emphasizing conduct, strives to be practical. "Ye shall live by them," the Bible legislator ordains,[3] referring to the commandments.

The Kingdom of God is not conceived in terms of the eschatologic, though eschatology is prominent in certain branches of Jewish thought and in limited areas of the Bible. Essentially, the Kingdom of God is a time when "the reign of arrogance shall have passed away from the earth," [4] and mankind live as children of God, under the sovereignty of the Eternal, the earth being the happy abode of all the children of man.

Holiness as experienced in human life is thus not other-worldly, nor supernatural; it is not to be sought in the sheltered places far removed from the traffic of life. The self, as we have noted in our delineation of man, is not originally sinful. Holiness does not require self-extinction nor self-abasement; rather, Jewish ethics seeks self-elevation under the wings of the Almighty, Who seeks primarily that man do justly, love mercy, and walk humbly with Him.

Third, Jewish ethics is particular in form and universal in content and aim.

The Ten Commandments are the heart of Mosaic law vouchsafed to Israel as "His own peculiar people;" but their content and reach are universal. They are not limited to Israel. Rabbinic fancy, we have noted, envisions Israel accepting the stewardship of the Law, and the Law was given in all the languages of mankind, since it is meant for all mankind. "These are the generations of the sons of Noah," is interpreted by the rabbinic sages to emphasize the principle of universality. "The principal races and nations known to the Israelites are arranged as if they were different branches of one great family. Thus, all the nations are represented as having sprung from the same ancestry. All men are therefore brothers. This sublime conception of the *unity of the human race* logically follows from the belief in the unity of God, and like it, forms one of the cornerstones of the edifice of Judaism. Polytheism could never rise to the idea of Humanity. . . . There is, therefore, no parallel to this chapter in the literature of any other ancient people. It has rightly been called a Messianic document." [5]

The Code of Holiness, directed to Israel, "Speak unto all the congregation of the children of Israel," stresses, "Thou shalt love thy neighbor as thyself." [6]

The Jewish sacred days, confined to Israel, are impelled by universal values: the Sabbath and its emphasis on rest for man and beast, the High Holy Days and the contemplation of all the forces determining human destiny, Passover and freedom, Shabuot and the Law, Sukkot and thanksgiving and social responsibility. The very concept of the "Chosen People," as we have noted, is basically universal—Israel the peculiar servant of the universal God. The *mitzvot* reduce themselves to the prophetic emphasis: "to do justly, love mercy and walk humbly with Thy God," and, ultimately, to faith in the universal God of righteousness.

BASIC PRINCIPLES

Basic principles are moral dynamics in the conduct of life as taught in Judaism. They are inherent in and organic to what has already been stated. We identify them more specifically for the purpose of clarity.

First is the love of God—*l'shem shamayin*—or, "for the glory of God." Sanctifying God's Name—*kiddush hashem*—is the highest reach of human virtue. The opposite is desecration of the Name—*hillul hashem.*

Man finds the motivations and the meaning of his life by doing God's will out of love. "Be not like servants who serve their master for condition of receiving a gift, but be like servants who serve the master not on condition of receiving a gift. And let the fear of heaven be upon you. . . . Make His will thy will, so that He may make thy will His will. . . ." [7] So teach talmudic sages. Reverence, humility, truthfulness, love, justice, compassion issue directly from the imitation of God's holiness. By observing these out of love, God's name is sanctified, and human life is lifted to exalted levels.

Second, basic in the Jewish conception of man is the sanctity of personality.

Made in the image of God, holding within itself a spark of divine fire, the human personality is sacred. He who destroys a single life is as one who destroys a whole world; he who saves a single human life is as one who saves a whole world. Man is a microcosm. "One man is equal to the whole of creation." [8] "Man was first created a single individual to teach the lesson that whoever destroys one life, Scripture ascribes it to him as though he had destroyed the whole world; and whoever saves one life, Scripture ascribes it to him as though he had saved the whole world." [9] Rabbi Akiba sees the basic principle of the Torah in the commandment "Thou shalt love thy neighbor as thyself," for the reason that it is based on respect for personality. "You should not say that inasmuch as I am despised let my fellow man be despised with me; inasmuch as I am cursed, let my fellow man be cursed with me." "If you act thus," said Rabbi Tanhuma, "know whom you despise, namely, a being made in the image of God." [10]

Suicide is viewed with abhorrence. Euthanasia is rejected as a moral evil. Only God gives life; only God may take it. This doctrine is expressed vividly in the martyrdom of Hananiah ben Teradion. When this martyr was suffering the agonies of slow death, his disciples urged him to hasten his death by breathing deeper the flames that were slowly consuming him. He replied, "It is better that He should take (the soul) who gave it, and let no one do violence to it himself." [11]

Respect for personality means respect for the differences in human beings. God's wisdom is registered in the differences that obtain in the personalities of men. The individuality of every human being "declares the greatness of the Supreme King of Kings, the Holy One, blessed be He; because a man strikes many coins from one die and they are all alike. But the Holy One, blessed be He, strikes every person from the die of the first man, but not one resembles another." [12]

Men differ intellectually. These differences too are of God. He reveals Himself to every man in keeping with the various capacities of men.

Third, the election of Israel, as we have noted in our discussion of the Chosen People, is an ethical dynamic in the life of Jewry. A special covenant obtains between God and Israel. Right conduct is, therefore, demanded. Idolatry is viewed as a breach in ethics; idolatry means adultery, for Israel is wedded to God:

> I will betroth thee (Israel) unto Me forever;
> Yea, I will betroth thee unto Me in righteousness and justice,
> And in lovingkindness and in compassion;

I will betroth thee unto Me in faithfulness,
And thou shalt know the Lord.[13]

If Israel is to know the Lord, Israel must practice righteousness, justice, lovingkindness, compassion, faithfulness. Amos
expresses it succinctly: "You only have I known of all the
families of the earth; therefore, I will visit upon you all your
iniquities." [14] *Noblesse oblige!* Isaiah, defining the Servant of
the Lord, describes him in ethical terms: a just, compassion-
ate, peace-loving, redeeming influence in the world.[15]

It is every Jew's duty to bring honor to the Jewish name by
exemplary conduct, for that way the name of God is glorified.
"Be ye clean, ye that bear the vessels of the Lord." [16] Further,
Israelites are responsible one for the other, for all form one
holy brotherhood. Life's circumstances have given special
weight to this doctrine of the rabbinic sages.

Fourth, the Golden Mean. Striving to guide practically the
every-day life of normal men and women, Judaism avoids extremes and hypnotic vagaries. Neither self-abnegation nor
self-centered greed nor altruism to a point where one undoes
himself and renders himself unfit to meet life's duties are its
points of emphasis; rather, it seeks the happy medium. To find
and effect the balance is the problem facing every sensitive
person.

Hillel gave classic expression to this principle: "If I am
not for myself, who will be for me? If I am for myself (only),
what am I? And if not now, when?" [17] The self must not be
crushed by the many; neither must the self be lawless anarchy.
And this adjustment of the one to the many must take place
within the swiftly moving days of our years. Hillel expressed,
further, this harmonious adjustment of the one to the many in
terms of the sanctity of personality as being the very center of
the Torah: "What is hateful unto thee do not do to your neighbor." [18] This version of the Golden Rule he considered the
whole Law; all the rest is only commentary. Of course, this
doctrine applies to all sorts and conditions of men—rich and
poor, Jew and non-Jew, even the criminal condemned to
death.

Within one's own self balance must be sought. Maimonides, following Aristotle's "The Mean," summarizes: "Good deeds are such as are equibalanced, maintaining the Mean between two equally bad extremes, the *too much* and the *too little*. . . . Likewise, liberality is the means between sordidness and extravagance; dignity, between haughtiness and loutishness; contentedness, between meanness and profusion. Gentleness is the Mean between irascibility and insensibility to shame and disgrace; and modesty, between impudence and shamefacedness. So it is with all other qualities." [19]

In the book of Proverbs the matter is put succinctly: The sage prays to be delivered from extremes. "Give me neither poverty nor riches." If he is too rich he is likely to degenerate and turn vulgar; if too poor, he may be driven to steal.[20]

The normal human instincts and desires are good. The good life accepts these and devotes them to the glory of God. "He who subjects himself to needless self-castigations and fasting, or even denies himself the enjoyment of wine, is a sinner." [21] Life and health and good cheer are the gifts of God; it is man's duty to enjoy them decently. Celibacy is thus decried. Man should marry and raise a family. Sex-life is normal and good. That was ordained of God. It must not be cheapened or vulgarized. "He who lives without a wife lives without joy and blessing, without protection and peace." [22] He is not a complete man, and he leads a thwarted life.

Fifth, man is a free moral agent, as we have noted in our discussion of man in the light of Jewish doctrine; he does have the freedom and the capacity to order his life in keeping with his desires. Whither a man wants to go there he is led. "The conviction that man's will is unfettered is therefore seen to be the foundation of rabbinic ethics. The nature of his life is moulded by his desires. He can misuse life's opportunities if he so wishes; but in no circumstance would it be agreed that he must misuse them. The evil impulse constantly tempts him; but if he falls, the responsibility is his and his alone." [23]

The base of Jewish ethics is man as a free moral agent, endowed with the capacity to tell right from wrong, and endowed, further, with the capacity to choose the good and reject the evil. Unless man does have this freedom of the will it is neither logical nor just to hold him responsible for any of his actions. "Stand on thy feet, son of man, and I will speak unto thee," [24] the prophet Ezekiel hears God speaking to him. Man does have the capacity to stand on his feet and hearing the voice of God, and when he does, as an upright human being, God speaks to him and teaches him his duties.

Jewish ethics is centered in God and implemented in man and man's world.

XIII. SOCIAL IDEALS

No man lives unto himself. No normal human being wants to. Every man's life is interbound with the lives of others and the life of society. The fate of the individual is dependent upon the fate of the group. Society, therefore, has responsibilities by the individual and the individual has duties by his society. In Judaism these social ideals and personal duties are of the fiber of the faith.

The talmudic masters stress it in law and homily, in legend, poetry, and prayer. "It is like unto a company of men on board a ship. One of them took a drill and began to bore a hole under him. His fellow travellers said unto him, 'What are you doing?' Said he to them, 'What does that matter to you? Am I not boring under my own seat?' They retorted, 'The water will come up and flood the ship for us all.'" [1]

To create a harmonious relationship between the individual and society basic principles must stand sure. These we sketch from the standpoint of Jewish teaching.

It should be borne in mind that Judaism is consistently pragmatic, particularly in the sphere of ethics. It does not debate, What is truth? What is justice? What is love? It has come to accept these major social and personal ideals in its discovery of the moral nature of the world. They are divine commandments, not merely subjects for academic discussion.

Rabban Simeon ben Gamaliel gives us a formula of social ideals that has become standard in rabbinic teaching. In *Abot* his formula is stated: "By three forces is the world preserved: by truth, by justice, and by peace; as it is said, Judge ye the truth and the judgments of peace in your gates." [2]

TRUTH

Grounded as Judaism is in the moral order of the universe, truth becomes, in the words of the talmudic masters, "the seal of God." [3] That is primary to everything that has to do with human life, personal and social. The talmudic sage thus cites truth first. And there is no gap between revealed truth and rational truth. The rational is a channel of the revealed.

Truth is more than a social necessity; we should be truthful whether it pays or not, for truth is of the essence of God and of the structure of the universe. Thus natural morality rises to the level of ethical religion. "Truth in Judaism, both ethical and theological, is not a matter of divine fiat, but rather an expression of a rational universe and its just God." [4]

The literature of the synagogue, from the Bible through the Talmud, and the vast rabbinic writings, repeat endlessly the holy character of truth and condemn the liar and hypocrite. The hypocrite brings God's wrath upon the world. His prayers are an abomination. Man cannot live with himself, nor with his fellows, nor at peace with God unless he reveres the truth. "Keep thee far from a false matter," the biblical legislator commands.[5] Prophet, Psalmist, sage and rabbi repeat the emphasis with renewed vigor. Who is worthy to stand before God? The Psalmist's reply is practical, as it is lofty: "He that hath clean hands and a pure heart, who hath not taken My Name in vain and hath not sworn deceitfully. . . . He that speaketh truth in his heart." [6] The rabbis were quick to note that not even in one's own mind may one contemplate falsehood. Only a truthful person is worthy of studying the Torah. Falsehood is more than inconsistency with facts; falsehood is theft. The first question asked on the Judgment Day is: "Have thy dealings with thy fellow man been in truthfulness?" [7]

JUSTICE

The second principle in the formula for the stability of the world given by Simeon ben Gamaliel, classic in rabbinic Judaism, is *din,* which is more than justice or judgment in abstract; it is justice and law.

Law, as we have noted in our consideration of *halakah* and the *mitzvot,* is the distinctive and authoritative channel of

Judaism. The revelation to Moses was not in terms of parables or dark sayings or mystic visions; it was in terms of commandments. "These are the ordinances which thou shalt set before them." [8] The prophets of Israel were not philosophers of justice but its impassioned protagonists. They spoke not as theologians or philosophers to their learned colleagues, but as divinely-inspired reformers to every man in terms of specific evils harassing their society. The rabbis are the true heirs to the prophets in carrying forward this emphasis.

Justice, like truth, is an attribute of God; hence it is a norm for human conduct. The righteous Judge deals justly with man. He rewards the righteous and punishes the wicked.

Justice is far more than social reciprocity or a mechanical "measure for measure." It is more than enforcing the accepted rights and duties of the individual. It is all this and more. It is the primary principle on which our world rests and by which it is sustained. Lawgiver, prophet, Psalmist, sage vie with each other in glorifying justice as divine will. "Justice, justice shalt thou pursue," the Deuteronomist exhorts.[9] "He judges the world in righteousness and the peoples in equity," chants the Psalmist.[10] "Righteousness and peace have kissed each other." [11] "Let justice well up as water and righteousness as a mighty stream," Amos pleads,[12] and gives expression to the dominant passion of Hebrew prophecy. Micah makes it the first essential in his interpretation of God's will; his words have become classic in the ethical traditions of the Western world:

> It hath been told thee, O man, what is good,
> And what the Lord doth require of thee:
> Only to do justly, to love mercy, and to walk humbly with thy
> God.[13]

Isaiah, like all the prophets, spurns ritualistic religion as an abomination unless the worshipper comes to the sanctuary with clean hands:

> Wash you, make you clean;
> Put away the evil of your doings
> From before Mine eyes;
> Cease to do evil;

Learn to do well;
Seek justice,
Restrain the oppressor,
Judge the fatherless
Plead for the widow.[14]

Understanding and knowing the Lord, Jeremiah insists, means practicing mercy and justice and to delight in these.[15]

The talmudic and later masters are unanimous in accentuating this prophetic emphasis. Rabban Simeon ben Gamaliel speaks for the entire rabbinic tradition in making justice one of the three pillars of the world. "The sword comes upon the world for the delay of justice, and for the perversion of justice. . . ." [16]

Justice is impartial. It knows no favorites, native-born or alien. "Ye shall do no unrighteousness in judgment; thou shalt not respect the person of the poor, nor favor the person of the mighty; but in righteousness shalt thou judge thy neighbor." [17] The rabbis are emphatic; justice must take its course, no matter what the obstacles be: "Let the law cut through the mountain." [18]

Justice is more than legal regularity. Beyond the technical is the moral claim, for ultimately justice is divine will.

Justice must be seasoned with mercy; but the rock-base is justice.

Righteousness and justice are the foundation of thy throne;
Mercy and truth go before Thee.[19]

Mercy crowns justice; it must not dethrone it. "Execute true judgment, and show mercy and compassion every man to his neighbor." [20] By the combined attributes of justice and compassion was the world created; neither one alone would make for an enduring, viable world. The midrashic masters of the synagogue express it in a vivid allegory: God's creation of the world "may be compared to a king who had some empty glasses. Said the king, 'If I pour hot water into them, they will burst; if cold, they will contract (and snap).' What then did the king do? He mixed hot and cold water and poured it into them, and so they remained (unbroken). Even so, said the

Holy One, blessed be He: 'If I create the world on the basis of mercy alone, its sins will be great; on the basis of justice alone, the world can not exist. Hence I will create it on the basis of justice and mercy, and may it then stand.' " [21]

PEACE

Significantly, Rabban Simeon ben Gamaliel adds peace as the third principle in his formula of the world's stability, predicating it on truth and justice. When truth and justice operate in a society peace follows; unless there be truth and justice peace will not be maintained. "All three are one, for where there is justice, there is also truth and peace." [22]

The peace sentiment in Judaism grew with the centuries, impelled by prophetic fire from within and the cruelties of the world without. For centuries only the helpless victims caught in the wars of the nations, not participants blinded by nationalist frenzy, the Jewish masters could dream the dream of universal peace as moral teachers. The accepted procedure among nations, war is accepted as such in the Bible itself and viewed as the punishment of God for the sins of the nation. "Holy wars" recur in Bible pages. The ark is taken into battle. Priests sound the *shofar* and bless the warriors. The prophets too see in war the weapon of God's wrath. The warring Assyrians are only "the rod of His anger."

However, the prophets looked to a time of universal peace based on God's righteousness. Isaiah's vision of universal peace, when nations shall beat their swords into plowshares and learn war no more, lured and comforted Israel.[23] That day would surely come; "it shall come to pass at the end of days." And peace would come as a result of social and national righteousness. "The work of righteousness shall be peace, and the effect of righteousness quietness and confidence forever." [24]

The peace sentiment dominates Jewish tradition; always it is associated with truth and justice. The traditional Hebrew salutation is *Shalom*, peace! The liturgy of the synagogue holds yearning prayers for peace. The priestly benediction

concludes with the word "peace," as the climax of God's blessings.[25] "Great is peace; all the benedictions end with peace,
because benedictions are worthless unless they be attended
by peace." [26] Even the angels in heaven and the dead in the
Beyond are in need of peace. The traditional Jewish sentiment
on committing a loved one to his eternal rest is "may he rest in
peace." The choice fruit of the tree of Torah and faith is peace.
The peace of God is serenity in one's own life and harmony in
the life of society.

The yearning for peace did not harden into a pacifist dogma,
however. In Jewish teaching peace is not a dogma resting on
an isolationist basis. Dependent as it is upon truth and justice,
it is to be achieved by the necessary sacrifices in its behalf.

Non-resistance never became an organic part of Judaism.
There are values dearer than peace, for peace is something
more positive than the absence of war. "Resist not evil" never
became a dogma in Judaism. Jewish tradition emphasized,
rather, "Thou shalt remove the evil from the midst of thee."
"Thou shalt not stand idly by the blood of thy neighbor."
"Whoso sheddeth man's blood by man shall his blood be shed,
for in the image of God made He man." [27] To go along with
forces that violate the sanctity of the human personality,
pervert truth and justice, attributes of God Himself, is to reduce peace to something immoral. With all its abhorrence of
war, the synagogue does not, therefore, encourage the con-
scientious objector.

CHARITY

The Hebrew word for charity—*zedakah*—in its primary
sense means justice. Here we have the basic characteristic of
the Jewish conception of charity.

In the Bible, and in later rabbinic Judaism, charity is obligatory and statutory. Biblical legislation requires that the
corners of the field be left unharvested; the forgotten sheaf
must not be retrieved. The olive trees and the vines must not
be gleaned too meticulously. That must be left for the poor,

the widow, the alien—for those who have no harvests to gather. That is the motivation of the Sabbatical year, "that the poor of thy people may eat." [28] Charity is thus more than personal liberality, or voluntary benefaction. It is statutory, commanded in sacred text.

The rabbinic masters carried forward this emphasis. They considered assisting the poor and needy as an act of social justice, and as an expression of faith.

And it is more than a legal requirement to be discharged impersonally. True charity must partake of personal sacrifice. In the vocabulary of the synagogue is a special term for this aspect of charity—*gemilut hasadim*—loving-kindness. It includes the personal and sacrificial elements in discharging one's obligations. Say the sages: Deeds of love are worth more than almsgiving. Charity is done at the mere sacrifice of money; deeds of love are performed with one's money and with one's person. Charity is only for poor; deeds of love are for poor and rich.[29]

Nicety of consideration for the recipient is required. He should not be humiliated; he should not know, if at all possible, the personal source of the benefaction.

Charity is more than personal benevolence: it is the duty of the community. By the end of the second century of the Common Era a communal system was started for the collection and distribution of philanthropic funds. This communal chest functioned on a broad base.[30]

Who had a claim on the community? The following: The poor of the town, in need of food and clothing, especially for the Sabbath and the other holy days. The transient was provided with temporary lodging. Orphan children and the bride in need of an outfit, dowry, or wherewithal for a decent wedding were entitled to assistance. Girls were given priority over boys. The poor in need of burial were a communal responsibility, as were captives needing ransom. Attention was given to the social position and the former manner of life of the recipient.[31]

In Jewish tradition charity is a basic tenet of the faith, an act of worship, and a basic aspect of social justice. A fine sense of values and techniques were evolved in the course of the centuries. Maimonides gives as good a summary of these as we may find in Jewish literature.

There are eight degrees in almsgiving, one higher than the other.

> Supreme above all is to give assistance to a co-religionist who has fallen on evil times by presenting him with a gift or loan, or entering into a partnership with him, or procuring him work, thereby helping him to become self-supporting.
>
> Inferior to this is giving charity to the poor in such a way that the giver and recipient are unknown to each other. This is, indeed, the performance of a commandment from disinterested motives.
>
> Next in order is the donation of money to the charitable fund of the community, to which no contributions should be made without the donors feeling confident that the administration is honest, prudent and capable of proper management.
>
> Below this degree is the instance where the donor is aware to whom he is giving the alms but the recipient is unaware from whom he receives them.
>
> Inferior to this degree is the case where the recipient knows the identity of the donor, but not *vice versa*.
>
> The next four degrees in their order are: the man who gives money to the poor before he is asked: the man who gives money to the poor after he is asked: the man who gives less than he should, but does it with a good grace; and lastly he who gives grudgingly.[32]

In the course of the centuries Jewish philanthropy became a social science. Under the pressure of need created by crises in history Jewish philanthropic endeavor assumed huge proportions on a world-wide scale.

LABOR

Living on charity, however, is something to be sternly avoided. Every man should be self-supporting, and should train his sons to be self-supporting. Better to do the most menial work than to resort to charity. The traditional grace after meals includes the petition: "We beseech Thee, O Lord our God, let us not be in need either of the gifts of flesh and blood (i.e. human beings) or of their loans, but only of Thy helping hands." [33]

Labor is a high ideal. It is a man's duty to work, earn his own livelihood, support his family, and contribute to the community. Even the scholar should work with his own hands. It sobers his learning. Further, labor dignifies the worker and the worker exalts his work. [34] "When thou eatest the labor of thy hands, happy shalt thou be and it shall be well with thee." [35] By labor man subdues his environment and rises to a level of life above that of the beast. "Therefore choose life," the biblical lawgiver asserts, and the rabbinic teachers add, "learn a handicraft." [36] The wife should do a good measure of her housework even if she be provided with many servants, because "idleness leads to lewdness and lewdness leads to mental instability." [37]

LOVE

The supreme affirmation of Judaism is the verse from Deuteronomy proclaiming the unity of God: *sh'ma yisroel adonoy elohenu adonoy echod*, "Hear, O Israel, the Lord our God, the Lord is One." [38] This is followed by the commandment; "Thou shalt *love* the Lord, thy God, with all thy heart, with all thy soul, with all thy might." Love enters into every divine and human relationship and exalts it.

"Mercy," "loving-kindness," "compassion" are synonyms for "love" in the vocabulary of Judaism. All these are attributes of God and patterns for human virtue. God is spoken of as "The Father of Mercies."

To live and love, labor and worship, motivated by and dedicated to the love of God, is, we have noted, primary in Jewish ethics. Man's love of God and God's love of man is the magic of the religious life. "Beloved is man," says Rabbi Akiba, "for he was created in the image of God: but it was by special love that it was made known to him that he was created in the image of God." [39] It was God's special love that gave man not only his divine endowment, but also the consciousness of his divine nature.

Reciprocal divine love is the essence of true religion as understood in the synagogue. Hence it is man's duty to love his fellow man, for every man is the child of God, and, further, every man must imitate God. The admonition to love God by obeying His commandments in our dealings with our fellow man recurs in the Written and Oral traditions of the synagogue. "Therefore thou shalt love the Lord thy God, and keep His charge, and His statutes, and His ordinances and His commandments, always." [40]

Love is not restricted to one's own group; love knows no restrictions. The Code of Holiness containing the commandment "Thou shalt love thy neighbor as thyself," contains the further command, "The stranger that sojourneth with you shall be unto you as the home-born among you, and thou shalt love him as thyself; for ye were strangers in the land of Egypt." [41]

The rabbinic masters emphasized it endlessly in their own way. The Hebrew word for stork is *hasidah*, which means "pious one," or "faithful one." At the same time the stork is listed among the "detestable" birds, not to be eaten by a faithful Israelite. A Hasidic teacher sees in this a rebuke to the limitations of love set by men. The stork, according to this homily, has one basic fault: it is good and faithful to its own kind only. Hence it is unclean in the sight of God. God's love through His faithful servants is meant for every man of whatever race or creed. [42]

FRIENDSHIP

The sweetness of friendship issues from the response to a basic need in human nature. One needs friends, companions, to supplement the intimacy of family relationships if his life is to be complete. The rabbis give us a parable expressing the need of friendship in human life. An ascetic by the name of Honi fell asleep one day and slept seventy years. On awaking he found himself alone in the world. All his friends had passed away. His immediate family was no more. His grandson did not know him. He went to the Academy, where he had been in the habit of studying and passing time with his colleagues and friends. He heard the rabbis discuss a difficult verse. One recalled that Honi used to resolve such difficulties in past years. Honi introduced himself; but no one believed him. He was alone and lonely, and prayed for death. Hence arose the proverb among the talmudic sages: "Either companionship or death." [43]

XIV. PERSONAL VIRTUES

The attributes of God and the social ideals as understood in Judaism are the standards of virtue for the individual. They become real as they are transformed into personality.

Central to the human personality, as we have noted, is the capacity to achieve "the image of God." The good life cultivates its capacities to their highest point of development. Personal virtue is "to do justly, love mercy, walk humbly with thy God." Every ideal, precept, commandment we have noted as indigenous to the pattern of faith in Judaism is transmuted into personal duty. "The word is very nigh unto thee, in thy mouth, and in thy heart, that thou mayest do it." [1] The master term in the religious life is "the fear of the Lord." "The fear of the Lord is the beginning of wisdom." [2] Weighing all the gains and pleasures of life, finding all things "a chasing after the wind and folly," Koheleth, nevertheless, comes to the conclusion, "fear God and keep His commandments, for this is the whole man." [3] Spoken by "the gentle cynic," or by a later pious editor, as some scholars believe, it is the authentic stamp of Judaism. "Fear of God" means a sense of reverence, dedication, humility, integrity. Justice, mercy, and compassion; love, truth and honor; hospitality, courtesy, and good manners are threads in the tapestry of the good life.

In the book of Job we have as complete a picture of the virtuous life as Scripture affords:

. . . I delivered the poor that cried,
the fatherless also, that had none to help him.
The blessing of him that was ready to perish came upon me;
And I caused the widow's heart to sing for joy.
I put on righteousness, and it clothed itself with me;
My justice was as a robe and as a diadem.
I was eyes to the blind,

And feet was I to the lame.
I was a father to the needy;
And the cause of him that I knew not I searched out.
And I broke the jaws of the unrighteous,
And plucked the prey out of his teeth.[4]

Personal virtue, in Bible and in post-biblical Judaism, is not passive resignation, abstention, self-abnegation, meekness in the face of unrighteousness; rather, it is positive, active, aggressive in opposition to evil. "Thou shalt not stand idly by the blood of thy neighbor;" "Thou shalt not follow a multitude to do evil." [5]

Job repeats his conception of human excellence and high integrity. He made a covenant with his own best self so to live as to bring upon himself "the heritage of the Almighty from on high:"

If I have walked with vanity,
And my feet hath hasted to deceit . . .
If my step hath turned out of the way,
And my heart walked after mine eyes . . .
If my heart hath been enticed unto a woman,
And hath lain wait at my neighbor's door . . .
If I did despise the cause of my man-servant,
Or of my maid-servant when they contended with me . . .
If I have withheld aught that the poor desired,
Or have caused the eyes of the widow to fail,
Or have eaten my morsel alone,
And the fatherless hath not eaten thereof . . .
If I have seen any wanderer in want of clothing,
Or that the needy had no covering . . .
If I have made gold my hope,
And have said to the fine gold:
    'Thou art my confidence,'

If I rejoiced because my wealth was great,
And because my hand hath gotten much . . .
If I rejoiced at the destruction of him that hated me,
Or exulted when evil found him . . .
If after the manner of men I covered (up) my transgressions,
By hiding mine iniquity in my bosom—
Because I feared the great multitude,

And the most contemptible among the families terrified me,
So that I kept silence, and went not out of the door—

Such violation of courage, manliness, duty, justice in every-
day life deserves the righteous punishments of God, "for I
should have lied to God that is above." [6]

Characteristically Hebraic, the sins negated and the virtues
extolled by Job are in terms of personal integrity in the sphere
of social relationships. They are not the virtues of the recluse
and the unworldly.

The sage in the book of Proverbs characterizes the conduct
of the wicked:

> There are six things which the Lord hateth,
> Yea, seven which are an abomination unto him:
> Haughty eyes, a lying tongue,
> And hands that shed innocent blood;
> A heart that deviseth wicked thoughts,
> Feet that are swift in running to evil;
> A false witness that breathed out lies,
> And he that soweth discord among brethren. [7]

The Psalmist gives us the ultimate formula of human virtue:
the man worthy to stand before his God is "he that hath clean
hands and a pure heart." [8]

To the personal virtues distinguishing the good life, at least
two further characteristics must be added, as evolved in Jewish tradition.

Filial piety holds a place of dominant importance in the
Jewish conception of personal virtues. "Honour thy father and
thy mother" is part of the Ten Commandments. The Code of
Holiness repeats the precept; the talmudic masters emphasize
it in every way at their command. Jewish family life is distinguished by filial piety.

Further, learning is an imperative quality in the distinguished Jewish personality. Study of His Law is a mode of
worship. "This book of the Law shall not depart out of thy
mouth, but thou shalt meditate therein day and night, that
thou mayest observe to do according to all that is written
therein." [9] The commandment became a compelling reality.

Judaism being a revealed religion, based on a sacred text, Jewry needed a body of learning on which to support itself. The Pharisaic emphasis of every man being a priest, disdaining an exclusive ecclesiastic hierarchy as the custodian of the faith, every man had to be versed in the heritage entrusted to him. The study of the Law became an exalted and exalting duty and privilege, as well as a practical necessity. "An ignorant man cannot be pious," says Hillel.[10] Respect for teachers is on a par with respect for parents. This emphasis saved Judaism from degenerating into a mystery cult. Learning, and the application of learning to everyday life, is an exercise in reason and practicality. When all roads of culture and opportunity were blocked to the Jew across the long stretches of history, when all the temples of culture were closed to him, he meditated in his Torah, studied His word, and made studying the ways of God the supreme ideal in human aspirations. Jewish folk fancy endowed this learning with sentiment, reverence, legend; it became a form of piety. Jewish infants were rocked to sleep to lullabies extolling the study of the Law, and aged men breathed their last sure that they would study the Law at the feet of the Master in the Academy on High for ever and ever. Thus the study of the Law outweighs all virtues and crowns life with grace.

INSTITUTIONS AND RITUALS

XV. JEWISH PRAYER BOOKS

The prayer-literature of the synagogue issues from the same historic circumstances that produced and moulded the synagogue itself. It voices the mind of the synagogue. The two are one. One is revealed in the other.

Like the synagogue, the Jewish prayer books are a folk creation. The prayers express the hopes, fears, frustrations and aspirations of the Jewish masses. They are the articulated longings of historic Jewry for the sacred. In turn, they have been endowed with a sacred character and divine inspiration. God Himself, affirms a talmudic observation, revealed to Moses on Mount Sinai the *Seder Tefila,* the order of the prayers.[1]

Like the synagogue, too, Jewish prayer-literature is the creation of many ages. The same forces that evolved the synagogue determined its liturgy. Like the Talmud, and the Bible itself, the prayer book represents many centuries, a varied historic landscape, a diversity of idealism within the framework of the sacred as understood in Israel, many minds, many moods, many authors and editors. Unlike the Bible and Talmud, the Jewish prayer-literature has never been closed. It is a growing, expanding sacred literature; new prayer books and new editions of old prayer books are being produced in our time.

The synagogue system was established probably soon after the return from the Babylonian exile. It took on form in the shadow of the second Temple. A number of the practices and forms of the Temple were adapted in the meetinghouse (synagogue) programs of devotions. Thus the reading of the Law, arranged by Ezra, became part of the synagogue worship. Psalms were used extensively in the second Temple; the Psalter may be considered as the hymnal of the Temple. The

Sh'ma and the Ten Commandments were recited daily in the Temple. At least a portion of the Eighteen Benedictions are of pre-Maccabean origin. The very hours of synagogue worship were set to correspond to the hours of the daily sacrifice in the Temple. References to these sacrifices are made in the prayers of the synagogue. The worshipper faced the East and Temple in his devotions. Thus, taking root in the shadow of the second Temple, the liturgy of the synagogue was largely influenced by the Temple cult. When, in the year 70, the Temple fell before the Roman legions, the synagogue took its place, and the prayers of the synagogue replaced the sacrifices of the Temple.

Jewish liturgy, as embodied in the prayer books and practices of the synagogue, reflects the religious life of the historic Jewish community from the days of Ezra-Nehemiah to the present. "This historical development of the Prayer Book," Israel Abrahams testifies, "has been the cause of some of its most conspicuous merits. Here and there perhaps its horizon is somewhat contracted, but, as the expression of the Jewish spirit throughout the ages, it reflects every mood of the human soul, it breathes a spirit of invincible faith, an earnest desire to be in harmony with God and to understand and do His will, and it offers in praise and gratitude to the Most High the homage of genuine heart-service. Taken as a whole it is a not unworthy sequel to the Psalter from which it has drawn so much of its inspiration." [2]

The idea of a prayer book, embodying the living faith, meant for every man, is a profound contribution Judaism made to the religious life of mankind. It is second only to the Bible itself.

Other religions had produced sacred texts and collections of sacred poetry. These, however, were meant for the priests or official functionaries of the various cults. They were not for the masses; to the laymen they were sacred secrets. Judaism produced something new. From the heart of Jewry came, in the course of the ages, a prayer-literature meant for every man; the Jewish prayer book became the book of devotions and the textbook of Judaism. The biblical doctrine that Israel is "a nation of priests and a holy people" and the democratic impulse implemented by the Pharisees in rabbinic law, did away altogether with the lay and ecclesiastic; every layman is a priest learned in the Law, and every priest is a learned layman. Thus Judaism avoided mystery cults and ecclesiasticism and sought religious forms in terms of every man's free status before his God. The Jewish prayer book is the expression of this grand doctrine.[3]

Church and mosque borrowed from Judaism the idea of a fixed prayer book. Thus the synagogue influenced the modes of worship of normative Christianity and Mohammedanism. Extemporaneous services are discouraged in Judaism; individualistic programs of worship, attempted at certain periods in the history of the synagogue, when old forms were challenged by the new, flourished for brief periods. In time they yielded to a more authoritative prayer book.

The contemporary synagogue follows several prayer books. We note the following basic prayer books or collections of prayers.

The *Seder Tefila* (order of service, popularly called Siddur, order) is the basic prayer book of the Orthodox synagogue.

Orthodoxy itself follows several different prayer books. Basically they are of two rites or usages (*minhagim*): the *Ashkenazic*, and the *Sephardic*. The latter is followed by the Spanish-Portuguese and some southern European Jews, and a few isolated congregations elsewhere in the world; the former (German), is the more popular, followed largely by Jews all over the world. In structure and form there is considerable divergence between the two. "The arrangement varies, the substance is not identical in every part, and the phraseology is often unlike in passages otherwise the same in contents." [4] These differences go back to early Palestinian and Babylonian usages. "But on the whole the rites contain the same features which were fixed once for all by the Gaonim." [5] The Gaonim were the heads of the academies in Babylon and Palestine, who succeeded the *Amoraim*, the compilers of the

Babylonian Talmud in the fifth century. The Gaonim were the dominant religious authorities of their time. About the year 875 the Gaom Amram made the first authoritative compilation of the Siddur. In its basic elements the present Siddur is in the general agreement with this first edition.

The major differences between the Ashkenazic and the Sephardic rites are in the *piyyutim,* sacred poetry, produced in the Middle Ages.

The *Mahzor* is a term commonly applied to the prayer book for the High Holy Days. The word means "cycle" and was applied to the calendar, later to poetic insertions and anthologies of sacred poetry, supplementing the regular prayer book. Several such collections were produced in France. Like the Siddur, the Mahzor follows the same lines of development in the Ashkenazic and Sephardic traditions,[6] differing primarily in the type of piyyutim.

The Reform movement in modern Judaism produced a great number of prayer books. The fathers of Reform, in its early stages, struggled with the problem of revising the historic liturgy. Inevitably a large number of rabbis in Germany and in the United States produced their own prayer books. In time they yielded to the present *Union Prayer Book for Jewish Worship,* in two volumes: one for the Sabbath, daily devotions, the Three Festivals, and prayers for various occasions; and another for the High Holy Days. Produced by the Central Conference of American Rabbis, it represents the mind of the Reform rabbinate of America.

The Conservative synagogue has followed the policy of adapting freely the Orthodox prayer book; in 1945 they published their own prayer book. The various abbreviations and revisions used in some Conservative synagogues are the individualistic efforts of the editors.[7]

The prayer-literature of Judaism is not limited by any means to the daily or holiday prayer book. The following compilations represent a far-flung field of sacred writing.

HAGGADAH is a name given to the special ritual prayer book for Passover Seder use. It utilizes the story of the exodus from Egypt, orders the Seder rites, contains considerable poetry and music, and the basic prayers associated with a holiday festivity. It is especially aimed at children and is a magnificent folk creation. It has undergone a great many editions and translations, and has been richly illustrated. The Reform rabbis made their own revision in keeping with the major lines of Reform theology.[8]

SELIHOT represent the special penitential prayers for fast days and pre-High Holy Day devotions. "The literature of supplications, generally called 'Selihoth,' is enormous. For about fifteen hundred years Israel continued to create poetry expressing inner contrition and distress, and disasters and persecutions which came from without. Communities which were left more at ease, as the European Sephardic group, have a scanty Seliha-literature, while others, and these constitute the great majority of groups, which went through the turmoil of the dark ages, gave vent to their wounded souls, writing Selihoth with the blood of their hearts." [9]

KINOT are elegiac poems, started in Gaonic times, meant for the observance of the Ninth Day of Ab, commemorating the fall of Jerusalem in the year 70. The material is drawn from Lamentations, the Psalms and the prophets, and from later rabbinic lore.[9]

TEHINOT are personal prayers for private devotions. They are intensely personal, expressing the feelings of the individual who spoke them. In time some of them became embodied in the established liturgy. The earliest ones are in Hebrew. Since the sixteenth century they are in Judeo-German, Judeo-Spanish, Judeo-Greek, Judeo-Italian. Most of Judeo-German tehinot were spoken by pious women who were unfamiliar with Hebrew. These are recited as improvised prayers in connection with the established liturgy, or may be spoken by the praying heart expressing its own burden in its own way at its own occasion. The Hasidic movement in modern Judaism, with its emphasis on the spontaneous, personal, emotional, inspired a large body of *tehinot*. These represent sincere, ardent, folk piety at its best.[10]

ZEMIROT are table songs for the Sabbath, sung by the family at dinner. They breathe the serene joy of the Sabbath, converting the very meal into a religious experience. The custom of singing hymns at the table goes back to the early talmudic period. In the medieval period the custom received special impulse from the Kabbalistic movement, and, later, from the Hasidic. Many compilations of *zemirot* were made in Amsterdam and Constantinople in the sixteenth century. Most of these songs were absorbed into two major collections, one for the Sabbath eve and one for the Sabbath afternoon. The dominant characteristic of zemirot is the glad rejoicing in the Sabbath. Hymns, in the form of psalms in Bible times, in intricate verse in the Middle Ages, enriched Jewish worship. In modern times hymnology received new impetus from the Reform movement. The *Union Hymnal* is the official hymnal of the Reform synagogues of America, supplementing the *Union Prayer Book*.

The PSALTER, throughout the ages, has been the never-failing fountain of devotions. Breathing a spirit of intense personal piety, it sustained Jewry as a people and every religious Jew personally in every hour of need. Much of Jewish prayer-literature, as we have noted, is drawn from the Psalms; special groups dedicated to the recitation of psalms were active in the synagogue in every age. Schedules of Psalms were developed for the pious to follow. Every major event, joyous or tragic, was met with a psalm. Into the ancient words every prayerful heart poured its own feeling and communed with God, "for it is good to give praise unto the Lord, and to sing Thy praises, O Most High." [11]

XVI. WHAT IS PRAYER—AND WHY PRAY?

Nature of Prayer

The religious person prays for the same reason that the man of intellect thinks, the musician plays, the bird sings; for the same reason that the plant bends toward the sun, or the needle of the compass points north. Prayer issues from an inner compulsion. Deep calls unto deep, inevitably. The divine within man responds to the divine beyond. The soul thrilled or agonized will give expression to its emotion; no rationalization is needed, no justification desired. The bird wings and sings; the reverent person feels and prays.

Not to all men is the capacity for prayer granted, no more than the capacity for reason or song, of deep feeling or fine appreciation, are granted to all men. He who has the light of reverence within him, and thereby moves in God's world with a song of the sacred in his heart, will be driven by an inner compulsion to give it release. Our verbal expression of the sacred within us is prayer. The religious personality must hold communion with God.

For one to deny the reality of the urge toward prayer in all men for the reason that he does not find it within himself is irrational. The color-blind person may as well deny the reality of colors, or the deaf deny the reality of music.

"If I was a nightingale, I would act the part of a nightingale: if a swan, the part of a swan. But since I am a reasonable creature, it is my duty to praise God. That is my business. I do it." [1]

This inner compulsion is part of the will to live. The plant bends toward the sun for the reason that it needs the rays of the sun to flourish. The man in a fox hole, knowing extreme danger, instinctively mutters a prayer. To the well-fed, secure, comfortable—who has never known dire distress—it may be irrational; the compelling power, however, is not logic but instinctive self-preservation.

Prayer is the voice of faith, and faith is primarily the instinctive reaching out for the powers that sustain and redeem life. We have faith in ourselves and in our children. Normally, we confidently assume that they will grow into competent men and women. We have no "scientific proof" of that at all. We have no proof whatever that the future holds a decent measure of life's sweetness for us. We assume that. We take it on faith. To assume the contrary is to paralyze the will and disintegrate life, or to covet madness. Thus men pray because they want life—life abundant, life eternal, for themselves and their race.

Instinctive, issuing from the non-rational areas of the personality, and expressing itself particularly in times of crisis, prayer may be primitive invocation and incantation of every demon, coarse as the screams of fear in the jungle; nonetheless, it is real and elemental. As we advance in the scale of civilization, our prayers—like our speech, our music, our arts, our medicine—are lifted and refined.

Prayers move on various levels: from the swampy regions of the jungle to the spacious firmaments of the Psalmist enraptured by the wonders of the universe, awed by its power, humbled by its infinity:

> The heavens declare the glory of God
> And the firmament showeth His handiwork.[2]

Savages offer savage prayers; warriors ask God to smash the enemy. Foolish men speak foolish prayers. The rabbinic masters have a phrase for that: *tephilah shel tiphla*—irrational petitions.[3] Wise men offer wise prayers; lofty minds speak lofty prayers.

The instinct to prayer is in the nature of man; the contents of our prayers are determined by the passions and fears, hopes and aspirations in the heart of man. Out of the heart are the issues of life; and out of the heart are the prayers we utter. As our passions and fears, hopes and aspirations are disciplined and refined by a growing understanding, our prayers are accordingly refined and ennobled.

TYPES OF PRAYER

Jewish prayer—like the prayers of all ethical, developed religions—fall into several categories. These types have been recognized by scholars.

Religion is primarily a sense of dependence on the Everlasting Arms. Prayer is a conscious appeal for help from on high. Thus prayers of *petition* are the earliest and the most basic type of prayer. The worshipper may petition for physical things for himself in the hour of his need, or for personal, spiritual or social values, or he may petition the Almighty in behalf of some one else. Petitionary prayers may therefore be gross and primitive, or idealistic and truly spiritual, depending upon the objects sought by the worshipper.

In the life of the individual and in the history of the race physical needs came first. Crashing thunder, lightning rending the heavens, raging floods, dreaded plagues, droughts, wars, wild beasts—these terrorized primitive man. He petitioned for deliverance. He even sought to coerce the gods or the demons with magic. Hence the elemental form of prayer: petition for help from on high.

Spiritual values and social needs emerged as man beat his way out of the jungles. Understanding the elements better, harnessing some of them to his will, man still found himself in need. Social needs evoked prayers for guidance and power. Fears still haunted him: fears issuing from his social environment and fears arising from the frailty of human life. Fears of tomorrow, old age, death; the yearning for deliverance from frustration, bereavement, loneliness, inner conflict, insecurity; the longing for peace of mind, emotional stability, composure in the face of the elemental forces harassing human life—

these evoked the profoundest prayers in the liturgies of the ethical religions. "Out of the depths I cry unto Thee, O Lord." [4]

Jewish liturgy includes petitions for prosperity, for rain and dew, for physical health, for deliverance from physical danger and social violence. The overwhelming emphasis, however, is for spiritual and social values. What may be cited as the most characteristic example is taken from the Amidah, the most solemn portion of the daily and holy day liturgy:

> Thou favorest man with knowledge, and teachest mortals understanding. . . .
>
> O favor us with knowledge, understanding and discernment from Thee. Blessed art Thou, O Lord, gracious giver of knowledge.
>
> Cause us to return, O our Father, unto Thy Law; draw us near, O our King unto Thy service, and bring us back in perfect repentance unto Thy presence. Blessed art Thou, O Lord, Who delightest in repentance.
>
> Forgive us, O our Father, for we have sinned; pardon us, O our King, for we have transgressed. . . .
>
> Look upon our affliction and plead our cause, and redeem us speedily for Thy name's sake; for Thou art a mighty Redeemer. Blessed art Thou, O Lord, Redeemer of Israel.
>
> Heal us, O Lord, and we shall be healed; save us and we shall be saved; for Thou art our praise. Vouchsafe a perfect healing to all our wounds; for Thou, Almighty King, art a merciful Physician. Blessed art Thou, O Lord, Who healest the sick of Thy people Israel.
>
> Bless this year unto us, O Lord our God, together with every kind of produce thereof, for our welfare; give a blessing upon the face of the earth.
>
> Give dew and rain for a blessing upon the face of the earth.
>
> O satisfy us with Thy goodness, and bless our year like other good years. Blessed art Thou, O Lord, Who blessest the years.[5]

The *Amidah* continues petitions to the Almighty for Israel's deliverance from the yoke of the oppressor, for restoration of

Zion, for God's favor upon all the just and righteous in Israel and upon "the righteous gentiles."

Petitionary prayer may rise to heights of spiritual nobility.

Gratitude for the gifts we treasure most is natural to sensitive people. We plow the earth and plant the seeds; but harvests come by the will of God. His good earth, His sunshine and rain, dew and wind, make harvests possible. Man is a co-worker with God. Alone he produces no harvests. Every man thus receives unearned increment from a bounty not of his own making. And every man is the recipient of spiritual harvests to which he contributes little in comparison with what he receives. Pioneers, who cleared the spiritual jungles as well as the physical, and extended the frontiers of civilization—prophets, scientists, social workers, physicians of the body and the mind, champions of justice, truth, mercy, freedom—have dowered every man with a rich heritage. Every man receives more than he gives. Man's very body, mind, and will, come to him from his sires. The thoughtful life will praise God for His infinite goodness. Hence the second type of prayer: prayers of *thanksgiving*.

Jewish liturgy thus contains many prayers of praise and thanksgiving. Most of the psalms of praise are recited in the course of Jewish devotion. "Praised be Thou, Lord our God. . . ." is a characteristic refrain. As an example of this type of prayer the following may be cited:

> We gratefully acknowledge, O Lord our God, that Thou art our Creator and Preserver, the Rock of our life and the Shield of our help. We render thanks unto Thee for our lives which are in Thy hand, for our souls which are ever in Thy keeping, for Thy wondrous providence and for Thy continuous goodness, which Thou bestowest upon us day by day. Truly, Thy mercies never fail and Thy lovingkindness never ceases. Therefore do we forever put our trust in Thee.[6]

Captivated by the awesome majesty of the universe about him, seeing in it the power of Him who called the world into being, the reverent person yields himself to it in a mood of adoration. *Adoration* may be considered the highest form of worship. Its mood is glad self-surrender before the power and the glory of the Creator and Redeemer.

Observing the sunrise over Mount Blanc, noting the miraculous beauty about him, Coleridge chants a hymn of praise:

> O dread and silent Mount! I gazed upon thee,
> Till thou, still present in the bodily sense,
> Didst vanish from my thought: entranced in prayer
> I worshipped the Invisible alone . . .
>
> .   .   .   .
>
> Motionless torrents! Silent cataracts!
> Who made you glorious as the Gates of Heaven
> Beneath the keen full moon? Who bade the sun
> Clothe you with rainbows? Who, with living flowers
> Of loveliest blue, spread garlands at your feet?
> God! let the torrents, like a shout of nations,
> Answer! and let the ice-plains echo, God!
> God! sing ye meadow-streams with gladsome voice!
> Ye pine groves, with your soft and soul-like sounds!
> And they too have a voice, yon piles of snow,
> And in their perilous fall, shall thunder, God! [7]

Thus Ralph Waldo Emerson, reflecting on prayer, observed truly when he wrote: Prayer "is the soliloquy of a beholding and jubilant soul. It is the spirit of God pronouncing his works good." [8]

The Psalms and later Jewish liturgy are replete with this type of prayer.

> O Lord, our Lord,
> How glorious is Thy name in all the earth!
> Whose majesty is rehearsed above the heavens. [9]

But the majesty of God is not only in nature touched by the supreme Artist, but, also, in human nature inspired by the supreme Teacher. The heavens declare the glory of God; the Moral Law restores the soul of man. Contemplating one as well as the other, the reverent soul bows in adoration. Hence the adoration prayers in Jewish liturgy celebrate the loftiest ideals, personal and social, envisioned in Judaism. The classic adoration prayer in Jewish worship is the *Alenu* prayer. As given in the Union Prayer Book, the prayer celebrates the glory of God in nature, and proceeds to extoll the greatness of God as revealed in the dream for His moral kingdom on earth:

> Let us adore the ever-living God, and render praise unto Him who spread out the heavens and established the earth, whose glory is revealed in the heavens above and whose greatness is manifest throughout the world. He is our God; there is none else.
>
> We bow the head in reverence, and worship the King of kings, the Holy One, praised be He.
>
> May the time not be distant, O God, when Thy name shall be worshipped in all the earth, when unbelief shall disappear and error be no more. Fervently we pray that the day may come when all men shall invoke Thy name, when corruption and evil shall give way to purity and goodness, when superstition shall no longer enslave the mind, nor idolatry blind the eye, when all who dwell on earth shall know that to Thee alone every knee must bend and every tongue give homage. O may all, created in Thine image, recognize that they are brethren, so that, one in spirit and one in fellowship, they may be forever united before Thee. Then shall Thy kingdom be established on earth and the word of Thine ancient seer be fulfilled: The Lord will reign forever and ever.
>
> On that day the Lord shall be One and His name shall be One.[10]

The glory of God is not only in the sunrise; it is just as surely in the sunset. "Man is duty-bound to praise God for the evil as well as the good," [11] teach the rabbinic masters. Hence in Jewish liturgy there are prayers of thanksgiving and adoration, for funeral and memorial services. Death is an awesome mystery; it reflects the Fountain of life. What may be considered as the prayer most freighted with Jewish sentiment and piety is the *Kaddish*. Spoken in memory of the departed, when a loved one is lowered to his eternal reward, or at a memorial service,* it is essentially a prayer of adoration, a

* Originally it had no such function.

heroic affirmation of the greatness and goodness of God even when our eyes are dimmed with tears and our hearts broken with bereavement.

Another type of prayer is the *didactic*. Its purpose is to teach the wisdom of God, the major lessons of the faith. It is basic especially to historic religions such as Judaism.

The word of God is a light upon our way. "For the commandment is a lamp, and the teaching is light." [12] In Judaism, prayer has a teaching function as well. The desire is to shield the light and preserve the truth. Hence the Jewish prayer book contains much material which is not all devotional in a technical sense: citations from the Bible, such as the Ten Commandments; portions from the Talmud, ethical and ritualistic; formulations of the faith, such as Maimonides' Thirteen Principles; hymns of a didactic nature, such as the *Yigdal* and *Adon Olam;* rules for the interpretation of the text of the Law, such as the Thirteen Rules of Rabbi Ishmael. The reading from the Pentateuch and the prophets are lessons in Judaism and form an organic part of worship. The traditional Jewish prayer book is thus a text book of Judaism, and study of the word of God may be considered a superior mode of worship. Zeal for learning is a form of religious enthusiasm.[13]

Prayers may be spoken in private, in the solitude of one's own heart; and they may be spoken publicly. Both forms are basic to the Jewish conception of prayer. Private prayers may be more spontaneous, and have a larger emphasis of personal devotion; public prayers have values which private devotions lack: they unite the individual with the community, contribute to the social force of prayer, and make the individual more effective in the communal expression and cultivation of his religion and his social ideals.

CONDITIONS OF PRAYER

True prayer requires certain qualities in the life of the one who prays. What the quality of the soil means to the plant, the mood of the worshipper is to the life of prayer.

Primary is the quality that is best designated by the Hebrew word *kawwanah*. It is concerned with the intention and attention of him who speaks the prayer—the intention of the heart and the attention of the mind. "The value of the words depends upon the attention of the mind," say the rabbinic teachers.[14] Sincerity, enthusiasm, direction toward God, faith, love, understanding,—all these are embodied in *kawwanah*.[15]

The following citations, taken from rabbinic sources, will convey an appreciation of this primary condition for prayer:

> The Merciful One desires the heart.[16]
>
> We should not rise to pray in the spirit of gloom or of idleness, of levity or idle talk; but only in the joy of religious duty.[17]
>
> Prayer should not be recited as if a man were reading a document. R. Aha said, 'A new prayer should be said every day.'[18]
>
> R. Ammi said, 'Man's prayer is not accepted unless he puts his heart in his hands.'[19]
>
> Let him who prays cast his eyes downward, but turn his heart upwards.[20]
>
> A man must purify his heart before he prays.[21]
>
> When thou prayest, regard not thy prayer as a fixed mechanical routine, but as an appeal for mercy and grace before the All-present.[22]
>
> R. Elazar said, 'Always let a man test himself: if he can direct his heart, let him pray; if he cannot, let him not pray.'[23]
>
> Rab said, 'He whose mind is not quieted should not pray.' R. Hanina was wont not to pray when he was irritated.[24]

With *kawwanah* goes humility. Man subordinates himself to a Power beyond himself. Glad self-surrender, self-realization as a finite creature touched by the Infinite, is the mood true prayer requires and evokes. God's will, not man's, must obtain. A prayer spoken by R. Eliezer, recorded in the Talmud, is a noble example of true religious humility—i.e., not self-abnegation but self-realization by losing one's self in God: "Do Thy will, O God, in the heavens above, and grant composure of spirit to those who revere Thee below, and do Thou what is good in Thy sight. Blessed art Thou, O Lord, who hearest prayer." [25] A popular inscription over arks in synagogues is, "Know before whom thou standest." [26] Humility is thus bringing our own lives and aspirations into perspective with the Lord of all.

Prayers must be *intelligently* spoken. "If the mind knows not what the lips utter, what profit hath a man of all his prayers?" [27] Even in the case of prayers spoken in a classic tongue understood imperfectly or not at all by the worshipper, meaning is read into the ancient forms.

Further, prayer requires *selflessness* and *generosity*. The best in man is released; the worst is mastered. Standing before the majestic, the petty vanishes. The magic touch of the sacred dissolves the crass. "Whoever has it in his power to pray on behalf of his neighbor, and fails to do so, is called a sinner." [28]

True prayer requires *ethical preparation* as well as the proper personal mood. In Judaism, the prophetic drive expresses itself in prayer as well as in legislation and exhortation. Isaiah attacks prayer and sacrifice when they are substitutes for justice.

> And when ye spread forth your hands
> I will hide mine eyes from you;
> Yea, when ye make many prayers,
> I will not hear;
> Your hands are full of blood.[29]

The powerful denunciation of prayers when spoken by hypocrites and exploiters, as given in the fifty-eighth chapter of the book of Isaiah, is the prophetic lesson of the Day of Atonement. Prayers are acceptable to God only when spoken in justice and contrition. Personal and social justice renders prayer true and worthy to be heard by God. "Then thou shalt call and the Lord will answer." [30] Jeremiah, man of prayer, demands of his hearers: "Will ye steal, murder, and commit adultery, and swear falsely, and offer unto Baal, and walk after other gods whom ye have not known, and come and stand before Me in this house, whereupon my name is called, and say: 'We are delivered.' . . ." [31] The Psalmist has given the classic definition of the ethical prerequisite for prayer. Who is fit to stand before God in the sanctuary? "He that hath clean hands and a pure heart." [32] The later rabbis proved themselves true heirs of the prophets and psalmists when they taught their disciples that prayers of atonement may absolve one only in the sphere of his relationship to his God; but in matters between man and man, no such absolution is possible. Every man must first right the wrongs of which he is guilty before he may seek forgiveness of God.[33]

THE VALUES OF PRAYER

The metaphysical validity of prayer did not disturb the minds of the rabbinic builders of Judaism. Their thinking issued from the unquestioned conviction that a just and loving Father rules the universe, Who, consciously and lovingly, hears men's prayers. That is taken on faith.[34]

In our discussion of the nature, types, and levels of prayer, the values of prayer are intimated.

Prayer regenerates, restores, unites, and harmonizes the individual personality and the group.

It is reported of the American poet, Oliver Wendell Holmes, that when asked by a friend why he went to church on Sunday morning, especially since he was of a sceptical turn of mind, he replied that a plant called reverence grew in his heart, and that he went to church once a week to water it. If we may borrow a metaphor from mechanics, we might describe prayer as charging our batteries. In the traffic of life, prayer—particularly public prayer on a sacred day—affords us an island of refuge where we may pause and regain our personal and social idealism.

Prayer brings us back to the center of stability in our lives as people who cherish the sacred. It restores balance. Isaiah spoke a profound religious truth when he observed, "Thou wilt keep him in perfect peace whose mind is stayed on Thee." [35] Praying people are strong people; they are invincible in the face of every calamity.

Prayer flings a vision before us and unrolls far horizons. Addressed to God, it lifts us out of the ordinary, mediocre, selfish, earthy. Finite man catches at least a broken ray of the Infinite. And that becomes a magic power which transforms personality.

> Who has known heights shall bear forevermore
> An incommunicable thing
> That hurts his heart, as if a wing
> Beat at the portal, challenging;
> And yet—lured by the gleam his vision wore—
> Who once has trodden stars seeks peace no more. [36]

Prayer gives us perspective, and thus brings life into proper focus. In one of the earliest prayers of the synagogue we have a good example of prayer adjusting the worshipper to himself and to the universe from the standpoint of the eternal:

> What are we? What is our life? What is our piety? What our righteousness? What our helpfulness? What our strength? What our might? What shall we say before Thee, O Lord our God and God of our fathers? Are not all the mighty men as nought before Thee, the men of renown as though they had not been, the wise as if without knowledge, and the men of understanding as if without discernment? For most of their works are void, and the days of their lives are vanity before Thee, and the preeminence of man over the beast is nought, for all is vanity. [37]

Public prayer has an additional value: it becomes a bond of union, transforming the worshippers into a community. It creates an inner unity and an inner source of strength. Further, it stretches the social horizon and expands the communal responsibilities of the individual. Thus Jewish prayer is in the plural: *Our* God and God of *our* fathers; not *My* God and God of *my* fathers, excepting in special instances.

Historic prayers have a still further value: they unite the

generations, preserving a community that defies the ages. The experiences of the fathers yield meaning to the children and children's children. Memory is invoked; the perspective of the ages comes into the personal life. Mortal man ceases being like a driven leaf; he stands rooted like a mighty oak. He receives and transmits. "He who called the generations from the beginning" thus becomes a personal reality through historic prayers.[38]

XVII. CUSTOMS, CEREMONIES, INSTITUTIONS

Jewish life is distinguished and sanctified by religious observances, customs, and ceremonies. Orthodox, Conservative, and Reform Judaism view them from the peculiar standpoints these three divisions of contemporary Judaism take toward all tradition; but all value customs and ceremonies as basic to any practical observance of Judaism. For the most part, Orthodox Judaism, operating with a divinely revealed Law, treats the customs and ceremonies of Judaism as rites; Reform, functioning in terms of a religious evolution, views them as sacred pageantry; Conservative Judaism temporizes between the two.

Religious ceremonies are a language of faith. The majesty of the sacred, the baffling mysteries of the Unknown as they impinge on the individual mind and conscience, the tender sentiment of faith, the intuition of the mystic, the yearnings and the passions of life do not lend themselves for easy expression in words. Man needs further vehicles to articulate the longings and apprehension within him. He finds it in music, in gestures, in art, in pageantry. Without a body of sacred ceremony, religion is stripped of the poetic, the tender, the deeply human which touches the divine. In a historic religion such as Judaism, these ceremonies crystallize into historic modes and customs, and often, especially in Orthodoxy, assume the force of law.

THE JEWISH HOME

The Jewish home is a religious home. It is a sanctuary dedicated to the Holy One of Israel. Every person is a priest; every person observes his faith in home and synagogue personally. "The Torah commanded us by Moses is the heritage *of the congregation of Jacob;"* [1] it is not the special endowment of any one ecclesiastic class. It cannot be observed vicariously.

In our discussion of the Sabbath and holidays we call attention to the various ceremonies associated with the observance of these sacred days. These observances transformed the Jewish home into a sanctuary and made it the nursery of religious idealism.

In addition to the ceremonies there described,[2] the following must be noted.

MEZUZAH

The observant Jewish family will dedicate its home upon moving into it, especially if it built or acquired its own house. No prescribed form is specified in the Talmud. The service usually includes a prayer, a psalm or two—Psalm XV, XXX, CI, etc.—and the traditional formula: "Blessed be Thou, Lord our God, King of the Universe, Who has sustained us in life, has preserved us, and brought us to this season." The *mezuzah* is fixed to the upper part of the right doorpost with the benediction: "Blessed be Thou, Lord our God, King of the Universe, Who hast commanded us to affix the *mezuzah*." It is customary to affix the *mezuzah* at an angle, the upper part pointing inward.[3]

The *mezuzah*—Hebrew for "doorpost"—is a small tube or case, made of wood or metal, containing a parchment, upon which is written in Hebrew in Torah script, Deuteronomy 6:4–9 and 11:13–21. Through a small opening in the upper part of the *mezuzah* is seen the Hebrew word *Shaddai*, God.

The purpose of the *mezuzah* is to fulfill the biblical command: "Thou shalt write them (the words of the Law) upon the doorposts of thy house and upon thy gates." [4] At certain periods, in various localities, the *mezuzah* came to be associated with amulets and charms. Such an interpretation is an abuse of the real intent. In contemporary Judaism it serves as a silent witness that the home is Jewish and God-fearing.[5]

TZITZIT—TALLIT

Orthodox Jews are required to wear fringes on their persons. These fringes—tzitzit—white threads, woven in keeping with rabbinic formula, were in Bible times attached to the four corners of the robes the men wore in daily use "that you may look upon it and remember all the commandments of the Lord and do them." [6] The robe was called *tallit*, a square piece of woolen cloth. Thus the *tzitzit* was the peculiar badge of the Jews, separating him from the non-Jew. In the course of time, as the Jew found himself in foreign lands, he was compelled by circumstances to abandon this biblically prescribed garment. To fulfill the law, traditional Judaism resorted to a small, four-cornered cloth worn by men under their street dress, to which the traditionally woven fringes are attached. The *tallit* has been preserved as the prayer shawl, worn by observant Jews—adult, male only—in their morning prayers. Reform Judaism has abandoned this institution. The *tallit* is retained, however, in some Reform synagogues as the surplice over the gown worn by the rabbi in worship. [7]

TEFILLIN

According to Orthodoxy every male adult, from the age of thirteen, is required to wear *tefillin* when speaking his week-day morning prayers. The word is derived from the Hebrew for prayer, *tefillah*. They are two square black leather boxes, containing on parchment four biblical passages: Exodus 13:1–19; 13:11–16; Deuteronomy 6:4–9 and 11:13–21. One is worn on the left arm and one on the forehead, where the hair-growth starts, held in place by leather straps. Like the *mezuzah* it is in fulfillment of the biblical command: "Thou shalt bind them (the words of the Law) for a sign upon thy hand and they shall be for frontlets between thine eyes." [8] Again like the *mezuzah*, the tefillin were given superstitious interpretations at various periods in Jewish history. This, plus the cumbersomeness of the objects and literalistic interpretation of Bible text, led the Reform fathers to abandon the custom.

Before and after meals the observant Jew speaks a prayer of thanksgiving to God for the bounty of the earth. On the Sabbath and holidays the blessings are more elaborate.[9]

DIETARY LAWS

Jewish dietary laws, decreed in the Bible, extended and integrated into the structure of Judaism in the Talmud, have been a powerful agency in keeping the Jewish community distinct and apart in the non-Jewish world. In keeping with their aim of separating and sanctifying Israel as the priest-people among the nations, the talmudic masters forged their most effective instrument in the dietary laws.

The various laws, to the last detail, the rabbinic teachers asserted, were divinely ordained. "Our Father in heaven decreed that we should abstain from it (forbidden food)" declares an ancient rabbinic teacher.[10] Modern interpreters of Orthodox Judaism concur. "There is no other reason for all the dietary laws than that God gave them." [11] "The dietary laws are exactly the same now (1896) as they were in the days of Moses." [12]

The Jewish diet, as prescribed in rabbinic law, is in terms of *Kosher* and *terefah,* permissible and forbidden, ritually fit and ritually unfit.

In Leviticus 11 and Deuteronomy 14 we have the Bible sources for the permitted and forbidden foods. Of mammals, those may be eaten that meet a double test: have cloven hoofs and chew the cud. Of marine life only those fish may be eaten that have fins and scales. Thus oysters, lobsters, crabs, eels are prohibited. All kinds of fowl are permitted excepting birds of prey, specifically identified in the Bible. Insects and reptiles are prohibited, excepting certain kinds of locusts, listed in the Bible. Flesh of diseased animals, or of animals that died a natural death (*nebelah*), or were torn by beasts or birds of prey (*terefah*), are forbidden.[13]

Of the permitted (*Kosher*) animals certain parts are prohibited: Blood and abdominal fat may not be part of the Jewish diet in any form. The Bible is emphatic: "It shall be a
perpetual statute throughout your generations in all your
dwellings, that ye shall eat neither fat nor blood." [14] "For
whosoever eateth the fat of the beast, of which men present
an offering made by fire unto the Lord, even the soul that
eateth it shall be cut off from his people. And ye shall eat no
manner of blood, whether it be of fowl or beast, in any of your
dwellings. Whosoever it be that eateth any blood, that soul
shall be cut off from his people." [15] Blood was considered life
itself. "Only be steadfast in not eating the blood; for the blood
is the life; and thou shalt not eat the life with the flesh." [16] The
prohibition against certain kinds of fat is not clear in its motivation. Forbidden, also, is the sirloin and tenderloin, unless
the sinew of the thigh vein is carefully removed. [17]

The biblical legislation was implemented by the rabbinic
masters in an elaborate system of *kashrut*. The prohibition
against eating blood led to two special requirements: special
method of slaughtering the animal and preparation of the
meat for cooking. The slaughtering must be done by a quali-
fied person according to rabbinic prescription. The gullet and
windpipe are slashed with a meticulously prepared knife to
assure of two requirements: all blood must be drained, and
as little pain as possible inflicted on the animal. The meat is
soaked and salted by way of further draining it of blood.

Rabbinic law extends the system of *kashrut* still further
by requiring different cooking utensils and dishes for meats
(*fleishig*) and dairy foods (*milchig*)—milk, butter, cheese,
etc. All other foods—permitted fish, all vegetables, fruits, etc.
—are neutral (*parve*), and may be combined with either
meat or dairy menus. Six hours must elapse before the pious
Jew may eat dairy foods after having eaten meat; a shorter
period is sufficient before eating meats after having eaten
dairy foods.

The principle of not mixing meats and milk foods is based
on the biblical injunction, "Thou shalt not seethe a kid in its

mother's milk." [18] This has been translated, "Ye shall not eat flesh with milk." [19]

Orthodox law requires, further, that special cooking utensils and dishes be used for the festival of Passover. The principle here is that no leaven must be used on the holiday; dishes in use throughout the year, are ritualistically unclean for the Passover.

In a special class of forbidden food is wine used in idolatrous worship, or made, or in any way handled, by an idolator. In case of illness or emergency these laws are relaxed.[20]

Orthodox Judaism insists on the scrupulous observance of the laws of *kashrut*, though, under the pressure of contemporary life, Orthodox Jews may take liberties with them. Reform Judaism treats the dietary laws as part of the ceremonial law, most of which it considers obsolete in modern times. Further, not sharing fully Orthodoxy's insistence on segregation and separatism as a principle, Reform Jews have allowed the entire Kosher code to lapse. Conservative Judaism officially stands upon the historic interpretation of *kashrut*. A further emphasis is made by Conservative rabbis and teachers: *survival value*. Seeking to live as a distinct, historic community in a non-Jewish world, these interpreters of Judaism place high value on any custom, ceremony or institution that tends to shield Jewry against assimilation and disintegration. In practice, however, many Conservative Jews follow Reform in disregarding the dietary laws.[21]

THE COVERING OF THE HEAD

Orthodox and Conservative Judaism require the covering of the head for all men when performing any religious duty, when reciting prayers, or when entering a synagogue. There is no law in the Bible or Talmud prescribing the requirement. The practice of covering the head is a custom (*minhag*); the insistence upon it as a religious standard developed in comparatively modern times. So great a rabbinic authority as Elijah, the Gaon of Vilna, states: "According to Jewish law it is permitted to enter a synagogue and to pray without covering one's head." [22] Modern scholars concur: "The practice of covering the head when entering a synagogue, and when reciting prayers or performing any other religious ceremony, is not based on any talmudic law and cannot be supported by any express statement in the Talmud. Many express statements and implied teachings of the Talmud rather point to the contrary. This practice is merely a custom that first appeared among the Jews of Babylon. In the course of time it spread to other countries and gradually became a generally observed custom among Orthodox Jews. Its origin probably goes back to a non-Jewish source." [23] In Orthodoxy, however, established custom acquires the force of law.

The purpose of the custom is to express reverence. The uncovered head, in the countries where the custom arose, expresses arrogance. To make the observance easier, a skull cap may be worn (*yarmulke*).

As late as the seventeenth and eighteenth centuries the practice was debated by rabbinic authorities. The principle of separatism was a basic consideration in establishing the custom, though in Mohammedanism the same practice obtains. In 1845 the Reform congregation in Berlin adopted the custom of praying bareheaded. In the subsequent polemics on the issue, Orthodoxy became all the more insistent on its requirement. The Reform practice of removing the hat is based on the consideration that in the Western world respect is shown by removing the hat. Reform, however, does not make its own interpretation a requirement of faith or practice. It treats the matter as a minor detail. Conservative Judaism has not deviated from Orthodoxy in this matter.

IN THE SYNAGOGUE

Every synagogue, however modest, has certain ceremonial objects.

In the eastern wall of the synagogue is the *Ark*, which holds the *Scrolls of the Law*. The congregation faces the Ark and the east (*mizrach*) in prayer. The custom of standing in prayer toward the east and Jerusalem (in western countries, west, south or north, elsewhere, as the case may be) dates back to the fall of the Holy City to the Babylonian invaders. The Scolls of the Law are especially prepared by consecrated and competent scribes. They are handwritten in square Hebrew letters, on the parchment of ritually clean (*kosher*) animals. The slightest error in the text disqualifies the Scroll. The two rollers to which the parchment is attached are called the *etz chayim* (tree of life). Discs at the upper and lower ends of the *etz chayim* keep the rolls straight. A band tied around the Scrolls holds it together. Various ornaments may be used in beautifying and honoring the Scrolls: a specially prepared mantle, on which may be embroidered the Ten Commandments, a crown of the Law, the names of persons memorialized, etc., a silver or gold breastplate, and crown, after the manner of the breastplate and crown worn by the ancient High Priest, may adorn the Scroll further. A pointer (*yod*) in the form of a closed hand with an extended index finger, in silver, gold, or wood, is used as an aid to the eye in reading from the Scroll. A curtain usually adorns the doors of the Ark (*Parochet*). A Ten Commandment tablet may be part of its decoration.

The Torah scroll is read as part of the morning services on the Sabbath, on all holidays, and on Mondays and Thursdays. The Pentateuch is divided into sections corresponding to the Sabbaths of the year (*sidrot*). Thus the Five Books of Moses are read through annually. Originally the Torah was read through in three years. The annual cycle, however, originating in Babylon, became the established custom. The prescribed portion from the Pentateuch is supplemented with selections from the Prophets (*haftarah*). Men from the congregation assist in the reading from the Torah, pronouncing a blessing before and after the reading. Being called up to the reading or assisting with the handling is a coveted honor. Men experiencing a special event in their lives—*bar mitzvah*, anticipating marriage, observing an anniversary, etc.—are especially honored by being called up to the last part of the Torah portion for the week (*maftir*). After reading, the Scroll is lifted so that the entire congregation may see it (*hagbeh*). The primary reason for reading from the Scroll is to expound the Law and the prophets. Thus religious study is part of worship.

Above and in front of the Ark is a Perpetual Light (*ner tamid*), symbolizing the eternal light of God and His Torah, in keeping with the biblical command: "Command the children of Israel . . . to cause the lamp to burn continually . . . before the Lord." [24] Flanking the Ark are seven branched *menorahs*.

In Orthodox synagogues a special section—usually the gallery—is reserved for women, for, traditionally, women are segregated from men in the synagogue. Reform Judaism, enfranchising woman for the first time in Jewish history, has done away with the segregation of the sexes in the synagogue. Conservative Judaism has not revised the traditional laws but has permitted the segregation to go by default.

The reader's and preacher's desks may be on a platform facing the congregation or—following the ancient and hence established custom adhered to in Orthodoxy—in the center of the synagogue, with the pews built around it. Originally the reading of the Law was the central feature of the service; hence the central position accorded the reader's desk (*almemar*, Arabic, *al-mimbar*, speaker's pulpit; or *bema*, Greek for speaker's tribune). Reform Judaism, emphasizing the sermon, moved the speaker's desk to the front. Conservative and many Orthodox synagogues have adopted this practice.

The various symbols and furniture described above are usually found in synagogues. Without some—the Scrolls of the Law, for instance—the synagogue can hardly function. But they are not required by law. In addition to those listed many more may be found in the well-situated synagogues—such as stained glass windows, memorial plaques, flags, various religious art objects. Other synagogues may be bare of most of these. The sanctity of the synagogue is determined not by what is in the synagogue but by what is in the hearts and minds of the worshippers. "Ye shall build me a sanctuary that I may dwell among them," [25] the Bible commands. The rabbinic teachers interpret it to mean: "Ye shall build me a sanctuary that I may dwell in the lives of those who build it." "When ten people sit together and occupy themselves with the Torah, the *Shechina* abides among them, as it is said, 'God standeth in the congregation of the godly.' " [26]

Ten men (*minyan*) are required to constitute a congregation for Orthodox or Conservative public worship. The service may be conducted by any one of them. Reform accepts women on equal terms with men in the conduct of a service.

XVIII. FROM CRADLE TO GRAVE

NAMING OF CHILD, CIRCUMCISION, REDEMPTION,
BAR MITZVAH, CONFIRMATION, MARRIAGE AND DIVORCE

From the cradle to the grave Jewish life is distinguished and consecrated by religious duties and observances, customs and ceremonies.

Girls are given their names in the synagogue services on the Sabbath nearest to their birthday, when one or both parents may be present in the synagogue. The father is usually called up to the Torah. Boys are usually named at the circumcision. Both girls and boys may be named in the synagogue. The name is of the parents' choice. In early talmudic times the custom developed of naming children after deceased relatives. In medieval times the custom developed, further, of avoiding naming children after living relatives, though it did not obtain among Spanish Jews. In contemporary Jewry the naming of children after living relatives, including fathers, is quite common.[1]

Male children are circumcised on the eighth day after birth, even if the day happens to be a Sabbath or the Day of Atonement. Circumcision may be postponed if the health of the child requires it. In Orthodoxy, a professional functionary (*mohel*), must perform the operation. Reform Judaism permits a physician to perform circumcision; under special circumstances a non-Jew too, may perform the operation. The custom goes back to the earliest of days in Jewish history, antedating Abraham, practiced by many non-Hebrew peoples. The rite is known as *brith milah*.[2]

The first born child, if a male, must be "redeemed." The service is known as the "redemption of the son." It finds its origin in very early Bible legislation; "Sanctify unto Me all the first-born, whatsoever openeth the womb among the children of Israel, both of man or of beast." [3] Redemption is achieved by paying a sum of money to a *Cohen* (i.e., a descendant of the Aaronic priesthood). Reform Judaism has abandoned the rite on the grounds that it is a primitive practice associated with the outmoded laws of primogeniture and dedication, and even of the sacrificing of the first-born to the deity. The Conservative synagogue has not spoken its mind in the matter.[4]

Young children beginning their school careers may be inducted with a special blessing, usually on the last Day of *Sukkot*, or *Simchas Torah*, the festival dedicated to the rejoicing over the Torah.[5]

Upon reaching the age of thirteen the Jewish boy is inducted into adulthood, and full responsibility as an adult in the household of Israel, with a special service of *Bar Mitzvah* (son of duty). The service is held on the nearest Sabbath or shortly thereafter. The boy is called up to the Torah, after the manner of an adult; he speaks the appropriate blessing, may read from the Torah and the Prophets, and may address the congregation or offer a special prayer. It is a happy event in the life of the family. The ceremony of *Bar Mitzvah* is of comparatively late origin. It seems to have originated with German Jewry, probably not earlier than the fourteenth century. Reform Judaism, placing women on equal footing with men, and, further, seeking to extend the boy's career in the religious school, has introduced the ceremony of *Confirmation* in place of *Bar Mitzvah*, for girls and boys alike, and not necessarily at the age of thirteen.[6] Both *Bar Mitzvah* and Confirmation are practiced in some Reform and Conservative congregations.

MARRIAGE LAWS, RITES AND CUSTOMS

Judaism has dowered marriage with all the sanctity at its command. It sees in marriage the central and most sacred institution in human life. Marriage is a consecration of man and woman for the furtherance of God's will on earth. Judaism disapproves of celibacy. "It is not good for man to be alone"; [7] therefore, God created woman. Man is incomplete without woman; a woman is incomplete without man, and both are incomplete without the presence of God.

In Bible times Hebrew marriage was polygamous. Gradually it shifted toward monogamy. The rabbinic masters could not categorically outlaw polygamy for the reason that it is sanctioned in the Bible; but they discouraged it in every way at their command. In 1040 Rabbi Gershon ben Judah virtually abolished polygamy among Ashkenazic Jewry. Bible law recognizes, also, concubinage as a form of polygamy.

Marriage is a sacred contract. Only they may enter into any contract who are fit and able to fulfill its terms. The same applies to a marriage contract. Hence, minors and mentally incompetent may not marry (idiots and insane). Special provision is made for deaf and dumb people to express themselves in the sealing of the contract. Sexually impotent people, eunuchs, and castrates may not marry.

Marriage is permitted only if parties to it meet specific requirements. To be valid both parties must enter into it on their own free will. Jewish marriage requires that both parties be Jewish. Intermarriage is prohibited. When the non-Jewish party is officially converted to Judaism the impediment is removed. The objection to intermarriage rests on religious, not racial grounds. The prohibition is removed and the marriage may be solemnized according to the established Jewish sanctions when the non-Jewish party is officially converted to Judaism. In every sense such a marriage has the same status as any other Jewish marriage.

Civil marriages are sternly discouraged in all branches of Judaism. Once they take place, however, they are binding. The offspring of such a marriage are considered legitimate.[8]

A table of prohibited marriages is established in rabbinic law, which is an extension and elaboration of biblical law, in the principles of consanguinity.[9] The principle of consanguinity is set aside in the cases of first cousins, and uncle and niece, these being sanctioned in the Bible.[10]

In all cases where there is a discrepancy between rabbinic and secular state law, the practice is to follow the stricter law.

The present marriage ceremony is a combination of two ceremonies, corresponding to two distinct stages in contracting a marriage in former times. The first stage was *Erusin,* or betrothal; the consummation of the marriage, a year later, was the *Nissuin,* when the bride was brought to the husband's home. The *Huppah,* wedding canopy, used today in Orthodox and Conservative marriage services, represents the bridegroom's chamber into which the bride was led.* From a legal standpoint the marriage began with the betrothal. Only a divorce could separate one from his betrothal. In the Middle Ages these two stages were combined into one service.

Reform Judaism has minimized the necessity of the *Huppah. Wine,* symbol of joy in Judaism, is used. In Orthodox and Conservative services the benediction over the wine is spoken at two points in the service, a survival of the earlier forms of marriage. The groom places a ring on the bride's finger and speaks the marriage formula, in Aramaic, which seals the contract:

"Behold, thou art consecrated unto me with this ring according to the law of Moses and Israel."

The use of the ring in the Jewish marriage service is of post-talmudic times. Orthodox and Conservative Judaism objects to a jewelled ring, preferring a plain gold band. The *Shulkhan Aruk* gives the following reason: "If he marries her with an object, with regard to the value of which it is easy to err, such as precious stones, it is necessary to make an evaluation. Therefore, it is the custom to marry with a ring that has no stone." [11] The ring was thus, in whole or in part, a purchasing price. That has lost all meaning in modern times when the ring

* Another explanation is offered. "What we today call the Huppah, namely a cloth held by four staves over the bride and groom, may be derived from the medieval custom of covering the bride with his tallit." (Freehof, p. 89.)

is a symbol only. In Reform services, therefore, any ring may be used. In Reform, also, the custom is followed by the bride placing a ring on the groom's finger, if so desired, as a symbol of the equality of men and women in the marriage. Orthodox and Conservative Judaism does not permit it.

At Orthodox services a *Ketubah* is read. This marriage contract is a reform measure introduced in the first pre-Christian century by Simeon ben Shetah, and had as its primary purpose the safeguarding of the rights of woman. It sought to put a check on arbitrary divorce, since a man could divorce his wife without her consent. In time the *Ketubah* underwent considerable modification, covering the business relationships, property rights, mutual responsibilities of husband and wife. It represents the legal part of marriage. Gradually, as the social, economic and political settings of Jewish life changed, and the state took over the legal aspect of marriage, bringing to it its own far securer safeguards of rights and duties, the *Ketubah* lost its reality. It figures in a marriage service today only as a bit of ritual. "The function of the *Ketubah* in our day is practically no other than to perpetuate an ancient tradition. Its effectiveness in actual questions of law, even Jewish law, is very slight, since it is stereotyped and reduced to the very minimum of specifications. Every *Ketubah* is exactly like every other *Ketubah*. In former days, its effectiveness as a document of rights and guarantees was real." [12]

Following the benediction, concluding the marriage service, a glass is crushed by the bridegroom in Orthodox and Conservative weddings. Reform has abolished the rite.

The ceremony of breaking the glass, the bridegroom stepping on it, is ancient. Officially, from the standpoint of Orthodoxy, it symbolizes the Jew's mourning for the destruction of Jerusalem. Modern scholars trace the custom back to superstitious origins. It is a survival of primitive efforts to ward off the demons that are bent on disrupting human happiness. "It is the belief that the evil spirits or demons are jealous of human happiness and therefore seek to spoil it or to harm the happy individual. The bride and the groom about to be married are,

accordingly, the objects of the envy of the demons and liable
to be harmed by them. It was believed that the bridegroom
was especially exposed to such danger. For the evil spirits, like
the arch demons or the fallen angels of old, notice the beautiful daughters of men and desire them." [13] The breaking of the
glass is a survival of a rite to ward off the demons. The custom
of veiling the bride, it is believed, is part of the same magic:
the aim is to hide her beauty from the evil powers.

Jewish marriages may not be solemnized on certain days.
Orthodoxy has developed an elaborate structure of forbidden
dates. Conservative Judaism has not revised it. Reform has
removed the prohibition from most of these.

No marriages may take place on the Sabbath nor on the first
days of the holidays, according to Reform practice. Most Reform rabbis will not officiate at weddings on *Tishe B'ab,*
though the fathers of Reform abolished the fast. Orthodox
and Conservative Judaism prohibits marriages on the following days: the Sabbath and all holidays (excepting Hanukkah,
Purim), fast days, half holidays, first through the ninth day of
the month Ab, commemorating the siege and fall of Jerusalem
to the Romans in the year 70; (very pious Jews will abstain
from marriage three weeks before the ninth of Ab), the Ten
Days of Penitence, between New Year and the Day of Atonement, and the "Omer" period between Passover and Shabuot.
The ban is lifted on the thirty-third day of this period (*Lag
Ba'omer*). The Omer period is prohibited because, according
to tradition, many of Rabbi Akiba's students died of the plague
during this period. The plague, according to legend, ceased on
the thirty-third day.

The prohibition of marriage on holidays rests on a double
basis: marriage involves a legal as well as a religious aspect.
No business may be transacted on sacred days. Further, the
joy of the marriage must not be confused with the joy of the
holiday.[14]

Marriages should not take place during the first thirty days
of mourning for parents.[15] However, the law recognizes
special circumstances and the general rule may be modified. A

widow is required to wait three months after her husband's death before remarrying. The primary purpose of the regulation is to leave no doubt as to the paternity of the possible offspring of the second marriage. Specific regulations require widowers to wait a varied period before remarrying. Reform encourages a thirty-day-period of waiting.[16]

Levirate marriage was practiced by many primitive peoples and is required in Bible legislation. The brother of a man who dies and leaves a widow but no male child is obliged to marry the widow. The first-born of this marriage carries the name of the deceased, "that his name be not blotted out in Israel." [17] The marriage was obligatory only when there was no male issue and when the same brothers had been living on the same estate. The surviving brother could free himself from the obligation by subjecting himself to the ceremony of *Halizah*. The Talmud considered levirate marriage objectionable; the shift to monogomy negated the institution.[18] Halizah was transformed from an evasion to a duty.

Divorce is an ancient institution in Judaism, established in Bible and regulated in talmudic and post-talmudic law. Because of the disability of woman in Hebrew law—as in practically all laws of antiquity—the right to divorce rests with the husband. Under talmudic law he may—at least in theory—divorce her at will. The wife may not divorce her husband, though under restricted circumstances the husband may be compelled to grant her a divorce. Various devices were employed in safeguarding the wife's rights. The *Ketubah*, as we have noted, was instituted and revised to meet this need. The principle, however, remains in Orthodox and Conservative Judaism: the right to divorce rests with the husband. Reform Judaism, for the first time in history, enfranchised woman and thereby placed marriage and divorce on the basis of absolute equality of the sexes before the law. Reform rabbis therefore accept civil divorce as final, and will officiate at the marriages of people divorced by the laws of the state, without requiring a traditional Jewish divorce (*get*). In Orthodox and Conservative Judaism woman's disability stands; a person civilly divorced cannot remarry without a Jewish divorce in addition to the civil.

Because divorce must originate with the man, and because, further, there is no presumption of death in Hebrew law, a special hardship is experienced by women whose husbands have disappeared. In periods of social dislocations, such as in times of war, where no official reports of death is made, the wife remains an *Agunah*, merely a deserted wife. She may not remarry according to the laws and practices of Orthodox and Conservative Judaism. Reform follows the civil laws in the matter.[19]

BURIAL AND MOURNING

Burial and mourning rites and customs arise from inner needs and the external environment. Judaism, developing as it did in many ages and in many lands, reflects in its mourning rites and customs the constant human instinct of solemnity and awe, and the yearning for consolation and reassurance, when facing the ultimate fact of death. The folklore of many peoples color many a rite and custom considered in Orthodoxy a divine decree by God to Moses on Mount Sinai.

Some practices are debated. On the whole, Orthodoxy stands on its central principle of divine revelation and seeks to justify the various practices on the basis of authoritative Jewish tradition in Bible, Talmud, or the Oral Law; Reform takes its stand on its own central principle of a progressive revelation, forever growing and forever responding to human needs, holding itself free to adjust its standards to various shifting circumstances. Conservative Judaism, finding itself between Orthodox dogma and folk feeling on the one hand and the pressure of the new environment, intellectually as well as socially, on the other, temporizes between Orthodoxy and Reform.[20]

Autopsy is forbidden in Orthodoxy, except in specific instances; it is permitted in Reform. The same applies to embalming: Orthodoxy prohibits it, excepting where the law of the land requires it; Reform has no religious objection to it. Immediate burial, required in Orthodoxy, is not required in Reform. Orthodoxy insists on shrouds and bare pine coffins; Reform is indifferent to it and permits people to follow whatever standard obtains in any given environment. Funeral services may not be conducted on sacred days, and not after sundown. Flowers are discouraged in Orthodoxy as an alien practice; Reform has no objections. Cremation is forbidden in authoritative tradition; "dust thou art and unto dust returnest," is followed literally. Reform permits cremation. Jewish people are buried in Jewish cemeteries; non-Jewish members of a Jewish family may or may not be permitted burial in Jewish cemeteries, depending on special considerations; Orthodoxy opposes it in principle. Disinterment is discouraged, but permitted under special circumstances. The practice of covering the mirrors of a house where a death took place is folkloristic and has no basis in law; however, from the standpoint of Orthodoxy such practices acquire the status of law. Reform is indifferent to this practice. Rending a garment, or cutting into it (keriah), is based on biblical example, and is mandatory in Orthodoxy. When news of Joseph's death was brought to his father, "Jacob rent his garments and put sackcloth on his loins." [21] Wearing sackcloth and putting dust on one's head never became an established custom; but cutting into a garment did. Reform is indifferent to the rite. Dark clothes as gesture of mourning is usually observed. A light is kept burning in the house of mourning for the first week of mourning. It is probably inspired by the association of light with the spirit of man; "the spirit of man is the lamp of God." [22] Public worship is held in the home for the week (Shivah). The requirements in official observation of mourning are eased as the year advances. Mourning practices are eased on the Sabbath and the other sacred days, for the joy of the sacred days must not be marred.

On the first Sabbath after the funeral, the mourners attend divine services at the synagogue. The Kaddish is recited by mourners at all services, for eleven months in Orthodoxy and for a year in Reform. An annual observance of the death of a loved one is observed (*Yahrzeit*) with the kindling of a light in the home, which burns from sundown to sundown.

The *Kaddish*, originally, had no association with death and mourning. It is a hymn of praise, extolling the majesty of God and avowing faith in Him, serenely accepting His will. "It was in the first instance a doxology at the conclusion of the reading of the Bible or of a sermon. 'The Kaddish has a remarkable history. Originally, it had no relation whatsoever to the prayers, and still less to the dead. It was the doxology recited by the teacher or preacher at the close of his discourse, when he was expected to dismiss the assembly with an allusion to the Messianic hope, derived especially from the prophets and the Psalms.' It was composed in Aramaic, for this was the language spoken by the Jews after the Babylonian exile, and it was held desirable that the doxology should be understood by those who were present at the discourses, but were little acquainted with the Hebrew." [23] The prayer is ancient; the responses are biblical, mainly from the book of Ezekiel.

There are several versions of the Kaddish, for various occasions and places in public worship. The Reform version is a combination of the several, with slight adaptations. Basically the following version from the daily service is standard:

> Magnified and sanctified be his great name in the world which he hath created according to his will. May he establish his kingdom during your life and during your days, and during the life of all the house of Israel, even speedily and at a near time, and say ye, Amen.
>
> Let his great name be blessed for ever and to all eternity.
>
> Blessed, praised and glorified, exalted, extolled and honoured, magnified and lauded be the name of the Holy One, blessed be he; though he be high above all the blessings and hymns, praises and consolations, which are uttered in the world; and say ye, Amen.
>
> May there be abundant peace from heaven, and life for us and for all Israel; and say ye, Amen.

He who maketh peace in his high places, may he make
peace for us and for all Israel; and say ye, Amen.[24]

In addition to the *Yahrzeit*, the departed are memorialized
on the Day of Atonement and the last days of the Three
Festivals—Pesach, Shabuot and Sukkot—with special memorial (*Yizkor*) prayers. The Reform synagogues have en-
larged the memorial service on the Day of Atonement; some
Reform synagogues do and other do not recite the *Yizkor* on
the Festivals.

Each of the practices cited above needs fuller exposition.
The student is referred to the literature indicated in the notes.

HOLY DAYS

XIX. INTRODUCTORY

Judaism, like all religions, celebrates a number of sacred days. Its basic teaching and unique character are expressed and fostered through these holy days. Each has its own distinctive philosophy, its own history, and its special ceremonial.

Two characteristics mark the whole cycle of Jewish holidays.

First, they are religious in character. The Bible ordains them as "feasts of the Lord," "holy convocations," "the appointed seasons of the Lord." There are no secular holidays in Judaism. What might have remained as secular events in history became religious institutions. The Passover might have remained merely an event in Israelitish history; tribes of slaves escaped their masters, as so many other tribes have done in the history of mankind. Pentecost might have remained only an event in history, a sort of "Constitution Day." Sukkot might have remained a farmer's frolic. In Israel, however, these were transformed into holy days, fostering sacred truth for the Israelite and mankind.

Second, all Jewish holidays revolve around the people Israel. They commemorate events in the life of the whole people; they do not celebrate any event in the life of any one personality in Jewry. Here is a further manifestation of the folk character of Judaism. Passover thus commemorates the time when all Israel found release from servitude; Shabuot memorializes the giving of the Law to all Israel; Sukkot reminds us of the harvests the Judean masses gathered; Purim recalls the time when all the Jews were delivered from disaster; Hanukkah extolls the valor of the Maccabees and the restoration and rededication of Jewry's central shrine. The Sabbath, New Year, and the Day of Atonement do not memorialize any historic event in the history of Israel; but they rest on a broad, universal basis.

In Jewish experience the holy days have yielded a double boon. They have been a bond of union, contributing mightily to the preservation of the Jewish people under circumstances that might have undone them. Being an extra-territorial group, Jewry always needed strong inner ties. The holy days have been such ties. They have kept the past alive in the souls of Israel; they have been rousing Jewry to its duties, exciting it with eternal hopes and uniting it with the bonds of historic sentiment, customs and ceremonies. They have radiated a holy light in every observant Jewish home and sanctified it. "The children of Israel shall keep the Sabbath and observe it throughout all generations. It is a sign between Me and the children of Israel forever." [1] And while the children of Israel preserved the Sabbath and the other sacred days, they found themselves preserved by them.

But the sacred days did more than merely preserve Jewry; they breathed the sacred into Jewish life and endowed it with religious idealism. What Ezekiel said of the ministry of the Sabbath in Jewish life defines the influence exerted by the rest of the Jewish sacred days: "I gave them My sabbaths to be a sign between me and them, that they might know that I am the Lord that sanctifieth them." [2] A characteristic sentence in Jewish liturgy is "Blessed art Thou, Lord our God, who hast sanctified us by Thy commandments." Thus have the holy days preserved Israel as "a nation of priests and a holy people."

In contemporary Judaism a difference obtains as to the number of days that are observed as sacred. Orthodox and Conservative Judaism observes the number established in law and custom: New Year, two; Day of Atonement, one; Passover, eight; the Feast of Tabernacles, nine; Pentecost, two. These represent rabbinic modifications of biblical requirements arising from the difficulties of the calendar. The synagogue follows the lunar calendar. The proclamation of the new moon involved considerable difficulties in Bible and in early

talmudic times. Sentinels watching for the appearance of the
new moon would report to the Sanhedrin in Jerusalem. The
Sanhedrin would receive the news, officially declare the new
month, and dispatch heralds throughout the Jewish world to
convey the tidings. Within the borders of Palestine the news
could be reported within the day; to carry the news to far flung
Jewish communities outside Palestine required more time.
Hence, an extra day was added to each holiday, except the
Day of Atonement. It would impose too harsh a discipline to
observe a fast for two consecutive days. The second day holiday is thus a Diaspora institution necessitated by the primitive
calendation methods of the time. Reform Judaism abolished
the second day for the reason that we are no longer confronted
with the difficulties of observation and proclamation of the
new moon, thus reverting to the number of days prescribed
in the Bible.*

All Jewish holidays begin with the sunset of the preceding
day, for the day, according to the Hebrew calendar, begins
with the evening. "And there was evening and there was
morning the first day," reads the account of Creation in Genesis. The formula is maintained throughout the chapter. The
evening is stated first; hence, it is reasoned, the day begins
with the evening.

Home and synagogue are the scenes of the observance. The
mother kindles the lights in the home and speaks a blessing.
The father pronounces the *Kiddush* and blesses the children.
Even the menu of the day contains some dish traditionally
associated with the holiday, thus reflecting the folk character
of Judaism. Much sentiment, poetry, and music have evolved
around each of the holidays.

Jewish holidays are basically joyous. The Days of Awe are
solemn, serious, disturbing the conscience; but they are not
sad. "Thou shalt rejoice before the Lord thy God, thou, and
thy son, and thy daughter, and thy manservant and thy maid-

* The New Year was observed as a two-day holiday in Palestine as well as
in the Diaspora.

servant, and the Levite that is within thy gates, and the stranger, and the fatherless and the widow that are in the midst of thee. . . ." [3]

The rest of the holidays are decidedly joyous. The Sabbath call to worship may be taken as expressive of the spirit of all Jewish holidays: "Come, let us sing unto the Lord; let us shout for joy to the Rock of our Salvations." "Serve the Lord with gladness; come before Him with singing." [4] A cup of wine is blessed on the eve of each of the holidays (excepting, of course, on the eve of the Day of Atonement, which is a fast day), wine being a symbol of joy. The holidays are commandments of the Lord; hence, they must be observed in joy. "Ever let a man fulfill the commandments of the Torah in joy, and it will be accounted unto him for righteousness." [5] "R. Eliezer said, 'On festivals let a man eat and drink, or sit and study.'" [6] "R. Joshua said, 'Divide your time; devote half to God and half to yourself.'" [7] R. Eliezer quoted Nehemiah 8:10, *Go your way, eat the fat, and drink the sweet and send portions unto him for whom nothing is ready; for this day is holy unto the Lord; neither be grieved, for the joy of the Lord is your strength.* But the enjoyment must be refined and chastened by the sense of the sacred. "The Holy Spirit does not rest where there is idleness, or ribaldry, or empty talk, but only where there is joy."

XX. THE SABBATH

The Sabbath is one of the oldest holidays in the history of Judaism. Its origin is unknown. The theories as to its beginnings are still debated by scholars. It has exerted a powerful spiritualizing influence in Jewish life from the earliest days to the present.

Several passages in the Bible serve as its basis. In the second chapter of Genesis we are told that the Sabbath was ordained by God upon the completion of Creation. Thus the Sabbath is part of the cosmic scheme of things. It was ordained by Him Who called the universe into being. The very universe would be incomplete without it. The Decalogue establishes it in law. The two versions of the Decalogue give it a double motivation. In Exodus it is impelled by the imitation of God:

> Remember the Sabbath day, to keep it holy. Six days shalt thou labour and do all thy work; but the seventh day is a Sabbath unto the Lord thy God; in it thou shalt not do any manner of work, thou, nor thy son, nor thy daughter, nor thy man-servant, nor thy cattle, nor thy stranger that is within thy gates; for in six days the Lord made heaven and earth, the sea, and all that in them is, and rested upon the seventh day; wherefore the Lord blessed the seventh.[1]

In Deuteronomy it is inspired by social justice:

> . . . that thy man-servant and thy maid-servant may rest as well as thou. And thou shalt remember that thou wast a servant in the land of Egypt, and the Lord thy God brought thee out thence by a mighty hand and by an outstretched arm; therefore the Lord thy God commanded thee to keep the sabbath day.[2]

The rabbis saw no conflict between these two versions of the commandment; rather, they considered one version as supplementing the other.

173

The Sabbath was given man to reclaim and redeem him physically and spiritually. This is the central aim of the day. The charge of austerity and legalistic rigor made against the Jewish Sabbath rests on an external and alien understanding of the Jew's love for his Sabbath. The rich sentiment, lofty prayer, exalted music, sacred poetry and deep humanity the Sabbath inspired in the life of Jewry is ample refutation of this charge.

The Jew spoke of the Sabbath as a bride come from heaven to grace his home with the beauty of holiness.[3] A Sabbath song popular in every observant home the world over since the seventeenth century welcomes "the ministering angels, the messengers of the Most High."[4] The Pharisaic masters make the joyous character of the Sabbath obligatory. Every man should enjoy three good meals on the day, and the poor must be helped to observe this requirement. The best silverware, china, linen should be used; one should wear his best clothes. Wine, symbol of gladness, is peculiarly appropriate to the day, since "wine maketh glad the heart of man."[5] One must not mourn his dead on the day; memorial services are excluded from the Sabbath ritual. Fasts falling on the Sabbath must be observed a day later. The only exception to this rule is the Day of Atonement. Only happy events are associated with the Sabbath. *Bar Mitzvah* is therefore placed on the Sabbath closest to the boy's thirteenth birthday. Family gatherings on the day are encouraged. Guests—particularly men of learning —grace the home. Thus did the rabbinic masters fashion the Sabbath as "a foretaste of the world to come."[6] The pious observers enjoyed "a special soul" on the holy day.[7] Commenting on the verse, "And ye shall keep the Sabbath for it is a holy day unto you," the rabbinic teachers observe, "The Sabbath is given to you but you are not surrendered to the Sabbath."[8]

The modes of Sabbath observance vary in contemporary Judaism. Orthodox Judaism, following the *Halakah*, adheres to the established laws and practices as stated in the authoritative lore of the synagogue; Reform Judaism, under the pressure of contemporary life, and impatient with ancient cere-

monial laws in the modern world, seeks to capture the spirit
of the Sabbath, taking bold liberties with law and time-
honored usage. Conservative Judaism is officially committed
to the *Halakah* and the traditional forms, but in practice follows for the most part the ways of Reform.

Orthodox Judaism interprets the Sabbath as a day of complete rest and absolute cessation of all work. The day is devoted to the spiritual life as prescribed in detail in rabbinic
law. The Sabbath is at once restrictive and spiritual.

No work must be done on the day. Worldly pursuits are
banned. The prohibition of physical labor means that no Jew
may kindle a light or prepare food on the day. That must be
done before the Sabbath eve. "Ye shall kindle no fire throughout your habitations upon the Sabbath day." [9] One must not
ride, write, carry ought in his pocket, nor walk beyond the
limits permitted by rabbinic regulation. In emergencies, when
life is at stake, or when danger threatens a community, or in
time of war, the Sabbath restrictions are lifted. A physician
may treat his patient in case of serious illness, "for the laws
of the Torah," says Maimonides, "are not laws of vengeance
against the world, but laws of pity, mercy, and peace." [10]

The day begins with sundown. The time is set to the minute.
To create a margin of safety, lest the Sabbath be violated, the
hour or two before the exact minute is considered as introductory to the Sabbath. Sabbath lights are kindled in the home
at sundown; divine services in the synagogue begin at the
same time. The ritual of the day is determined in law and
custom. Nothing is omitted from the historic prayer book; in-
troductions are permitted but reluctantly and sparingly. The
prayers are entirely in Hebrew, with some portions in Aramaic.

On his return home from the synagogue the observant Jew
finds his home transformed into a sanctuary. He blesses his
children and recites the "virtuous woman" portion of the
thirty-first chapter of Proverbs in praise of his wife. He recites
the *Kiddush* over a cup of wine or fresh loaves of white bread
before partaking of the Sabbath eve meal. The meal itself is

partly ritualistic in character. Certain dishes are associated with the Sabbath. The table has a festive appearance even in the most modest home. Table songs—*zmiroth*—may be chanted between courses, or before grace is spoken.

The central feature of the Sabbath morning service in the synagogue is the reading from the Torah. Each Sabbath is known by its Torah portion. A number of Sabbaths are designated as special or distinguished Sabbaths.[11]

Reform Judaism observes the Sabbath with a view of making it yield its spiritual significance rather than scrupulous correctness of ritual. Thus it will permit writing, riding, carrying things on the Sabbath, if it is done reasonably. It recognizes frankly that because of the contemporary social and economic circumstances most Jews must attend to their businesses on the Sabbath. It has moved the Sabbath eve services to a late hour in the evening, following the meal at home, thus making Sabbath worship more possible for the larger number of people. It has abbreviated the service, rendering most of it in the vernacular, on the theory that the worshipper should have a clear understanding of what he is saying in his prayers. It has restated the contents of the liturgy in keeping with its understanding as to what is basic and what secondary in Judaism, and has given the sermon a place of prominence in the service.

Conservative Judaism observes the Sabbath in much the same manner as does Reform, though officially it has not departed from the Orthodox theology. Most Conservative synagogues hold late Sabbath eve services, abbreviate the liturgy, enjoy instrumental music and mixed choirs. Like Reform, Conservative Judaism is emphasizing the importance of the sermon as a feature of divine services.

Israel's life and destiny are peculiarly bound up with the Sabbath, observe the talmudic masters. This states a historic fact and defines the central problem in the life of religious Jewry. The institution that has endowed the life of the Jew with the beauty and the power of holiness is inundated by the waves of secularism that are overpowering all ancient landmarks.

XXI. DAYS OF AWE

NEW YEAR AND DAY OF ATONEMENT

The most solemn days in the Jewish calendar are New Year (*Rosh Hashanah*) and Day of Atonement (*Yom Kippur*). They mark a period of ten days known as *Ten Days of Penitence.* Stricter observance of religious duties and a larger measure of thoughtfulness generally distinguish these days. The intervening Sabbath is known as *Sabbath of Repentance,* deriving its teaching from the fourteenth chapter of the book of Hosea, read in synagogues on this Sabbath: "Return, O Israel, unto the Lord thy God, for thou hast stumbled in thine iniquity." [1] Several days before the New Year special prayers of supplication (*S'lichoth*) are recited in Orthodox and some Conservative synagogues at the break of day. It is customary to visit the graves of loved ones during these penitential days. Orthodox Judaism prohibits weddings on these days. Most Conservative congregations adhere to this restriction. Reform has declared it void on the ground that while these days are earnest they are not mournful; hence the prohibition is unwarranted.

New Year and Day of Atonement are usually spoken of as Days of Awe (*Yomim Noraim*). The designation is derived from the contents and spirit of these sacred days. They are the most universal holy days in the calendar of the synagogue, appealing to the human rather than to the distinctively Jewish.

Awe is a complex mood; it is an experience of wonder, veneration, fascination, fear. The harp of faith has many strings: awesome contemplation, dependence, gratitude, hope, despair, remorse, penitence, adoration. On Rosh Hashanah and Yom Kippur these strings are struck with might. The worshipper then stands before the sacred. He is fascinated and overwhelmed, lifted and exalted. Awe beats at his heart with powerful wings challenging.

On the Days of Awe the observant Jew contemplates his mortality and his destiny. Deep, elemental forces are aroused in his breast, for "God hath placed eternity in his heart" and "deep calls unto deep." He meditates on the complicated bundle of life with its tangled threads of birth and death, memory and hope, joy and sorrow, duty and honor, the swiftly moving procession of the days of his years with their sunshine and shadow. The shuttle flies back and forth in the loom; soon the pattern is finished and the thread is broken. The worshipper is before the throne of the Almighty; the judgments of God are about to be pronounced and his fate sealed.

New Year

New Year comes on the first day of Tishri, the seventh month in the Hebrew calendar. It falls, usually, in the latter part of September.

The new moon was a sacred occasion in ancient Israel. Many Bible passages refer to it as a solemn festival marked by the cessation of work, special sacrifices and the blowing of the *shofar* in the sanctuary. The earliest biblical sources couple it with the Sabbath. The seventh new moon was an especially sacred occasion, since seven was considered a sacred number. The seventh day was a sacred day, the Sabbath; the seventh year was a Sabbatical year; seven Sabbatical years culminated in the Jubilee. The seventh New Moon, accordingly, became the most important of the New Moon festivals, and developed into the New Year.

Just what the contents of the New Moon were the Bible references do not reveal. Presumably the waxing and waning of the moon evoked thoughts and apprehensions of man's mortality. Man, child of dust, is only a stranger and sojourner on earth. The tides swept on inexorably; man sought comfort in the shadow of the Eternal. This impulse beats with powerful rhythm in the Days of Awe.

Two strands determine the contents of New Year.

First, it is a *Day of Memorial.* The Bible speaks of it as a "memorial of blowing the trumpets," and a "day of blowing the trumpets." [2] The meaning and purpose of this blowing of trumpets is not clearly stated. The interpretation given in Jewish tradition, and established in Judaism, is that it is an occasion when memory is aroused, when the past is recalled, the future envisioned, and inventory taken.

Second, it is a *day of judgment.* This strand was woven into the texture of Judaism in later times. In the historic prayer book for the High Holy Days (*Machzor*) the idea of judgment is given emphatic expression. The worshipper is before the tribunal of the Judge of all the earth. The past is recalled so that honest judgment may be pronounced:

> *Reader.* And thus may the sanctification ascend unto thee; for thou art our God and King.
>
> *Cong.* We will celebrate the mighty holiness of this day, for it is one of awe and terror. Thereon is thy dominion exalted and thy throne is established in mercy, and thou sittest thereon in truth. Verily it is thou alone who art judge and arbiter, who knowest and art witness; thou writest down and settest the seal, thou recordest and tellest; yea, thou rememberest the things forgotten. Thou unfoldest the records, and the deeds therein inscribed proclaim themselves; for lo! the seal of every man's hand is set thereto.
>
> The great trumpet is sounded; the still, small voice is heard; the angels are dismayed; fear and trembling seize hold of them as they proclaim, Behold the Day of Judgment! The host of heaven is to be arraigned in judgment. For in thine eyes they are not pure; and all who enter the world dost thou cause to pass before thee as a flock of sheep. As a shepherd seeketh out his flock and causeth them to pass beneath his crook, so dost thou cause to pass, and number, tell and visit every living soul, appointing the measure of every creature's life and decreeing their destiny.
>
> On the first day of the year it is inscribed, and on the Day of Atonement the decree is sealed, how many shall

pass away and how many shall be born, who shall live and who shall die, who at the measure of man's days and who before it; who shall perish by fire and who by water, who by the sword, who by wild beasts, who by hunger and who by thirst; who by earthquake and who by plague, who by strangling and who by stoning; who shall have rest and who shall go wandering, who shall be tranquil and who shall be harassed, who shall be at ease and who shall be afflicted; who shall become poor and who shall wax rich; who shall be brought low and who shall be upraised.[3]

Man's place in the universe, and every man's personal part in the drama of life, is thus the central theme of New Year. The prayers, music, scriptural reading, and sermon of the day are aimed at stimulating the imagination and rousing the conscience. Memory and conscience are alerted and life is chastened. A new chapter begins in the Book of Life.

But the individual life can find no meaning and no virtue unless it be as a harmonious part of a larger humanity. The social ideals proclaimed in Judaism are stressed on the sacred days. God being just, merciful, long suffering, ever true, man must imitate Him and thus achieve "the image of God." The voices of the prophets ring in the synagogue with peculiar power. The classic pronouncements of Hebraic idealism are repeated. God being one, mankind is one.

> All the world shall come to serve Thee
> And bless Thy glorious Name,
> And Thy righteousness triumphant
> The islands shall acclaim.

> And the peoples shall go seeking
> Who knew Thee not before,
> And the ends of earth shall praise Thee,
> And tell Thy greatness o'er.[4]

The kingdom of God, an ancient ideal in Judaism, is the morning star of the reverent worshipper. And "on that day the Lord shall be One and His name One." [5]

The Torah lesson for the day includes the story of the sacrifice of Isaac. Its lesson of faith in God and the readiness to obey His will, however difficult it be, however hidden His purpose, is peculiarly appropriate to the occasion. The reader of the Bible from a historic standpoint sees in it a further lesson, the protest to human sacrifice.

The essential teaching of the day may be summarized by reflecting on the significance of the *shofar*. The ram's horn, the symbol of Rosh Hashanah, is sounded in the course of the morning service. It is a dramatic moment in the devotions.

The shofar is a ram's horn, used in ancient Israel as a signalling instrument in the secular life of the people. In the course of time it was taken into the Temple and given religious significance. Three sets of notes are sounded. These are meant to sound a threefold message: the sovereignty of God, divine justice, and revelation. Upon the individual conscience is thus expressed the warning: "Awake, ye sleepers, and ponder your deeds; remember your Creator and go back to Him in penitence." [6]

Folk practices developed about New Year. The observances prescribed for the eve of all holy days take place in the home. The texts of the prayers spoken by the mother as she kindles the lights, and by the father as he recites the Kiddush and blesses the children, are adapted to the New Year. The custom developed of serving honey with the meal. As bread is dipped in honey the father says, "May it be His will that this year be a sweet one." In the afternoon of the first day of Rosh Hashanah the Orthodox perform the ceremony known as *Tashlich;* they empty their pockets into the river, lake, or sea, reciting a verse from Micah, "May God cast our sins into the depths of the sea." [7] Prominent authorities in the history of Judaism sought to discourage it; but the folk practice persists. Reform ignores this practice. The traditional greeting of New Year is *L'shanah tovah,* "May you be inscribed for a good year!"

DAY OF ATONEMENT

The Day of Atonement is the climax of the Ten Days of Repentance. It is decreed in the Bible as "a sabbath of sabbaths," a solemn day of God.

> "And it shall be a statute forever unto you: in the seventh month, on the tenth day of the month, ye shall afflict your souls, and shall do no manner of work, the home-born or the stranger that sojourneth among you. For on this day shall atonement be made for you, to cleanse you; from all your sins shall ye be clean before the Lord. It is a sabbath of solemn rest unto you, and ye shall afflict your souls; it is a statute forever." [8]

The day has undergone a radical transition since its biblical period; however, its message of repentance, confession, forgiveness, has remained constant. The word "atonement" is frequently made to express at-one-ment between a man and his neighbor and his God. This is the aim of the day.

The confessional of the synagogue is a strictly private matter between a man and his Maker. No confession is made to any earthly agent or intermediary. The rabbi does not hear confession; he can grant no absolution. Such a concept is entirely alien to Judaism. If the rabbi does listen to the confessions of those who wish to unburden themselves to him, he does it only as a friend receiving the confidence of a friend. In the secret places of one's own heart is confession made and atonement achieved, for

> "The Lord is nigh unto all them that call upon Him,
> To all that call upon Him in truth." [9]

The confessional prayers are motivated by the search for absolute integrity before Him who looketh into the heart. They run the whole gamut of human weakness and aspiration.

> "For the sin which we have sinned against
> Thee under stress or through choice;
>
> "For the sin which we have sinned against
> Thee openly or in secret;

"For the sin which we have sinned against
Thee in stubbornness or in error;

"For the sin which we have sinned against
Thee in the evil meditations of the heart;

"For the sin which we have sinned against
Thee by word of mouth;

"For the sin which we have sinned against
Thee by abuse of power;

"For the sin which we have sinned against
Thee by the profanation of Thy name;

"For the sin which we have sinned against
Thee by disrespect for parents and teachers;

"For the sin which we have sinned against
Thee by exploiting and dealing treacherously with our neighbor;

"For all these sins, O God of forgiveness,
bear with us! pardon us! forgive us!" [10]

Thus the worshipper stands before his God in contrition, confesses his mistakes and shortcomings, admits his sins of commission and omission, and seeks to bring himself into harmony with the will of God. He stands alone before His God, alone responsible for the quality of his life.

But he stands also as a member of the congregation of Israel. Jewry, on the Days of Awe more than at any other time, stands before the Holy One as a congregation, seeking unity with the Supreme Source of its being. The ancient ritual of the High Priest in Bible days making atonement for his people on the sacred day is recalled; the symbolism is freighted with sentiment, unifying scattered Jewry and uniting the centuries —even the generations yet unborn—with the mystic ties of a common destiny as the servant of the Holy One.

The Day of Atonement is a fast day. No food and no water is taken by the observant Jew from sunset to sunset. The institution of fasting derives its impetus from the biblical command, "ye shall afflict your souls." All schools in Judaism observe the tradition of fasting.

But fasting is something much more than merely afflicting one's soul; it is a means of achieving the spiritual sensitivity the day urges upon us. Even in Bible days it was viewed by the prophets as a means toward attaining nobility of spirit. The prophetic lesson for the day is the fifty-eighth chapter of Isaiah. The prophet's words, boldly spoken, are repeated in the synagogue.

"Wherefore have we fasted, and Thou seest not?
Wherefore have we afflicted our soul, and
    Thou takest no knowledge?—
Behold, in the day of your fast ye pursue your business,
And exact all your labours.
Behold, ye fast for strife and contention,
And to smite with the fist of wickedness;
Ye fast not this day
So as to make your voice to be heard on high.
Is such the fast that I have chosen?
The day for a man to afflict his soul?
Is it to bow down his head as a bulrush,
And to spread sackcloth and ashes under him?
Wilt thou call this a fast,
And an acceptable day to the Lord?
Is not this the fast that I have chosen?
To loose the fetters of wickedness,
To undo the bands of the yoke,
And to let the oppressed go free,
And that ye break every yoke?
Is it not to deal thy bread to the hungry,
And that thou bring the poor that are cast out to thy house?
When thou seest the naked, that thou cover him,
And that thou hide not thyself from thine own flesh?" [11]

The evening service inaugurating the Day of Atonement begins with the *Kol Nidre*. Few prayers in Jewish experience have had so powerful a grip on the Jewish consciousness. The prayer itself—if we may speak of it as a prayer—is a legal formula, written in terse legalistic terminology in Aramaic, petitioning the Almighty for the annulment of the vows, pledges, oaths that may mar our integrity "from this Day of Atonement to the next Day of Atonement." In the early period of its history its inclusion in the Day of Atonement devotions was strongly opposed by authoritative exponents of Judaism.

The will of the masses, however, prevailed and it became a deeply revered part of the liturgy. Jewish martyrdom in the course of the ages endowed the formula with awe. Victims of the Inquisition recited the formula and poured into it their bitter contrition for having taken false vows to an alien faith under cruel compulsion of the torture chambers. The music to which the formula is set has held enthralled the Jewish spirit, though it is of comparatively modern times. The supplicative, haunting melody is believed to have originated in southwestern Germany in the early part of the sixteenth century.

The Kol Nidre has been a source of grief as well as inspiration to the Jewish people. Anti-Semitic agitators have pointed to the prayer as proof that Judaism condones the breaking of one's word, and that, therefore, the Jewish word is not trustworthy.

The Kol Nidre issues from the sanctity in which vows are held in Judaism. The plighted word is sacred. "When a man voweth a vow unto the Lord, or sweareth an oath to bind his soul with a bond, he shall not break his word; he shall do according to all that proceedeth out of his mouth." [12] A classic example of the sanctity of vows in the religious life of ancient Israel is to be found in the story of Jephtah. Even so rash a vow might not be broken, not even when a precious life was involved.

The rabbinic masters have emphasized with all the power at their command that the formula deals with sins between a man and God; the vows referred to are the religious and purely personal. It is not applicable to man's relationship to his fellows. The Mishnah states explicitly. "The Day of Atonement and repentance atone for transgressions of man in his relation to God, but for transgressions between man and man there is no expiation on the Day of Atonement, until the wrongful act has been rectified." [13] "For him who says, 'I will sin and repent,' repentance is of no avail." "The Merciful One desires the heart." [14]

Accordingly, a very beneficent custom developed in Jewish life, which reveals best the true meaning of Kol Nidre. Every pious Jew sought to recreate harmony between himself and his friends and associates where harmony and good will may have been impaired. One should forgive all those who have wronged him, and be forgiven by those whom he might have wronged wilfully or unwittingly, before seeking forgiveness of God. "If thou hast sinned against thy brother first go and reconcile thyself to him, for otherwise the Day of Atonement cannot absolve thee." [15]

The prayers for the Day of Atonement continue throughout the day. Some of the elders may remain in the synagogue all through the night, chanting Psalms, reading sacred texts or otherwise engaging in meditation. The custom developed of kindling long candles in both synagogue and home. In strictly Orthodox synagogues the men may wear white robes; in Conservative congregations only the rabbi or those who lead in the service may wear the white robe. Most Reform congregations have allowed the custom to lapse.

So profound an experience as the Day of Atonement has been in Jewish life naturally led to the development of considerable customs and practices in preparation for the event. The order of the service includes a memorial service, when every worshipper recalls his beloved dead, or friend, or teacher. The congregation as a whole may recall the men and women who had enriched the life of the community and who had gone to their eternal rest within the year. In the course of the day the book of Jonah is read with its lesson in the universality of God and the efficacy of repentance. A prolonged call on the shofar sounded before the open Ark, while the congregation is standing in reverence, proclaims that the day of prayer is ended.

Thus the Days of Awe come annually to Israel. Jewry experiences the sacred. The sincere heart communes with its God and is comforted; an ancient people renews its youth by the fountains of inspiration. Voices from the past speak with divine compulsion and hope beckons: "Cast away from you all your transgressions, wherein ye have transgressed, and make you a new heart and a new spirit; why will ye die, O house of Israel?" [16]

"The sacrifices of God are a broken spirit;
A broken and contrite heart, O God, Thou wilt not despise." [17]

XXII. THE THREE FESTIVALS

In striking contrast to the Days of Awe are the Three Festivals, Passover, Pentecost (or Feast of Weeks), and Tabernacles—*Pesach, Shabuot* and *Sukkot*. They were gay, colorful pilgrim feasts in Bible days, when the Judean population journeyed to the national shrine bearing offerings, singing songs, celebrating their early or late harvests, and renewing the ties that bound them to their God and His sanctuary. "Three times a year shall all thy males appear before the Lord thy God in the place which He shall choose: on the feast of unleavened bread, on the feast of weeks, and on the feast of tabernacles; and they shall not appear before the Lord empty; every male shall give as he is able, according to the blessing of the Lord thy God which He hath given thee." [1]

From all parts of Judea these pilgrims journeyed to the central shrine on Mt. Zion. The Mishnah has preserved a vivid picture of these pilgrimages.[2] The country roads and mountain passes were crowded with the gay peasant throngs keeping holiday. Every pilgrim carried his own offerings on his own shoulders. These were the first olives, dates, figs, grapes, pomegranates, sheaves of wheat or barley, perhaps a pigeon or two. The rich gave more, the poor less. The wealthy would bring their first fruits in baskets of silver or of gold, while the poor would bring them in wicker baskets made of peeled willow-twigs. But every man made his offering "according to the blessing of the Lord his God," and that he did personally. The King carried his own basket, for there must be no vicarious observance of religious duty. Choice oxen, gayly decorated, drew carts heavily laden with the offerings of the rich. The leader, perhaps playing a flute, chanted pilgrim songs; the crowds joined in the chorus:

"I will lift up mine eyes unto the mountains:
From whence shall my help come?
My help cometh from the Lord,
Who made heaven and earth." [3]

Or,

"I was glad when they said unto me,
Let us go into the house of the Lord.
Our feet have stood
Within thy gates, O Jerusalem.
Jerusalem is built as a city
That is compact together:
Whither the tribes go up,
The tribes of the Lord,
Unto the testimony of Israel,
To give thanks unto the name of the Lord." [4]

Thus the processions moved from town to town. Before each town the procession halted. The leader invited the inhabitants to join. "Come, let us go up to Zion to the house of the Lord our God." The natives joined and the throng moved on. The landscape reechoed to their songs. Before the Holy City dignitaries met the pilgrims and welcomed them. "Our brethren, ye are welcome."

Before the Temple court the pilgrims halted. The Levites appeared, chanting "I will extol Thee, O Lord, for Thou hast raised me up, and hast not suffered mine enemies to rejoice over me." [5] The pilgrims then entered the Temple and joined in the rites of the festival.

The three Pilgrim Feasts were thus joyous occasions. Men rejoice when they gather their harvests; their prayers are in terms of thanksgiving, not litanies of repentance. And thou shalt rejoice in thy feast. [6] The spirit of the Three Festivals is best expressed in the *Hallel* (Psalms 113–118; 136). These are expressions of jubilant thanksgiving to the Guardian of Israel:

"The Lord is for me; I will not fear;
What can man do unto me?"

"I will give thanks unto Thee, for
Thou hast answered me,
And art become my salvation."

"This is the day which the Lord hath made;
We will rejoice and be glad in it."

The *first* characteristic distinguishing these festivals, then, is that they were gay pilgrim festivals in Bible days and they have preserved their sunny, joyous spirit to this day. The *second* characteristic we note is that their agricultural nature has come down to our own time.

In the course of time the Three Festivals acquired historic significances. This historic content pushed the agricultural into the background. Thus Passover, Pentecost, and Tabernacles have a common agricultural base; each has, further, its own distinctive historic significance. We must therefore study each of the Three Festivals separately.

Passover

Passover is the oldest of the Jewish holidays. In its present form it is the result of a long evolution. Two holidays observed by the primitive Israelites at the dawn of their history are at its roots.

One of these is the festival the shepherds observed long before the Israelitish deliverance from Egypt. The renewal of nature in the springtime of the year, and the reproduction of the flocks inspired celebration. The sacrifice of the firstlings of the flock was a common practice and the nomadic Israelites practiced it along with other peoples. The other is the festival of *matzot,* observed by the peoples of Canaan. When the Israelitish tribes entered Canaan and gradually adopted the ways of a settled agricultural community the pastoral sacrifice of the firstlings fused with the agricultural spring festival of unleavened bread. The Bible records unconsciously testify to this osmosis:

> "In the first month, Nisan, on the fourteenth day of the month at dusk, is the Lord's passover. And on the fifteenth day of the same month is the feast of unleavened bread." [7]

A third element entered the fusion when the eating of *matzot* was reinterpreted as being a reminder of the escape of the

Israelites from their Egyptian oppressors. The unleavened bread, a common food in the observance of the spring festivals by various peoples inhabiting Canaan, became "the bread of affliction," and "a memorial of the departure from Egypt."

> "And they baked unleavened cakes of the dough which they brought forth out of Egypt, for it was not leavened; because they were thrust out of Egypt, and could not tarry, neither had they prepared for themselves any victual." [8]

The nomadic shepherd festival and the Canaanitish spring festival fused into a distinctively Hebraic institution vested with historic memories of deliverance from Egyptian slavery. The Hebraic interpretation transformed the earlier festivals into a national feast of deliverance charged with spiritual dynamics.

In its Hebraic form too it underwent much transformation. In the seventh century B.C.E., as a result of the Reformation of Josiah, the Passover was reestablished as a national feast observed in the central shrine of the nation; in the days of the Second Temple it was the occasion for an elaborate system of sacrifice. But it retained its new historic content as a memorial of the exodus from Egypt.

Thus Passover acquired its classic meaning as Israel's Feast of Freedom—*z'man cherusenu mikro kodesh zecher lizias mizroyim,* "the season of our liberation, a holy convocation, a memorial of the departure from Egypt."

The memory of Egyptian slavery became a spiritual dynamic in Judaism. In the Deuteronomic version of the Ten Commandments it is the motivation for the Sabbath. Prophet and lawgiver invoked it as the premise for the logic of their social idealism. Because God had delivered Israel from Egyptian tyranny, argues Amos, a special responsibility rests on Israel to establish a just society.[9] The legislator made it part of the social legislation of Israel. "If a stranger sojourn with you in your land, you shall not do him wrong. The stranger that sojourneth with you shall be unto you as the home-born among you and thou shalt love him as thyself; for ye were strangers in the land of Egypt." [10] The rabbis embodied it in the ritual for synagogue and home on all significant occasions.

It is a joyous, colorful, buoyant festival. The chains of bondage are broken; the oppressed are free; the tyrant is crushed. God Himself hath thus decreed, for God is a God of freedom, and He wants his children to live as free men and women. Even nature rocks to the marching rhythm of man's emancipation from tyranny and is thrilled:

> "When Israel came forth out of Egypt,
> The house of Jacob from a people of strange language;
> Judah became His sanctuary,
> Israel His dominion.

> "The sea saw it, and fled;
> The Jordan turned backward.
> The mountains skipped like rams,
> The hills like young sheep.

> "What aileth thee, O thou sea, that thou fleest?
> Thou Jordan, that thou turnest backward?
> Ye mountains, that ye skip like rams;
> Ye hills, like young sheep?

> "Tremble, thou earth, at the presence of the Lord,
> At the presence of the God of Jacob;
> Who turned the rock into a pool of water,
> The flint into a fountain of waters." [11]

Coming as the holiday does at the springtime of the year, when nature appears reborn, the flowers and birds return, the days grow longer, and the sunshine stronger, the festival acquires additional impetus toward the colorful and cheerful.

The name "Passover" may have some association with the biblical report that the destroyer "passed over" the houses of the Israelites in inflicting the last plague upon the Egyptians. More likely, however, the name may be derived from *pesach*, "the Paschal Lamb," the sacrifice offered on the festival in its primitive bedouin days.

The holiday begins on the fifteenth day of the month of Nisan and is decreed as a seven-day festival. The rabbinic masters added an extra day because of the exigencies of the calendar, as we have seen. In Reform practice the festival is restored to its biblical requirement of seven days. Orthodox and Conservative Judaism celebrates the first two and last two days as sacred, the intervening days being a semi-holiday; Reform observes only the first and last days. The dietary regulations for the Passover are in force throughout the holiday.

The evening ushering in the holiday is a rich home celebration. The meal of the evening acquires a religious significance. It is known as the *Seder,* and follows a traditional form as given in the prayer book for the occasion, known as the *Haggadah.* The very food tells the story of God's deliverance of the oppressed. The symbolic foods are: *matzot,* "the bread of affliction," the central symbol of the feast; horse-radish, symbolizing the bitterness of slavery, wine expressing the sweetness of freedom, *haroses*—a mixture of almonds and apples—a reminder of the clay of which the Israelites made the bricks under the whips of the taskmasters. A hard-boiled egg, symbol of life, a roasted shankbone, reminder of the paschal lamb sacrifices, a spray of parsley, a touch of spring, and salt water are grouped in a ceremonial Passover dish. A goblet of wine for the prophet Elijah is in the center of the table, for Elijah, a roaming, generous spirit, is believed to visit every Jewish house on all happy occasions and share in the joy. As such he is expected to visit every Jewish house on seder night and bring his blessing. In the course of the seder service the door is opened to him and he is welcomed.

The father, or otherwise the head of the house, conducts the service with much dignity. All share in the recitations. Four cups of wine are consumed by each person. Dignified and religious, the seder is at the same time a gay, cheerful experience for all, especially for children. Historic romanticism is the essential spirit of the seder. The serious and gay, prayer and fun, mingle freely. The story of the exodus is retold leisurely in the prayers, recitations, music, and food of the evening, "indeed, to dwell at length on it is accounted praiseworthy," states the Haggadah. Nursery rhymes and legal formulae are organic parts of the same Haggadah. An occasion for the gathering of families and friends in the home of a loved one, the humanity and cheer of the seder is deepened by human affections as well as by divine redemption.

The seder is a home celebration, and has been observed as such since Bible days. Of recent years—largely because of the exigencies of city life—the custom is developing of holding congregational *sedorim* in the social quarters of a synagogue.

The prayers, Bible readings, music and sermons of the festival are in terms of man's search for freedom, personally and socially, with Israel's redemption as background and text. The Bible reading recalls the story of the exodus as told in the Pentateuch; the prophetic lesson reminds Israel of its divinely appointed destiny and summons every soul in Jewry to prove itself worthy of the heritage and equal to its responsibilities. The jubilant *Hallel* is chanted in the course of the devotions in the synagogue on the last day of Passover, memorial prayers for loved ones are spoken. The Passover hymn expresses the praise of God the redeemer of the enslaved and prays:

"Be with all who in thrall
To their tasks are driven;
By Thy power speed the hour
When their chains are riven;
Earth around will resound
Joyful hymns to heaven."

A great many customs and ceremonies are associated with Passover. Its ritual is the most elaborate on the Jewish calendar. The preparations for the festival have assumed a set form. The removal of all leaven from the strictly observant home follows a set and quaint ritual known as *b'dikas chometz,* "searching for leaven." Orthodox and most Conservative homes use only special dishes and kitchen utensils that have never been touched by anything leavened. Glassware and porcelain dishes may be rendered fit for use on Passover by being dipped in boiling water; metal vessels are rendered fit by being passed through fire. Reform and some Conservative Jews do not consider the change of dishes as important.[12]

With its ancient symbolism the Passover has been a never-failing fountain of living waters to Jewry, rousing Israel with its long, long memories and eternal hopes, and summoning every Jew to think and aspire in terms of freedom through law. Passover, as the Festival of Freedom, finds its realization in Shabuot, the festival that commemorates the giving of the Law to Israel on Mount Sinai.

SHABUOT

Fifty days after the first day of Passover is the festival of *Shabuot*, or *Pentecost*, or *Feast of Weeks*, as the holiday is variously known. These three names are synonyms. They identify the holiday from the standpoint of its date.

Biblical law prescribes "the counting of the Omer":

> "And ye shall count unto you from the morrow after the Sabbath, from the day that ye brought the sheaf of the waving; seven weeks shall there be complete; even unto the morrow after the seventh week shall ye number fifty days. . . ." [13]

The word Sabbath in this connection has been authoritatively established by the rabbinic masters, after considerable debate, as meaning a *day of rest* referring to the first day of Passover. The fiftieth day (*pentecost* in Greek), or on completion of seven weeks (*shabuot* in Hebrew) is the holiday. It falls on the sixth day of the month of Sivan.

The "counting of the Omer" specified in biblical law requires each Israelite to make a daily offering to the national sanctuary throughout the forty-nine-day period of a measure (*omer*) of barley, as part of the barley harvest sacrifice. In the course of time this period came to be associated with much sorrow in the life of Jewry—the persecution under Hadrian and the massacres by the Crusaders. Orthodox Judaism, therefore, prohibits weddings on these days. The one day on which the ban is lifted is the thirty-third day of the Omer (*Lag B'omer*), for the reason that a plague that had decimated the disciples of Rabbi Akiba ceased on that day. The day has therefore come to be known as "the scholars' festival." Reform Judaism ignores the ban on weddings in the Omer period. Conservative Judaism retains it.

In its agricultural stage Shabuot was a wheat harvest feast, and "the day of the first fruits." [14] In time it came to memorialize the revelation of the Torah to Israel through Moses at Mount Sinai, on the fiftieth day after the Israelites escaped from Egypt, and is accordingly designated in the tradition of the synagogue as "the season of the giving of our Law."

Synagogue tradition has preserved a vivid description of the first fruit offering. We have already called attention to it.*

The motivating sentiment of the first fruit offering is clear. In the words of the Psalmist, "The earth is the Lord's and the fullness thereof." [15] The farmer plowed and planted; but the harvest is of God, and man is dependent on His everlasting arms. Dependence on God and gratitude to Him motivated the Judean peasant, "for all things come of Thee, and of Thine own have we given Thee." [16] In prosperity as in adversity man must turn to God.

Enjoyment of God's blessings imposes responsibility. Man is not the absolute owner but the steward of the riches vouchsafed him. He must share it with those who have no harvests. This social responsibility must be expressed in a specific manner.

> "Seven weeks shalt thou number unto thee; from the time the sickle is first put to the standing corn shalt thou begin to number seven weeks. And thou shalt keep the feast of weeks unto the Lord thy God after the measure of the freewill-offering of thy hand, which thou shalt give, according as the Lord thy God blesseth thee. And thou shalt rejoice before the Lord thy God, thou, and thy son, and thy daughter, and thy man-servant, and thy maid-servant, and the Levite that is within thy gates, and the stranger, and the fatherless, and the widow, that are

* See Chapter XXII.

in the midst of thee, in the place which the Lord thy God
shall choose to cause His name to dwell there." [17]

The rabbinic teachers add:

"Bring the poor that are cast out to thy house and thou
wilt offer thy choicest first fruits to God." [18]

Shabuot is associated with Passover not only chronologically and externally; it has a deeper and more intimate association. Passover memorializes freedom; Pentecost speaks the
message of law and self-discipline. "All that the Lord hath
spoken we shall do and hearken." [19] There is no liberty, say
the rabbinic teachers, without law and discipline—more especially, divine law and self-discipline. The Hebrew slaves
did not achieve freedom by escaping their taskmasters. They
were only run-away slaves. Freedom and the dignity of free
men came only when they voluntarily embraced the Law.

The Torah portion read in synagogues on the holiday is
the revelation of the Ten Commandments as reported in the
book of Exodus. The book of Ruth, with its message of loyalty,
is read as the prophetic lesson.

With the rise of Reform Judaism, the tradition developed
of confirming Jewish children on the festival. The practice is
growing also in Conservative synagogues. Orthodox and Conservative Jews observe it as a two-day festival; Reform Jews
observe only one day.

TABERNACLES

The third of the Three Festivals is Tabernacles or *Sukkot*.
Like Passover and Pentecost, it is agricultural in origin. It is
decreed in the Bible as a harvest festival:

"On the fifteenth day of the seventh month (Tishri),
when ye have gathered in the fruits of the land, ye shall
keep the feast of the Lord seven days; on the first day
shall be a solemn rest, and on the eighth day shall be a
solemn rest. And ye shall take you on the first day the
fruit of goodly trees, branches of palm-trees, and boughs

of thick trees, and willows of the brook, and ye shall rejoice before the Lord your God seven days.

. . . .

"Ye shall dwell in booths seven days; all that are home-
born in Israel shall dwell in booths; that your generations
may know that I made the children of Israel to dwell in
booths, when I brought them out of the land of Egypt:
I am the Lord your God." [20]

The injunction to dwell in booths gave the holiday its name
and its symbolism. "Sukkah" means "hut," the temporary
abode of those who lived in the fields during the harvest-
gathering season. The plural, "sukkot," came to be the name
of the festival. Observant Jews to this day build a *sukkah,* out-
of-doors where possible, or in the synagogues proper. This is
made of scraps from field and forest and decorated with the
produce of the harvest. Much art and poetry has been inspired
by the family gatherings in the colorful sukkah. Every Jew
is enjoined to visit the sukkah, with his loved ones and friends,
and take at least one meal in it. On entering the sukkah he
speaks a blessing: "Blessed art Thou, Lord our God, King of
the universe, who hast sanctified us by Thy commandments
and has commanded us to dwell in the sukkah."

Rabbinic law specifies its construction. The controlling
principle is that the sukkah must symbolize all that is temporary and insecure in human life; the joy of the harvest must be
steadied by the realization of man's mortality and by his dependence upon God. It must not be built of solid masonry; it
must be dismantled after the holiday; the roof must allow the
stars to be seen and the rain to come through, reminding man
of God beyond. Only God and His will are the ultimate reality
and the basis of human security. The sukkah must be beautiful, for the commandments of the Lord must be observed es-
thetically.

Besides the sukkah, the traditional symbols of the holiday
are the *lulav,* a palm branch, the citron (*esrog*), myrtles, and
willows, based on biblical command. Their true meanings are
unknown, though homiletic meanings are given them. The ob-

servant Jew, holding the lulav and esrog in his hands, recites
the following benediction as part of the festival devotions:
"Blessed art Thou, Lord our God, King of the universe, who
hast sanctified us by Thy commandments and hast commanded us to take the lulav."

A harvest festival, the message of Sukkot is dependence
on God and thanksgiving, the same sentiments and the same
social duties that motivate the First Fruit festival. In time the
festival acquired a historic significance. The sukkah came to
symbolize the tents in which the Israelites dwelt in the wilderness as they journeyed from Egypt to the Promised Land, and
the conviction of God's providence—"that your generations
may know that I made the children of Israel to dwell in booths
when I brought them out of the land of Egypt." This is part
of the historic tendency in Judaism to emphasize the memory
of Egyptian servitude. Unlike Passover and Pentecost, however, Tabernacles retains to this day more of the agricultural
than of the historic significance, with all the color and joy of
the harvest.

Tabernacles lasts seven days. The seventh day is known as
Hoshana Rabba, for the reason that a prominent number of
the prayers for the day begin with the phrase, *hoshana*—
"help, O Lord!" Two sacred days follow, and have become
organic parts of the festival. The eighth day is *Sh'mini Azeret,*
"the eighth day, a festival." The specific meaning of the day
is not clear. Prayers for rain are part of its liturgy, a survival of
the water drawing celebration as it was observed in the days
of the Second Temple. The ninth day is *Simchas Torah,* the
rejoicing of the Law. It is of post-talmudic origin. It developed
in Babylonia in connection with the annual cycle of the reading of the Torah. This has become a festival dedicated to the
reading of the Law. The Scroll of the Law is completed and
begun anew on the day. The last portion of the book of Deuteronomy is read from one Scroll, and the opening verses of
Genesis are read from another, to symbolize the ideal that the
reading of God's word never ceases in Israel. It is a merry
holiday. Old and young abandon themselves to religious

romanticism. Processions and refreshments, the elders bearing the Scrolls, children waving banners, are part of the
devotions. The synagogue poet caught in words the folk spirit
of the holiday:

"The Angels came a-mustering,
    A-mustering, a-mustering,
The Angels came a-clustering
    Around the sapphire throne.

"A-questioning of one another,
    Of one another, of one another,
A-questioning each one his brother
    Around the sapphire throne.

"Pray who is he, and where is he,
    And where is he, and where is he,
Whose shining casts—so fair is he—
    A shadow on the throne?

"Pray, who has up to heaven come,
    To heaven come, to heaven come,
Through all the circles seven come,
    To fetch the Torah down?

" 'Tis Moses up to heaven come,
    To heaven come, to heaven come,
Through all the circles seven come,
    To fetch the Torah down!" [21]

XXIII. FASTS AND MINOR FESTIVALS

FASTS

Several fasts must be noted as part of the Jewish cycle of sacred days. They are observed by the especially pious. These are: *Tenth of Tebeth,* commemorating the siege of Jerusalem by the Roman legions in the year 70; the *Seventeenth of Tamuz,* marking the breach made in the wall by the besieging army; the *Ninth of Ab,* memorializing the destruction of the Temple; the *Third of Tishri,* recalling the murder of Gedaliah; and the *Fast of Esther,* observed in memory of the fast ordained by Queen Esther. The Ninth of Ab is the most important. It has come to be a day memorializing Jewish suffering throughout the ages. It has no biblical authority and rests entirely on tradition. The book of Lamentation is read in synagogues on the night of this fast day, the congregation assuming the form of mourning.[1]

PURIM

The two minor festivals are Purim and Hanukkah. Purim celebrates the delivery of the Jews from the plottings of Haman, as told in the book of Esther. The Persian tyrant issued a decree ordering the annihilation of the Jewish community on the fourteenth day of the month of Adar. The intended day of destruction turned into a day of salvation. Mordecai and his cousin, Queen Esther, are the heroes of the day. Folk fancy exalted them into glamorous figures. Purim is the jolliest day in the Jewish calendar. The holiday is essentially a folk festivity—largely in the manner of a Mardi Gras —in terms of masquerading, dancing, parties for children, staging of comic plays, with Haman as the villain, Mordecai and Esther as the saviours of their people. Exchange of gifts, in compliance with the injunction in the book of Esther for "sending portions one to another and gifts to the poor" (*shalach monos*), and the eating of *Hamantaschen,* triangular cakes filled with poppy seed and honey, are the characteristic ceremonials of the day. Much dramatics was inspired in Jewish life, particularly in the Medieval Ages. No special functions are ordained for home or synagogue excepting the recitations of a special prayer and appropriate psalms, and the reading of the book of Esther.[2]

HANUKKAH

Hanukkah commemorates the triumph of Judea under the leadership of the Maccabees over the Syrian-Greek tyrants in the year 165 B.C.E.

Upon the death of Alexander the Great in the year 323 B.C.E., the vast empire he had fashioned collapsed. His generals snatched pieces of it as their booty. Egypt came under the rule of the Ptolemies; Syria fell to the Seleucids dynasty. These two dynasties were in constant and bitter warfare for supremacy. Between them was little Judea. The fortune of war swayed back and forth, and Judea was the constant battle field, now under the rule of one contending power, now under the other. Until 198 B.C.E. Judea was under Egyptian domination; after that date it was under the heel of the Syrian-Greeks.

Judea was between the hammer and the anvil not only politically, but spiritually even more. Externally it was raked by the swords of both contending empires; internally it was torn by political and religious dissension. One section of the population was sympathetic to the Egyptians; the other favored the Syrians. Both groups were being transformed by the Hellenism which Alexander had unleashed upon the countries he had subjugated. The Hellenism that inundated Judea and eroded the very foundations of its Hebraic traditions was a degenerated Hellenism, not the Hellenism of the Greek philosophers or artists. Professor Cornill testifies:

"Greek history from the end of the Peloponnesian War to the time of Alexander the Great presents a truly depressing picture of abjectness and worthlessness. Very soon the average Greek had of civilization only the moral decay, of culture only the conceited arrogance. Only recall with what undisguised contempt the Romans looked down upon the Greeks when they first became acquainted with them. The Roman, who still retained the early Roman honesty and thoroughness, regarded every Greek as a mere blackguard, and 'Graeculus' became an epithet for the characterization of a windy, puffed-up, characterless, unreliable fellow.

"And this ethical dissolution which may be called absolute decay, made rapid progress; they were soon on the verge of complete moral bankruptcy. And so the Greeks became for the Orient the bearers of civilization indeed, but also the bearers of moral degeneration. Where they really predominated arose frivolity and skepticism and a moral laxity more repulsive under its varnish of culture than undisguised barbarism and untutored license." [3]

Hellenism in its nobler nature touched Judaism earlier on Egyptian soil and exerted a powerful influence. The first three Ptolemies were consciously Hellenizing the Jewish community. Alexandria became a historic center of a dazzling Hellenized Hebraism. A portion of the Jewish Bible was translated into Greek; one of the leading libraries of the ancient world was founded in Alexandria, and the Jewish writings were well represented. The book of Ecclesiastes and the Apocryphal book by Jesus Ben Sirach belong to this period. Judaism was in an enticing and dangerous embrace of a dazzling culture.

But the Hellenism that swept Judea at the time of the Maccabees by way of Syria was in a state of degeneration. Its chief sponsor was Antiochus IV, ruler of Syria, and one of the madmen of history. He took for himself the title *Epiphanes*, "God-incarnate," or "God visible"; bitter wit of the time changed it to *Epimanes*, "mad-man," and history has concurred in this version.

In the year 168 B.C.E. he issued his infamous decree that set

204 JUDAISM IN THEORY AND PRACTICE

off the revolt. His aim was the absolute totalitarianization of his empire. Judaism was outlawed; observance of any of its forms was punishable by death. The sacred writings were burned. All Jews were required to offer sacrifices to the Greek gods; the Temple at Jerusalem was turned into a shrine of Olympian Zeus. The blood of a swine was smeared over the holy of holies. The Jews were to turn Greeks. The highways and byways of Judea were crowded with Syrian-Greek soldiers enforcing the decree in every brutal manner known to them.

Furious rebellion broke loose. The signal for revolt was given by an aged priest in the village of Modin. The ancient chronicler gives us a vivid report:

"It was on the fifteenth day of the month of Kislev, that the messengers of King Antiochus set up an idol on the altar of God, and had incense burnt in its honor. And they gave order that the people of Judea should forsake the law and the covenant, profane the Sabbath and pollute the sanctuary. And many chose rather to die than to forsake the holy covenant. And the king's officers came to the city of Modin, and said to Mattathias, the son of John, the son of Simon the Hasmonean, a priest of the sons of Joarib who dwelt in Modin: Thou art a great man and strengthened with sons and brethren in this city. Come, then, and fulfill the king's command as all the heathen have done, and the men of Judah and they that remained in Jerusalem. And thou shalt be in the number of the king's friends. But Mattathias answered and spake with a loud voice: Though all the nations that are under the king's dominion obey him and fall away each one from the religion of his fathers, yet will I and my sons and my brethren walk in the covenant of our fathers. God forbid that we should forsake the Law to depart from our faith either to the right hand or the left. And when one of the Jews came in the sight of all to sacrifice to the idol, Mattathias was inflamed with zeal, neither could he forbear to show his anger, and he slew him, and also the king's officer, and the altar he pulled down. And Mattathias cried throughout the city with a loud voice saying: Whosoever is zealous of the law and maintaineth the covenant, let him follow me. So he and his sons fled into the

mountains, and they went about pulling down the heathen
altars, and they rescued the law out of the hands of the
Gentiles." [4]

For three years the rebellion raged. Pious men turned
warriors. Their heroism, martyrdom, and skill are one of the
miracles of history. Leadership was in the hands of Mattathias'
sons, particularly in the hands of the amazing character, Judah
the Maccabee, or Judas Maccabaeus, as he is usually designated in the history books. Priest, he fought with the enemies' sword with a daring, skill, and contagious enthusiasm
that have won the admiration of the subsequent ages. His
religious passion and military genius turned a mob into a
fighting machine. He must have been one of the great orators
of all time. His exhortations to the army on the eve of battle
raised the fighting spirit of men to a pitch of white heat:

> ". . . arm yourselves, and be valiant men, and see that
> ye be in readiness against the morning, that ye may fight
> with these nations, that are assembled together against
> us to destroy us and our sanctuary: For it is better for us
> to die in battle than to behold the calamities of our peo-
> ple and our sanctuary. Nevertheless, as the will of God is
> in heaven, so let Him do." [5]

Victory finally came to Judea.

On the twenty-fifth day of the month of Kislev, in the year
165 B.C.E. the Temple was cleared of its abominations and re-
dedicated to the Holy One of Israel.

It was more than a political victory, for it had been more
than a political war. Basically two philosophies of life and
destiny were in conflict. They are known to us as Hebraism
and Hellenism, the one a God-centered discipline of life as
developed in Israel, the other a man-centered interpretation
of all things as evolved in Greece.[6]

Hanukkah thus commemorates the first war in history for
religious liberty, and speaks the message of rededication to
God and duty as taught in Judaism versus the decrees of
the tyrants and their hedonistic philosophies. "Not by might
and not by power but by My spirit, saith the Lord." [7]

Legend has it that in cleansing the Temple of the idols a cruse of sacred oil was discovered which was expected to burn one day. By miracle this little oil burned eight days. The historic reason for the eight days is probably the reported fact that the festival was patterned after the festival of Tabernacles, which is observed for eight days.[8]

In the early ceremonial of the holiday much emphasis was given to illumination. Lamps were lit and placed in doors and windows. In time this illumination reduced itself to the kindling of a Hanukkah light on the first night of the festival and increasing the number of candles by one on each successive night. Prayers are spoken as the lights are kindled:

> "Blessed art thou, O Lord our God, King of the universe, who hast sanctified us by thy Commandments, and commanded us to kindle the light of Hanukkah."

> "Blessed art thou, O Lord our God, King of the universe, who wroughtest miracles for our fathers in days of old, at this season."

> "Blessed art thou, O Lord our God, King of the universe, who hast kept us in life, and hast preserved us, and enabled us to reach this season."

Like Purim, Hanukkah does not require the cessation of worldly pursuits. Exchange of gifts and merriment, the staging of special programs in religious schools, the recitation of the Hallel in the course of the regular devotions are the only special observances. In the thirteenth century a synagogue poet composed a Hanukkah hymn, *Mooz tsur,* recounting God's guardianship of Israel throughout the ages and in the days of the Maccabees. In its English form it is the standard hymn in all English-speaking synagogues. It is an admirable expression of the motivating spirit of Hanukkah:

> "Rock of Ages, let our song
>   Praise Thy saving power;
> Thou, amidst the raging foes,
>   Wast our shelt'ring tower.
> Furious, they assailed us,

But Thine arm availed us,
    And Thy word
    Broke their sword
When our own strength failed us.

"Kindling new the holy lamps,
    Priests approved in suffering,
Purified the nation's shrine,
    Brought to God their offering.
And His courts surrounding
Hear, in joy abounding,
        Happy throngs
        Singing songs
With a mighty sounding.

"Children of the martyr-race,
    Whether free or fettered,
Wake the echoes of the songs
    Where ye may be scattered.
Yours the message cheering,
That the time is nearing
        Which will see
        All men free,
Tyrants disappearing."

XXIV. BASIC QUESTIONS

Basic questions confront Orthodox, Reform, and Conservative Judaism. Thus far in our present volume the concern has been with the sympathetic and objective delineation of contemporary Judaism. In the following pages we are concerned with a critical appraisal by examining the basic questions confronting the leaders of each group.

Questions Facing Orthodoxy

Orthodox Judaism must cope with at least three basic questions upon which its destiny depends. They are peculiar to Orthodoxy.

First, how long can Orthodoxy resist the new learning—the new mind wrought by the new sciences and philosophies— and, at the same time, talk with integrity and conviction to the enlightened mind?

The heart will not adore what the mind disowns. That is basic to the religious life of the enlightened man. Judaism extolls the consistency of heart and mind as the will of God. "Thou shalt love the Lord thy God with all thy heart, with all thy soul, and with all thy might." That includes the intellect as well as the emotions. "Ye shall be whole-hearted with the Lord your God." The heart, to the biblical folk, was the seat of intelligence as well as of emotion. Orthodoxy cannot sweep away in indignation the natural sciences, nor the philosophies of the Western world; neither can it dismiss with a scornful gesture the science of philology and the critical approach to the Bible.

Orthodoxy may vindicate this or that dogma. The issue, however, is not saving one dogma or another. The central issue is, how can Orthodoxy vindicate its authority that rests on the dogma of a divine Bible supernaturally transmitted to Moses on Mount Sinai? How long will its imposing temple of faith rest on this corner stone, when the corner stone is badly impaired for Orthodoxy's own children?

Historically, Judaism, confronted with embarrassing questions issuing from the belief of an infallible Bible, found escape in one or another of its forms of Bible exposition. When the *simple meaning* of the text contradicted the mind, resort was had to the *allegoric,* or, if that gave no deliverance, to the *midrashic,* or the *mystic.* These four paths of Bible exegesis still are valid for what each has to offer; but they no longer offer escape from the findings of the scientists, philologists, historians. The primary question is, can Orthodoxy recapture—or retain, if it believes that it still holds the fort— the authority of the infallible Bible—supernaturally revealed, perfectly preserved—that is at the base of the whole rabbinic structure of Judaism according to *halakah?*

Second, how long can Orthodoxy maintain itself in religious isolation?

The world is one. East and West have met; their blood and tears have commingled. The blood rites of cruel ages have brought them together and made them one. Their hearts and their minds have met, in antagonism or in harmony, but they have met. No isolation is possible for very long.

The winds of alien doctrine from the four ends of the earth have always swept through the Jewish community and impregnated the mind of Jewry with new thought and aspiration. But there was a certain amount of isolation to Jewish life because of the restrictions made by a hostile environment. For centuries the ghetto walls served as a break on foreign ideas and alien customs. Now the ghetto walls are down. Jewry is exposed to all the philosophies and heresies of the world, and Jewry revels in the experience.

Geographically our world is small; spiritually it is vast. Every mystery solved by scientists gives birth to vaster mysteries. The radio and airplane, the printed page and the spoken word, penetrate to the remotest villages in Tibet. No

Himalayas are austere enough to block the spoken word. Jewry lives on the highways of the world. Her gifted children crowd the metropolitan centers and markets, the classrooms and laboratories everywhere. Judaism escaped the Copernican revolution for several centuries. Now it is the first to sense the impact of revolutions in the making. It is as sensitive to intellectual and moral disturbances as a seismograph is to an earthquake. Can Orthodoxy hold her children and retain her own integrity in a system of belief that makes spiritual isolation a cardinal principle of faith, particularly now when mankind is struggling desperately to achieve One World?

A *third* basic question confronts Orthodoxy. It has become an official allegiance, not a personal discipline, for vast numbers of Jews. They who observe the Sabbath, keep the dietary law, offer their daily prayers, are a shrinking minority. They violate the second commandment by claiming to be Orthodox. Still, Orthodoxy remains inactive, and when it does act, it acts usually in terms of denunciation and excommunication —weapons of an age that is long past.

QUESTION FACING REFORM

From the opposite pole comes the challenge to Reform.

Reform has sought to divest itself of the temporary, the local, and has striven after the fire of God as revealed in the prophet's majestic word. Bold, daring, Reform represents Judaism as an adventure. The cry of the prophet might have been emblazoned on its banner: "Clear ye in the wilderness a pathway for our God."

Soul needs body. A disembodied religion may be only a phantom of the mind. Judaism has been practical *and* idealistic. It has not negated the world; it has not drawn a sharp line between the secular and the spiritual. It harmonized the prophet with the priest, the universal with the particular.

Judaism has been a dynamic faith not in spite of its many customs, forms, institutions; these have rendered it real and effective. The true heirs to the prophets were the rabbinic masters, with all their legalism and all their minutia of ritual. They took the abstract word of God and made it the practical rule of everyday life for the individual and the community. True, at times they carried their rules and regulations to an unhappy extreme, and reduced the prophet's burning word to a mere bit of liturgy to be recited by rote; but such extremes were only the abuses, and every system of faith is vulnerable to abuse. The historic fact is that they gave the Word body, and planted Judaism in the soil of earthly reality as well as heavenly vision.

Can Reform divest itself of much of the ancient forms and institutions, shift from the ancient channel of *halakah* and authority to the channel of free inquiry and individual judgment, negate the nationhood of Israel, stress only the religious fellowship, expose itself joyously to all the forces of assimilation, and despite it all remain a distinctive prophetic Judaism? To raise the question is not to answer it in the positive nor in the negative; it is only to delineate the challenge. The fact is that idealism needs an idealist. Any idealism that destroys the idealist defeats itself. That is the challenge confronting Reform Judaism.

QUESTIONS FACING CONSERVATIVE JUDAISM

The Conservative synagogue is the youngest of the three branches of contemporary Judaism. It frankly confesses that it has not yet formulated its program and is a bit proud of this. Instinctively averse to a fixed system of belief, and viewing Judaism as a historic process rather than an organic system, it chooses the paths laid out by life rather than the blue-prints dictated by the intellect. However, an organic unity cannot be avoided nor evaded. Children reared on the discipline of Torah will seek inner harmony and spiritual consistency. They will not be satisfied with pious makeshift indefinitely. Thus the central question facing Conservative Judaism is, can it formulate a program and create the necessary instrumentalities that will give reality to its distinctive interpretation of Judaism?

Several questions issue from this central problem.

First, can Conservative Judaism adhere to tradition without making an idolatry of tradition?

Traditions are the forms through which the faith of the fathers expressed itself and was transmitted to their children. Primary is the fire of God, not the censer. The vehicles of faith are important, but they are of secondary value. The rabbinic masters spoke and legislated in terms of "a fence around the Law." The Law is primary; the fence is secondary. Conservative Judaism, shifting the center of gravity from the word of God to tradition, is in danger of reversing the values and turning tradition into an idolatry. Its primary emphasis is on the fence, rather than the garden.

In Orthodoxy and in Reform the driving power is, "Thus saith the Lord." The two schools differ sharply in the interpretation of the word of God, but the word of God it is. It is the highest reach of human idealism; it demands personal piety. Conservative Judaism has accepted the findings of the scholars to the effect that the Bible is a human document issuing from man's gropings up the mountain of the Lord; but it has refused to go beyond it in search of the word of God. It has concentrated on the forms at one time believed divine and which it admits are divine no longer. A new meaning is given to the divine when it is asserted that anything that comes out of "catholic Israel," or anything world Jewry has absorbed and assimilated, is divine and binding. Israel is thus a superior source of divinity than Sinai and God. In historic Judaism Israel is sternly subordinated to God and His will.

Second, can the traditions of past ages serve not only as sanctions but as statutes and ordinances for the present and the future?

Scholars of the Conservative synagogue have added much to the unravelling of the skein of tradition. They have traced the strands back to various ages, circumstances, personalities.

Thoroughly aware of this learning, can Conservative Judaism persist in treating Israel's lore as God's law, and maintain that the lore of the past is the law for the present and the future? That assumes a static world, as it assumes absolute wisdom for the fathers, and that is unthinkable. Jewry is part of mankind and mankind is on a new earth under a new heaven. Beyond all our yesterdays are the endless tomorrows, and the synagogue has encouraged the faithful to pray to the Lord of all worlds.

Third, can the Conservative synagogue establish a standard of values in its adherence to tradition and create the instrumentalities to integrate its values?

The garden of faith has weeds as well as flowers. Some of the weeds are decidedly bad. They are sheer rites in magic and superstition. Which tradition is good and which is not so good and which is bad? How shall one tell the primary from the secondary? What shall the norm be? By what standard shall new forms be rejected or admitted? To say, as a teacher of Conservative Judaism says, that he prefers to "stand aside and watch like Eliezer at the well," is to surrender to a timidity of mind that is akin to evasion of responsibility.

Conservative Judaism must find a norm to enable it to tell the flower from the weed, and it must establish an agency to implement its values once it has clarified them. The abortive attempt of the Rabbinical Assembly of America to deal with the problem of the deserted woman is a tragic example of the present impotence of the Conservative synagogue in making its central value of tradition respond to life.

Fourth, is it possible for one and the same scholar to operate with a non-Mosaic Pentateuch in his study and to defend in his pulpit the traditions that issue from and rest upon a Mosaic authorship of the same Pentateuch? Is there not here a double standard of thinking inevitably leading to doubletalk? Perhaps the justification for this inconsistency may be found in what is emphasized as "survival value." Jewry, being an extra territorial group, needs traditions—customs, folk ways, ceremonies, rites—to hold it together and preserve it, and these traditions serve that purpose. Hence, these traditions must be preserved, despite the findings of the scholars. In this reasoning the cardinal ideal of true religion is ignored: Judaism, like all spiritual religions, is a search for truth, and truth is the supreme ideal. "The seal of God is truth," say the rabbinic masters. Religion is at heart a daring adventure. It would storm the very heavens to find God's truth. It is not a mere hoarding of tradition. The Conservative synagogue cannot exchange personal integrity for "survival values." Personal piety, sincerity, the search for the divine must have God's truth as its morning star.

Fifth, can Conservative Judaism save itself from the embrace of nationalism?

Nationalism is an angry and jealous god. It is in the nature of nationalism to extoll itself as the highest good. Every value, every department of life, every sentiment is subservient to nationalism. It recognizes no law beyond itself. Carried to its logical conclusion nationalism is a reversion to primitive tribalism. Exclusiveness and intolerance are of its very nature. Supreme master of its domain, it subordinates to itself religion as well as education, art, literature, philosophy, science.

Much in Judaism is of national origin—common descent, national memories, language, holidays. Historically, Judaism has infused these values with religious significance and subordinated them to the will of God. Even Ezekiel, the most nationalistic of the prophets, visioned Israel restored to its own soil and independent life as a theocracy. Modern nationalism reverses the process. It takes ancient traditions and recreates them into a nationalism that is supreme, recognizing no law of God or man beyond itself.

Conservative Judaism is wedded to modern Jewish nationalism. The issue is once more between Ezra and the prophets. Ezra, it must be remembered, subordinated "the holy seed" to the Lord of all.

SUPPLEMENT

WHY THE JEWS REJECTED JESUS

The thoughtful Christian is puzzled by the question, "Why did the Jews reject Jesus?" It is a logical and earnest question from the Christian standpoint. Many Jews also raise the same question.

Jesus was a Jew. That is universally acknowledged, even by the hostile critics of Judaism. He was born to Jewish parents, was reared in an overwhelmingly Jewish community, scrupulously observed every detail of the ceremonial law, ministered exclusively to Jews, had nothing but disdain for non-Jews, never set his foot outside Jewish Palestine, spoke the Jewish vernacular, was steeped in Synagogue tradition, insisted upon the immutability of the Law, Written and Oral,—lived and died in the faith. Starting a new religion was farthest from his conscious intentions. "Go nowhere among the Gentiles, and enter no town of the Samaritans, but go rather to the lost sheep of the house of Israel . . . Salvation is from the Jews . . . I was sent only to the lost sheep of the house of Israel . . . Do not give dogs what is holy; and do not throw your pearls before swine." [1] A sympathetic student of the Gospels interprets the verse: "Though some commentators try to avoid the unpleasant conclusion, there seems little doubt that the dogs and the pigs are approbrious Jewish appellations for the heathen and that what is forbidden (even though the Evangelist did not so interpret the saying) is any preaching of the Gospel to the heathen or Samaritans." [2]

Faithful to the Law, Jesus was vibrant with the spirit of the Hebrew prophets, the faith of the Psalmists, and the visions of the Jewish apocalyptists. "The stern reproof of the 'First Isaiah,' the divine consolations of the 'Second Isaiah,' the

215

sorrows of Jeremiah, the soaring vision and stern wrath of
Ezekiel, the sighs and laments of the Psalms, the promises
foreseen in Daniel, together with those portions of the Pentateuch, full of love of God and the love of man—all moved
him to rapture and enthusiasms, penetrated his soul and enriched his spirit." [3] He was zealous for the ceremonial law and
followed the most rigid Pharisees in their interpretations of
the Law. "Think not I have come to abolish the law and the
prophets; I have come not to abolish them but to fulfill them.
For truly, I say to you, till heaven and earth pass away, not
an iota, not a dot, will pass from the law until all is accomplished." [4] "Even though they are in the language of Oriental
hyperbole," declares a Christian scholar, "they apparently
validate the entire ceremonial law." [5] And a Jewish scholar
observes: "This is rabbinism with a vengeance." [6] His disciples considered him a descendent of King David. His last
words on the cross was from the Psalms, in the Jewish vernacular of the day.

Why, then, did his own people reject him? Was it sheer
stiff-necked perversity or spiritual blindness, as has been
charged by generation upon generation of Christian preachers
and teachers?

The answer has several aspects, and they issue from two
major sources: the theological and the historic circumstances
of the time of Jesus.

THREE CONSIDERATIONS

At least three considerations must be borne in mind before
we undertake to answer the question before us.

First, we must note the varied meanings of two words. "Rejected," and its counterpart, "accepted," have special theologic meanings in Christianity which they do not have in Judaism. Christians and Jews using these terms in religious discourse move on different levels of meaning.

In Christendom, "accepting Jesus" means much more than
merely to receive an academic fact with a consenting mind,

as one accepts any other fact to be true; "rejecting Jesus" means more than merely refusal to accept in the ordinary meaning of the word "accept." There is theologic freight in these two basic words in the vocabulary of the Church. With acceptance goes salvation, redemption, status before God and eternal bliss; with rejection goes damnation, sin, and punishment in the hereafter. Jews using these terms employ them in the secular sense only. There is no tranforming grace and no sin in these words; they are academic terms only.

Second, it must be remembered, always, that we today know very little of Jesus that is not seriously questioned by competent and devout scholars. The records are inadequate. They come from confused ages; not one is from the pen of a man who knew Jesus personally; not one is concerned with history primarily—history was not the concern of the Gospel writers. The sources are sermons aimed at special groups with special theologic interests for partisan purposes. They are woefully incomplete and contradictory; they suffered much in transmission from generation to generation and from one language into another. Pious zeal, not historic accuracy, guided the pens of the authors, in an age when zeal for the faith was infinitely more important than good faith with historic facts. The efforts to harmonize the testimonies of the Gospels has been a prodigious and monumental effort; the constant stream of books issuing from the presses today is testimony that the harmonizations made thus far are not entirely satisfactory.

Third, it should be remembered that Jesus made only a slight impression in his own lifetime. His ministry was altogether too short—perhaps less than one year. Moses, according to tradition, led his people through the desert, and crisis after crisis, forty long years; Isaiah, Jeremiah, Ezekiel preached their convictions all through their adult lives, and left with their disciples written testimonies of their words. Jesus flashed through the black Judean skies like a meteor, and, like a meteor, disappeared. It was his very few disciples —Paul and the Gospel writers—who resurrected him in the life of his people and the world; but in this resurrection he was transformed. He was no longer Jesus, the humble Palestinian rabbi; he emerged as the Christ,—a supernatural, uniquely divine, Son of God.

In his own day he was only one of a great many roaming preachers, in a limited area of Palestine, attracting crowds— for a brief time—speaking to them in the open countryside or in the local synagogue, meeting with favor or with skepticism, as did other "Galilean intinerants," to which the rabbinic sources testify.[7] Whatever differences the crowds may have detected in his teachings were apparently only the differences between one Pharisee and another. He would preach his sermon, tell his parable to his chance audience; the poor, the sick, the diseased, the psychotic, the heavy-laden—and the land must have been filled with them in the wake of the Herodian butcheries, earthquakes, famine—were attracted to him as he moved through town. He spoke to them in vivid parables, not like the more learned and more formal expounders of the Law, revealing to them the teachings of their own faith. He won their hearts, healed some, had his exchanges with the local skeptics and the authorities and went his way. In less than a year—certainly not much more than a year—his career ended. No records preserved his words; no one personally associated with him wrote down the facts of his experiences. His death must have been as nameless as his life. Many were crucified as he was by the authorities of the Roman police state; he was only one more victim. He came from obscurity and went into obscurity. The references to him in the secular histories of the age—Josephus, Tacitus, Suentonius —granting their authenticity, are extremely meagre.

No official Jewish body—no Sanhedrin, no Rabbinical Council—met and deliberated whether to "accept" or "reject" Jesus. He was accepted or rejected by the masses as all other moral teachers were accepted or rejected. Some believed in him; some questioned his teachings; some dismissed him scornfully. There was no official rejection, no more than there was an official acceptance of, say, Isaiah or Jeremiah.

When, today, men ask: "Why did the Jews reject Jesus?"

SUPPLEMENT

we must remember the semantics and the historic circumstances involved: we must agree on the meanings of "rejected," and "accepted," and bear in mind that the facts are extremely meagre, and that, further, he made only a slight impression in his own brief career. The enormity of the decision, viewed from our time, was but a briefly-noted detail in his own time.

THE ANSWER FROM THEOLOGY

Seeds of Alienation

Jesus made no open break with the laws of Moses, not even with the Oral Tradition of the Pharisees. His quarrels with the Pharisees were on the grounds of their personal shortcomings, not with their teachings. Nevertheless, there "was in his teaching the nucleus of such a contradiction." [8] The seeds of alienation from the Judaism of his day were imbedded in his teachings and in his personality. His disciples nurtured these seeds and brought forth the fruits of contention and final alienation. What were these seeds?

Obsession with Messiahship

Jesus was deeply obsessed with the conviction that he was the Messiah, uniquely divine, supernatural, heavenly Messiah, so ordained by God Himself. It possessed and mastered him, and set him on a path of estrangement from his people.

The turning point in the life of Jesus was his baptism by John. "Now when all the people were baptized, and when Jesus also had been baptized and was praying, the heaven was opened, and the Holy Spirit descended upon him in bodily form, as a dove, and a voice came from heaven, 'Thou art my beloved Son; with thee am I well pleased (or, *to-day have I begotten thee*.)' " [9]

Granted that the actual words may be legendary, the experience was real and enormous; it left a deposit in his soul

that transfigured him. He was called. He was God's only begotten. The prophecies of Isaiah, the mystic phrases in the
Psalms, the visions of the apocalyptists over which he had
brooded came true. He was a man possessed of a supreme
secret. He shrank from his destiny, even as Moses did before
the burning bush, or Jeremiah when he was called to take his
place as "prophet unto the nations;" he doubted himself ("the
Satan tempted him"); but he had been lifted into a realm
above the human. Thus possessed, he spoke, taught, and acted
in a manner that created a widening gulf between him and his
people.

His Messiahship became the overwhelming force in his life,
whereas in the teachings of the Pharisees the coming of the
Messiah was a secondary belief, or one belief among many.
The ceremonial laws, which he had never repudiated, slipped
into the background of his teachings; to the Jewish masses and
their teachers they were primary.

Meaning of Messiah

There were two levels to the meaning of "Messiah." To
the Jewish masses and their teachers the Messiah was *King*—
Messiah, primarily a political liberator of the nation, who
overcomes the enemies of the nation by force and liberates
his people. Kings Saul and David were thus Messiahs,
anointed by God's priest to deliver His people from their enemies. The second level of meaning was the heavenly Messiah,
the supernatural, divine, come from heaven to redeem the
world. This second level of meaning was in the making. One
was primarily a human and political liberator; the other was
primarily a supernatural, apocalyptic figure. The line between
the two concepts was vague. The masses, deeply depressed
by the cruel circumstances of their age, were smarting under
Roman tyranny; while they yearned for deliverance from
their woes, it was largely for deliverance from Roman oppres-
sion that they prayed. But the vision that lured Jesus was the

heavenly, eschatologic kingdom. Here is another seed of alienation.

Other-Worldly Kingdom of Heaven

When Jesus summoned his disciples to assume the yoke of the Kingdom of Heaven, he summoned them to a supernatural, other-worldly Kingdom, not to the recreation of the human society in this world, as men understand this world. Albert Schweitzer testifies: "We must reconcile ourselves to the fact that Jesus' religion of love made its appearance as part of a system of thought that anticipated a speedy end of the world." [10] Claude G. Montefiore, a profound and deeply sympathetic student of the Gospels, states, "In the Gospels the Kingdom . . . is a sort of short-hand expression for the condition of beatitude and glory in which the righteous will find themselves after the Judgment, at the end of the present world order, and at the full inauguration of the next world order . . ." [11]

The Jewish masses yearned for deliverance from very practical Rome in their own immediate life-time, and prayed for a Messiah who would bring them this deliverance. Jesus' conception of the Messiah did not satisfy the depressed, submerged masses in the immediate present. Hence estrangement and alienation.

Other-Worldly Ethic

The ethical teachings of Jesus were primarily other-worldly. "Jesus was not thinking of public justice, the order of civic communities, the organization of states, but only how the members of his religious brotherhood should act toward each other and toward those outside their ranks. Public justice is outside his perview. Moreover, he believed that the old order was coming soon to a catastrophic end. What would even be the use of the old methods for the cure of evils? . . . In the

new order there would be no need for force, or for police-
men, for all the wicked would be safely prisoned in hell, and
those who would live upon the regenerated earth would be
all happy, righteous and peaceful." [12] Hence Jesus would ad-
vise, "Render to Caesar the things that are Caesar's, and to
God the things that are God's;" [13] the rich had no chance in
the hereafter; only the poor may enter the Kingdom. Men's
rewards were in heaven.

Most of the Jewish masses were left cold by these other-
worldly consolations. They had lived and suffered cruelly and
sought practical deliverance. Their Jewish ethical teachings
were this worldly and practical.

Lack of Sympathy for Human Nature

Jesus' emphasis on asceticism and the renunciation of
the world held no reality for the suffering Jewish masses.
"Blessed are you that hunger now, for you shall be satisfied
. . . Blessed are you that weep now, for you shall laugh . . .
Blessed are you poor, for yours is the Kingdom of God . . .
Rejoice and be glad for your reward is great in Heaven . . ." [14]
held no appeal to people crushed as they were under appalling
misery. It no doubt was spiritual comfort to some; but it
offered them no practical relief. The denunciation of wealth,
gaiety, and popularity as evil in themselves was a novel teaching. His attitude toward divorce followed the extreme view
of Shammai; it was Hillel's more lenient view that prevailed.
His emphasis on celibacy, martyrdom, non-resistance, turning the other cheek and love of enemies were, from the standpoint of the masses and their teachers, extreme views; it simply did not make sufficient appeal to be accepted. Jewish
ethics made more sympathetic allowances for the frailties of
human nature and the demands made by the environment.

The New Authority

Consciously or unconsciously Jesus set himself up as the
new authority, beyond Moses. If he believed himself to have

been the Messiah, it was a natural, even inevitable, development.

"You have heard that it was said to men of old . . . . . but
I say unto you," [15] were words carefully chosen by Jesus, or
by the disciples who record the words in his name. He does
not say, "Moses and the *Torah* say . . . but I say unto you;"
he is careful not to break with the religious tradition. The
break, however, was there, and a deep wedge was driven between Jesus and his people. " 'You have heard that it was
said . . . but I say unto you,' imply the abrogation of the
old Law of God and the introduction of the new law of Jesus
. . . The Christian as well as the Jew should bear in mind
the criticism of Jerome: The *verily I say unto you* of the New
Testament has replaced the *Thus saith the Lord* of the Old." [16]
"A rabbi cited authorities, and a prophet said, *Thus saith
Yahweh,* or oracle of *Yahweh.* Jesus, perhaps deliberately, dis-
penses with such locutions, either because of a sense of divine
inspiration or because the truth of his assertion should be
transparently clear. He certainly spoke as one having authority." [17] Encouraging his disciples to meet martyrdom, he motivates them by exhorting them to remember for whom this
martyrdom will be: "For my sake." That represented a new
emphasis. Jewish martyrdom was motivated by the *Santifica-
tion of God's Name;* the motivation and supreme justification
is God, not any one man—however revered a teacher or
prophet he may be. In his words and attitude revealed here
is a seed of alienation. The Gospel writers, developing this
attitude, set up Jesus as the new authority, in contrast to
Moses and the Torah. The gulf between Jesus and his people
was widening.

Miracles and Forgiving Sins

The rabbis looked askance at Jesus' preoccupation with
miracles, healing, exorcising demons, raising the dead. Some
Talmudic masters were alarmed by the spread of traffic with
demonology.[18] Miraculous healing was more or less normal

for the time; the Pharisaic masters too practiced it, and Jesus grants that they had the power to practice the art.[19] However, miracle working was entirely secondary to their calling; in the works of Jesus, from the Pharisaic standpoint, it was the primary endeavor, and they were deeply disturbed by it. The ethical, spiritual teachings of Jesus were no doubt obscured by the emphasis on the working of miracles. In the nature of things miracles are sensational affairs, they capture men's imaginations much more quickly and more completely than the speaking of a calm ethical truth.

With his miracle working Jesus allowed himself to forgive sins as the Son of God. That was a shocking experience to pious Jews. When, restoring a paralytic, Jesus said to him, "My son, your sins are forgiven," the scribes who stood by were astonished. "Why does this man speak thus? It is blasphemy! Who can forgive sins but God alone?" [20] That was the authentic Jewish view. The claim to Sonship—or, at least, the assumption of it—was blasphemous. The responsible Jewish masters recoiled from Jesus.

Scholars are not agreed on the authenticity of any of the verses we have cited in connection with the various matters that made for estrangement between Jesus and the Jews. But whether or not Jesus spoke the words as they are reported in the Gospels, the realities to which they give testimony were there. The seeds of alienation were there; nurtured by the disciples of Jesus they sprouted and grew.

The Answer from History

There was no sharp line between the theologic, religious on the one hand, and the crisis of the nation on the other. The two were one. But the national sorrows under Roman tyranny were a cruel, crushing experience, and Jesus had no interest in that.

Jesus ignored the national misfortunes at a time when martyrs without number laid down their lives for the preservation of their nation. His emphasis was on a disembodied faith and an abstract ethic, mainly in terms of the other-world. As we have noted, he was not particularly interested in civil life and its cruel injustices. He certainly was not interested in the nation as such. "The Judaism of that time," testifies Joseph Klausner, "had no other aim than to save the tiny nation, the guardian of great ideals, from sinking into the broad sea of heathen culture and enable it, slowly and gradually, to realize the moral teaching of the prophets in the civil life and in the present world of the Jewish state and nation." [21]

When Paul, and the other disciples, cultivated these seeds into vigorous plants, transforming the humble Galilean preacher into the Christ—supernatural, Son of God, over against Moses and the Torah, with an imposing system of supernatural and authoritative theology—the break was finally effected.

Why Do Not Jews Accept Jesus Today?

Jewish teachers are often asked, "Why do not Jews accept Jesus today? Granting all the difficulties from the standpoint of theology and history, what stands between Christian and Jew today in terms of Jesus?

Theologically it is just as unthinkable for the modern Jew to compromise the central watch word of his faith: *Hear, O Israel, the Lord our God, the Lord is One* now as it was then. Orthodox, Reform, and Conservative Jews alike find the Son of God dogma simply incomprehensible. The Jewish mind is shaped in terms of ethical monotheism.

If Jews cannot accept Jesus in the historic Christian interpretations, with any measure of spiritual integrity, why do they not accept him from the liberal Christian standpoint, seeing in him the supreme human personality but not a uniquely divine being?

Two considerations must be borne in mind.

First, to Christians, of all denominations, Jesus is the symbol of all that is pure of heart, sacred, poetic, lovely; to Jews he is the symbol of cruelty, bitterness, persecution, blood and tears. That is the tragedy in Jewish-Christian relations.

Jews do not hate Jesus; many of them fear him. He is associated in their minds, from childhood, with something ominous: Crusaders slaughtering thousands of Jews in his name, the inquisition and the torture chambers in his name; heresy hunting and expulsions, pogroms, yellow badges, "Christ-killer" cries, anti-Semitism.

Religious people—Jewish and Christian alike—do not fully appreciate the enormous fact that religion is not in books, not in Bibles, not in pronouncements by ecclesiastic authorities, not in cathedrals, but in the lives of the people who profess it. Jews know Jesus not on the basis of what the Gospel writers say, and not on the basis of what great spirits in Christendom have said or are saying today; they know Jesus by the conduct of the Christian community. And the Christian community, all through the centuries, branded the Jew as the Judas of history and placed a curse upon him and his children forever.

The traditional Christian version of the crucifixion is a pulsating pain in Jewish life. It is a poisoned well. Religious anti-Semitism flows from it constantly, persistently. The Christian community, for all its noble men and women in history and present-day life, has been a persecuting community. Jesus is its symbol. The Jews, inevitably, have recoiled from Jesus.

Second, to the liberal Christian, Jesus is central to his faith; to the liberal Jew—who has the same picture of Jesus from the standpoint of modern scholarship—Jesus is subordinated to a host of other teachers and preachers and martyrs of Judaism. He is not the unique teacher; he is one of a great many teachers. Jewish scholars today—Montefiore, Abrahams, Klausner, *et al*—are glad to pay tribute to Jesus as a supremely gifted human being, who taught mankind precious truth, but they will not make him the central figure among the masters in Israel. Tragically, Jesus the Christ is still the Great Divide between Christian and Jew.

ABBREVIATIONS

BIBLE

Cant.	Canticles	*Hab.*	Habakkuk	*Nah.*	Nahum
Chron.	Chronicles	*Hag.*	Haggai	*Nehem.*	Nehemiah
Dan.	Daniel	*Hos.*	Hosea	*Num.*	Numbers
Deut.	Deuteronomy	*Isa.*	Isaiah	*Obad.*	Obadiah
Eccl.	Ecclesiastes	*Jer.*	Jeremiah	*Prov.*	Proverbs
Esth.	Esther	*Josh.*	Joshua	*Ps.*	Psalms
Ex.	Exodus	*Judg.*	Judges	*Sam.*	Samuel
Ezek.	Ezekiel	*Lam.*	Lamentations	*Zech.*	Zechariah
Gen.	Genesis	*Lev.*	Leviticus	*Zeph.*	Zephaniah
		Mal.	Malachi		

MIDRASH

Mid   Midrash, usually preceding an abbreviation of a book of the Bible, e.g. *Mid. Ps.*, Midrash to Psalm.

R   after the abbreviation of a Bible book, *Rabbah*, e.g. *Gen.R.*, Genesis Rabbah.

TALMUD

Tractates of the Babylonian Talmud cited in this work; where reference is to the Jerusalem (or Palestinian) Talmud *Jer.* precedes the tractate title.

A.Z.	Abodah Zarah	*R.H.*	Rosh Hashanah
B.B.	Baba Batra	*San.*	Sanhedrin
Bek.	Bekorot	*Shab.*	Shabbat
B.K.	Baba Kamma	*Sheb.*	Shebi'it
Er.	Erubin	*Suk.*	Sukkah
Ket.	Ketubot	*Ta'an.*	Ta'anit
Mak.	Makkot	*Yeb.*	Yebamot
Meg.	Megillah		

OTHER

C.C.A.R.	Central Conference of American Rabbis Year Book.
H.E.R.E.	Hastings Encyclopedia of Religion and Ethics
H.U.C.A.	Hebrew Union College Annual.
J.E.	Jewish Encyclopaedia
J.P.S.	Jewish Publication Society
Sh.A.	Shulhan Aruk
Tan.	Tanhuma
Tos.	Tosefta
U.A.H.C.	Union of American Hebrew Congregations
U.J.E.	Universal Jewish Encyclopedia
U.P.B.	Union Prayer Book

NOTES

NOTES

I. THE SOURCES

1. The best English edition of the Babylonian Talmud is the Soncino, London. An English edition of the Mishnah in addition to above, is the translation made by Herbert Danby, Clarendon Press, Oxford, 1933.
   A good digest of Talmudic opinion is A. Cohen, *Everyman's Talmud*, E. P. Dutton, New York, 1932.
   An extensive and objective anthology of rabbinic lore, the talmudic and extra talmudic, covering the first five hundred years of the Common Era, is C. G. Montefiore and H. Loewe, *A Rabbinic Anthology*, Macmillan, London, 1938.
   No complete English translation of the Palestinian Talmud has as yet been made.
2. Abot 1:17.
3. A collection of the Agada of the Babylonian Talmud, *En Ya'akob*, made by Jacob ibn Habib, a Spanish refugee in Salonica in the early part of the sixteenth century, became popular with the Jewish masses the world over. An English translation was made by S. H. Glick, New York, 1916.
4. The midrashic literature is enormous, and much of it has appeared in English. The more important collections in English are: Louis Ginzberg, *Legends of the Jews*, 7 volumes, Jewish Publication Society, Philadelphia, 1909–38; *En Ya'akob*, cited above; *Midrash Rabbah*, 10 volumes, Soncino, London, 1940.
5. The following rabbinic quotations are borrowed from Bialik and Rabinitsky, *Sefer ha-Aggadah*, Tel Aviv, 1933, Introduction.
6. An abridged edition in English is Hyman E. Goldin, *Code of Jewish Law*, 4 volumes, Hebrew Publishing Co., New York, 1927.
7. See "Bible Exegesis" in U.J.E.
8. A standard one volume work in English on Jewish philosophy is Isaac Husik, *A History of Medieval Jewish Philosophy*, Jewish Publication Society, Philadelphia, 1930.
9. Freehof, Solomon B. *The Responsa Literature*, Philadelphia, Jewish Publication Society, 1954.
10. See Idelsohn, A. Z., *Jewish Liturgy and Its Historic Development*, N.Y., Holt & Co., 1932; *The Authorised Daily Prayer Book*, ed. Singer; Abrahams, Israel, *A Companion* to above (Orthodox, historic notes); *Services for the New Year and Day of Atonement*, and *Festival Services*, ed. Adler, H. M. (Orthodox), N.Y., Hebrew Publishing Co., 1927; *Sabbath and Festival Prayer Book* (Conservative), N.Y., Rabbinical Assembly of America, 1952; *High Holy Day Prayer Book* (Conservative), ed. Silverman, Hartford, Conn.; *Union Prayer Book*, Vol. I–II, Newly Revised (Reform), Cincinnati, Central Conference of American Rabbis; *Sabbath Prayer Book* (Reconstructionist), N.Y., 1945.
11. Cohon, S. S., *What We Jews Believe*, p. 67.

231

II. ORIGIN AND HISTORIC CHARACTERISTICS
OF THE SYNAGOGUE

1. For a different theory as to the origin of the synagogue, see Israel Abrahams, *Studies in Pharisaism and the Gospels*, I, p. 1 (Cambridge, 1917): "If it (the synagogue) was due to the diaspora at all, it must be attributed to the exiles in Babylon. This is no modern guess, for we have the statement of Justin (Dialogue with Trypho) that the Jews applied Malachi II:11–12 to the prayers of the Israelites *then* in dispersion. We may confidently assert (with W. Bacher, *Hastings' Dictionary of the Bible*, s.v.; G. A. Smith, *Jerusalem*, I, p. 364) that the synagogue was a Palestinian institution of the Persian period."

2. Moore, *Judaism*, I, p. 285.

3. *Ibid.*, pp. 281–307; art. *Prayer, Jewish* in H.E.R.E.; Kohler, *Origin of the Synagogue. and Church;* Baron, *The Jewish Community*, I, Ch. III.

IV. ORTHODOX JUDAISM

1. The term "Orthodox," it is believed, was first used by Abraham Furtado, President of the Jewish Assembly of Notables, convoked by Napoleon.

2. Abot 1:1.

3. Num. R., Naso, xiv, 10; Mid. Ps. on 78:1.

4. Ber. 5a.

5. Mishnah Torah, ed. Hyamson, p. 16, 34a.

6. Deut. 4:2.

7. E.g. The Babylonian Amoraim assumed the authority as judges and rabbis without Palestinian ordination; the Oral Law was codified in defiance of the very same Oral Law; the Maccabees permitted warfare on the Sabbath, etc.

8. Isserles to Sh. A., *Orah Hayyim*, 690, par. 17; *Yoreh Deah*, 376, par. 4.

9. Singer, p. 90.

10. Jung, U.J.E., art. *Judaism, Orthodox*. See also, Hertz, *The Pentateuch*, etc., p. 402; *Affirmations of Judaism*, Chapters II–III; Moore, *Judaism*, I, p. 235.

11. Pes., 7b.

12. Deut. 17:11.

13. See J.E. art. *Commandments;* Schechter, *Aspects*, Chapters VIII–IX; Maimonides, *The Book of Divine Commandments*, tr. Chavel; Jung, *Judaism in a Changing World.*

14. Gen. R., Wayera, 53:7.

15. Abot 3:18.

16. Ps. 119:12, 14–16.

17. Friedlander, *Jewish Religion*, p. 2.

18. Makkot 23b–24a.

19. On the creeds formulated by the Jewish thinkers in the Middle Ages, see Husik, *History of Medieval Jewish Philosophy:* Crescas, p. 372 ff.; Maimonides, p. 409 ff.; Albo, p. 410 ff. See, further, Schecter, *Studies*, I, Ch. VI; Neumark, *The Principles of Judaism in Historical Outline*, Cincinnati, 1929; M. Kaplan, *The Place of Dogmas in Judaism*, and discussions by Ginsberg, Rosenblatt, Goldman, in Proceedings, IV, pp. 280–312; S. S. Cohon, *Judaism and Christianity Compare Notes*, Part II, Ch. III.

20. *Mishnah Torah*, ed. Hyamson, p. 34a.

21. Singer, p. 89.
22. See Herzog, *The Main Institutions of Jewish Law*, p. 24 ff. "In the year 135 A.D., at the crisis of the disastrous revolt against Hadrian, a meeting was held at Lydda. The assembly was attended by famous rabbis (including Akiba), and the question was discussed as to the extent of conformity with Roman demands which might justifiably be made rather than face the alternative of death. . . .

"It was decided (Sanhedrin 74a) that every Jew must surrender his life rather than commit any of the three offenses: idolatry, murder, and *gillui arayoth*, a phrase which includes both, idolatry and incest." (Israel Abrahams, *Studies*, II, p. 74.)
23. See Lauterbach, C.C.A.R., Vol. XXXV, p. 373.
24. Cohen, *Everyman's Talmud*, p. xvii. See also, Hirsch, *Nineteen Letters of Ben Uziel*, seventh letter.

V. REFORM JUDAISM

1. See Marcus, *Israel Jacobson*, C.C.A.R., Vol. XXXVIII, p. 386 ff.
2. Quoted by Philipson, C.C.A.R., Vol. XX, pp. 252, 255.
3. *Ibid.*, 253.
4. Abot 2:13.
5. C.C.A.R., Vol. XX, p. 267.
6. *Ibid.*
7. *Ibid.*
8. Wise, *Reminiscences;* May, *Isaac M. Wise;* Philipson and Grossman, *Selected Writings of Isaac M. Wise.*

9. Proceedings of the Pittsburgh Rabbinical Conference, C.C.A.R. for 1923. See Philipson, *Reform Movement in Judaism.*
10. C.C.A.R., Vol. XLVII, p. 97 ff. See also *Revaluation of Reform* by Cohon, Levy, Rauch, Schulman and Silver, in C.C.A.R., Vol. XLV.
11. Liptzin, *Germany's Stepchildren.*
12. *Studies, Addresses, and Personal Papers*, p. 217.
13. Singer, p. 77.

VI. CONSERVATIVE JUDAISM

1. Ginzberg, *Students, Scholars and Saints;* also, art. on Frankel in J.E. and U.J.E., and Philipson, *History of Reform Judaism.*
2. Ginzberg, *ibid.*, p. 209.
3. *Ibid.*, pp. 205, 209.
4. *The Charter of the Seminary* in *Seminary Addresses*, p. 23.
5. Schechter, quoted by Bentwich, *Solomon Schechter*, p. 296.
6. *Studies in Judaism*, Series I, Introduction, pp. xvii–xviii.
7. *Tradition in the Making.*
8. Proceedings, Vol. IV, pp. 130–1.
9. Solomon Solis-Cohen, *Sabato Morais: Teacher and Leader*, p. 225.

10. Cohen, Shulhan Aruk as *Guide for Religious Practice*, Proceedings, Vol. VI, pp. 115–45. See also same author, *Canon of Interpretation of Jewish Law*, *ibid.*, Vol. V, pp. 170–88.
11. Finkelstein, *Things That Unite Us.* Proceedings, Vol. IV, pp. 48–9, 144.
12. *Ibid.*, pp. 48–9.
13. Proceedings, Vol. V, p. 185.
14. Ginzberg, *Students, Scholars and Saints*, p. 211.
15. Speaking officially the Conservative rabbinate affirms: "We desire to re-affirm our faith in our religious tradition which has al-

234   JUDAISM IN THEORY AND PRACTICE

ways associated with Palestine the fulfillment of the Scriptural promise: 'In thee shall all the nations of the earth be blessed.' This promise succinctly but adequately expresses our conception of the essence of Zionist aspiration and the national destiny of our people. "We re-affirm our historic claim to Palestine, as the land where for more than a thousand years our fathers lived a national life and built a religious civilization which has profoundly and beneficially influenced the course of history. This land, further sanctified by the vision and message of the prophets, by more than eighteen centuries of unfaltering hope and tear-drenched prayer, and by the blood and sweat of the modern Jewish pioneer and martyr, has become inextricably intertwined with our religious faith and has assumed a central and all important position in every program of practical action aiming to ameliorate the present plight of our people and our tradition." (Proceedings, Vol. V, pp. 388–400.)

16. A group within the Conservative rabbinate, impatient with the theologic conservatism of their colleagues, projected the *Reconstructionist* movement, with the aim of reconstructing the pattern of Jewish belief, practice, and social institutions. Its formula is Judaism as a civilization. Judaism is viewed not merely as a religion, in the Western sense of the word, but as a distinct civilization: an ethnic group; national memories and national aspirations; a national tongue, Hebrew; national holidays, the festivals are interpreted with emphasis on their national aspects; national folk ways, customs, ceremonies, literature, dance, drama.

The Jewish community of the world constitutes one international nation; the national home, Palestine. Since 1948, the protagonists of this school have been concerned with finding a formula that would enable American Jewry to establish special ties of loyalty, spiritually, with the State of Israel without compromising their American allegiance.

On the American scene the *Reconstructionist* disciples seek a corporate Jewish community, with corporate authority. Jewish education, to be true to itself, must indoctrinate the child not only with religious principles but with national folk-ways, customs, sentiments, loyalties. Interpreting American civilization in terms of "cultural pluralism," such an adjustment of the Jewish citizens, it is claimed, would add variety and depth to American life, rather than represent an alien strain in the American pattern.

See: Kaplan, *Judaism as a Civilization; Judaism in Transition; Reconstructionist Papers; Mordecai M. Kaplan, An Evaluation,* ed. Eisenstein and Kohn, *The Truth About Reconstructionism* in "Commentary," I, 2; Eisenstein, *What We Mean by Religion; Creative Judaism;* Dinin, *Judaism in a Changing Civilization;* Gordis, *The Jew Faces a New World;* Kohn, *Future of Judaism in America;* Steinberg, *A Partisan Guide to the Jewish Problem; Reconstructionist* files; Art, Proceedings, Vol. V, p. 195; Grossman, *A Civilization Within a Civilization?* (in "Commentary," I, 3); Cohon, *Conservative and Reconstructionist Judaism* in Reform Judaism: Essays by H.U.C. Alumni, p. 107 ff.

17. Hagiga 3b; Num. R., XV: 18.

18. *The Charter of the Seminary* in *Seminary Addresses,* p. 25.

NOTES   235

VII. BASIC UNITY

1. Cohon, *What We Jews Believe*, pp. 67–77.
2. For the meaning of excommuni-

cation in Judaism see art. *Excommunication* in J.E.

THEOLOGIC FOUNDATIONS

1. Zohar, Lev. 73a.

VIII. GOD—THE HOLY ONE OF ISRAEL

1. Deut. 29:29.
2. Ps. 42:7.
3. Job 11:7–9.
4. Ps. 29.
5. Art. *God* in H.E.R.E.
6. Deut. 6:4.
7. See Hertz, *The Pentateuch and Haftorahs* to this verse.
8. U.P.B., I, p. 98. For historic background see Abrahams, *Companion to the Daily Prayerbook*, pp. v–vi.
9. See Wolfson, *Notes on Proofs of the Existence of God in Jewish Philosophy*, in H.U.C.A., Vol. I, p. 575.
10. II:50; see also V:18, ed. Kaplan.
11. Singer, p. 29.
12. *Mekilta* 18:12, 59a.
13. Gen. R., XXVI:6.
14. Deut. R., II:31; Sanh. 74a.
15. Mech. to 19:18; 65a.
16. Ps. 148:13.
17. Midrash to Ps. 24:5.
18. Mech. to 17:6; 52b.
19. Singer, p. 291.
20. Ber. 13c.
21. Ps. 90:2.
22. See Montefiore, *Rabbinic Anthology*, p. 307.
23. Singer, p. 240.
24. 6:3.
25. Lev. 19:1.
26. 73:25.
27. 42:2.
28. Tr. by Nina Salaman, *Poems of Jehudah Halevi*, p. xxv.
29. Gen. 1:4, 31.
30. I.K. 18:39.

IX. TORAH—HIS TESTIMONY

1. Gen. R., 1:1.
2. Deut. 33:4.
3. Deut. 30:20.
4. Josh. 1:8.
5. Abot 1:13.
6. *Ibid.*, 2:9.
7. *Ibid.*
8. Ps. 1:2; 19:8.
9. Ps. 115:16.
10. Ps. 2:1, 4.
11. Ab. Zarah 17b.
12. I Sam. 17:45.
13. Mak. 3:16.

X. ISRAEL—HIS WITNESS

1. See *Jew* in an unabridged Webster's Dictionary, or in the Oxford Dictionary.
2. See Rawidowiez, *Israel* in Judaism: A Quarterly, Vol. 2, No. 1.
3. Exod. 19:5–6.
4. Is. 43:10.
5. Ps. 114:1.
6. E.g. Cant. R. to 1:4.
7. Jer. 31:32; 32:38 ff.
8. Hooton, *Up From the Ape*, p. 397.

236 JUDAISM IN THEORY AND PRACTICE

9. Fishberg, *The Jews;* Hooton, *Twilight of Man,* pp. 232–50.
10. Deut. 26:5.
11. 16:3.
12. Mtt. 23:15.
13. Num. 15:15.
14. See Hertz, *The Pentateuch and Haftorahs* to Gen. 5:1; also, Lauterbach, *Attitude of the Jew Toward the Non-Jew,* C.C.A.R. Vol. XXXI, p. 192 ff.
15. Sheb. 39a.
16. Yeb. 48b.
17. Singer, p. 48.
18. Is. 51:1–2.

19. Singer, p. 48.
20. Kohler, *Jewish Theology,* p. 323.
21. Is. 43:10.
22. Is. 42:1–8.
23. Amos 3:2; Jer. 7:23; 31:34–5.
24. Is. 43:1–3. See Abrahams, *Companion to Daily Prayer Book,* p. x–xi.
25. Cited by S. S. Cohon *Liberal Judaism,* May, 1946.
26. B.B. 24b; B.K. 113a; San 74a.
27. 29:5–7.
28. Micah 4:5.
29. Is. 12:2–3.

XI. MAN AND HIS CAPACITIES

1. Exod. 25:8.
2. Sifre, Deut. 306.
3. Lev. 20:25.
4. Ab. Zarah 20b.
5. Shab. 50b.
6. Gen. 1:27; 5:1.
7. Ps. 8:6.
8. Abot 3:18.
9. Singer, p. 5; U.P.B., p. 101.
10. Tan. Behukkotai, 56b.
11. Yoma 69b.

12. Toledot 138a.
13. Ezek. 18.
14. Deut. 30:15 ff.; 11:26–8.
15. Job 14:4.
16. Ecc. 12:7.
17. Is. 14.9 ff.
18. Ecc. 12:7.
19. Ps. 49:17.
20. Ecc. R., V:14.
21. Prov. 6:22; Abot 6:9.

XII. THE ETHICS OF JUDAISM

1. Lev. 19:2.
2. Deut. R., XI:22; XIII:5; Sota 14a.
3. Lev. 18:5.
4. Singer, p. 48.
5. Hertz, *Pentateuch and Haftorahs* to Gen. 10:1.
6. Lev. 19:2, 18.
7. Abot 1:3; 2:4.
8. Ab. R. N. XXXI.
9. Sanh. 4:5.
10. Gen. R., XXIV:7.
11. Ab. Zarah 18a; Gen. R., XXXIV:13; B.K. 91b.

12. Sanh. 38a.
13. Hosea 2:21–22.
14. Amos 3:2.
15. Is. 42, etc.
16. Is. 52:11.
17. Abot 1:4.
18. Shab. 312.
19. *Eight Chapters,* IV.
20. 30:8.
21. Ta'an. 11a; 22b.
22. Yeb. 62a, 63a.
23. Cohen, *Everyman's Talmud,* p. 101.
24. Ezek. 2:1.

XIII. SOCIAL IDEALS

1. Lev. IV:6.
2. 1:18.
3. Jer. San. I, par. 1, f. 18a, line 64

(Montefiore, *Rabbinic Anthology,* p. 307).
4. Wolk, art. *Truth* in U.J.E.

5. Exod. 23:7.
6. Ps. 24:4; 15:2.
7. Ber. 28a.
8. Exod. 21:1.
9. Deut. 16:20.
10. 98:9.
11. 85:9.
12. 5:29.
13. 6:8.
14. 1:16–17.
15. 9:23.
16. Abot 5:11.
17. Lev. 19:15.
18. Sanh. 6b.
19. Ps. 89:15.
20. Zech. 7:9.
21. Gen. R., 12:15.
22. Jer. Ta'anit 4:2.
23. Is. 2:2–4.
24. Is. 2.
25. Num. 6:26.

26. Num. R., 11:16.
27. Deut. 13:5; Lev. 19:16; Gen. 9:6.
28. Exod. 23:10.
29. Suk. 49b; B.B. 10b.
30. B.B. 8b–9a.
31. Ibid.
32. Yad, Mattenot Aniyyim, X:1–14.
33. Singer, p. 281.
34. Abot 2:2.
35. Ps. 128:2.
36. Deut. 30:19; Peah 15c.
37. Ket. 5:5.
38. Deut. 5:4.
39. Abot 3:18.
40. Deut. 11:1.
41. Lev. 19:34.
42. Newman, Hasidic Anthology, p. 130.
43. Ta'an. 43a.

XIV. PERSONAL VIRTUES

1. Deut. 30:14.
2. Prov. 1:7.
3. 12:13.
4. 29:12–17.
5. Lev. 19:16; Exod. 23:2.
6. 31:5 ff.
7. 6:12–19.
8. 24:4.
9. Josh. 1:8.
10. Abot 2:6.

XV. JEWISH PRAYER BOOKS

1. R.H. 17b.
2. Abrahams, Companion, p. iv.
3. See Freehof, The Small Sanctuary, Ch. I–III.
4. Abrahams, Companion, p. ii.
5. Ibid.
6. See Idelsohn, Jewish Liturgy, p. xiii ff.
7. Sabbath and Festival Prayer Book.
8. Haggadah, ed. Roth; Union Haggadah. The Reconstructionist Foundation produced an edition of its own, The New Haggadah.
9. Selihot and Kinot, ed. Roedelheim (Hebrew).
10. Idelsohn, Jewish Liturgy, Ch. VIII; Freehof, Devotional Literature in the Vernacular, C.C.-A.R., Vol. XXXIII, 375–415.
11. Ps. 92:2.

XVI. WHAT IS PRAYER AND WHY PRAY?

1. Epectitus, Moral Discourses, ed. Carter, Book I, Ch. CVI.
2. Ps. 19:2.
3. Tos. Ber. 7:5.
4. Ps. 130:1.
5. Singer, p. 46 ff.
6. U.P.B., p. 138.
7. Samuel Taylor Coleridge, Hymn Before Sunrise in the Vale of Chamouni.
8. Self-Reliance.
9. Ps. 8:2.
10. U.P.B., pp. 71–2.
11. Ber. IX:5.

12. Prov. 6:23.
13. See Nathan Isaacs, *Study as a Mode of Worship*, in *Jewish Library*, ed. Jung, Series I, p. 57 ff.
14. Meg. 20a.
15. On *kawwanah*, see Montefiore, *Rabbinic Anthology*, Ch. X.
16. Sanh. 106b.
17. Ber. 31a.
18. Jer. Ber. IV, par. 3, f. 38a, line 64.
19. Ta'an. 8a.
20. Yeb. 105b.
21. Exod. R. Beshalah, XXII:3.
22. Abot 2:18.
23. Ber. 30b.
24. Er. 65a.

25. Ber. 29b.
26. Ber. 28b.
27. *Sefer Hasidim*, ed. Wistinetzki, p. 389.
28. Ber. 12b.
29. Is. 1:15.
30. Is. 58:9.
31. Jer. 7:9–10.
32. Ps. 24:4.
33. Yoma VIII.
34. For a brief discussion of the metaphysical problem see Brightman, *A Philosophy of Religion*, p. 423 ff.
35. 26:3.
36. Mary Brent Whiteside.
37. Singer, pp. 7–8.
38. Is. 41:4.

XVII. CUSTOMS, CEREMONIES, INSTITUTIONS

1. Deut. 33:4.
2. See Chapters XX–XXIII.
3. Singer, p. 300.
4. Deut. 6:9.
5. See Idelsohn, *Ceremonies of Judaism*, pp. 64–5.
6. Num. 15:38–40. See Hertz, *Pentateuch and Haftorahs*, Notes.
7. See Idelsohn, *Ceremonies of Judaism*, p. 57.
8. Deut. 6:8.
9. Singer, p. 278 ff.
10. Sifra, Kedoshim, XI. Cited by Kohler, art. *Dietary Laws*, J.E.
11. Samson Raphael Hirsch. Cited *ibid.*
12. Friedlander, *The Jewish Religion*, p. 237.
13. Lev. 17:15; 22:8.
14. Lev. 3:17.
15. Lev. 7:25–27.
16. Deut. 12:23; also, Gen. 9:4; Lev. 17:10 f.; 19:26; Deut. 12:16; 15:23.
17. Gen. 32:33.

18. Exod. 23:19; 34:26; Deut. 14:21.
19. Targum Onkelos and the rabbis following.
20. The Chief Rabbi of England, Joseph H. Hertz, in 1939, decreed that Jewish children evacuated from London as a war measure, might eat non-Kosher foods, including meat and shell fish.
21. For further study the student is referred to the authoritative digest of rabbinic law, *Shulhan Aruk*, Yoreh De'ah, par. 87–97; Levin and Boyden, *The Kosher Code of the Orthodox Jew;* Cohen, *The Royal Table.*
22. Quoted by Lauterbach, C.C.-A.R., Vol. XXXVIII, p. 589 ff.
23. *Ibid.*, p. 590; Freehof, *Reform Jewish Practice*, p. 43 ff.
24. Exod. 27:20–21.
25. Exod. 25:8.
26. Abot 3:7; Ps. 82:1.

XVIII. FROM CRADLE TO GRAVE

1. See Lauterbach, *Naming of Children*, C.C.A.R. Vol. XLII, p. 322; Freehof, *Reform Jewish*

Practice, p. 111; *Rabbi's Manual*, p. 12.
2. Gen. 17:9–14. See Singer, p.

304, and Notes in *Companion.*
3. Exod. 13:2, 12–13; Num. 18:14–16.
4. See Singer and Abrahams above; art. *Primogeniture* in J.E.
5. See Freehof, *Reform Jewish Practice*, p. 26.
6. *Ibid.*, p. 24.
7. Gen. 2:18.
8. C.C.A.R., Vol. XIX, pp. 170–184; Kohler, *The Harmonization of Jewish and Civil Laws of Marriage and Divorce, ibid.* XXV, p. 374 ff.
9. *Rabbi's Manual,* pp. 156–7, and Notes, pp. 158–184. See Epstein, *Marriage Laws in Bible and Talmud;* S. S. Cohon, *Marrying a Deceased Brother's Wife,* C.C.-A.R., Vol. XXXV, p. 364 ff.
10. Isaac, for instance, married Rebekah, daughter of his paternal uncle's son, Gen. 24:15; Jacob married Rachel and Leah, his maternal uncle's daughters, Gen. 28:2.

11. *Eben Haezer,* 31:2. See Freehof, *Reform Jewish Practice,* p. 93.
12. Epstein, *Jewish Marriage Contract,* p. 5.
13. Lauterbach, H.U.C. Annual, II, p. 355.
14. See Freehof, *Reform Jewish Practice,* p. 72 ff.
15. *Moed Katan,* 23a; Freehof, *ibid.,* p. 80.
16. Freehof, *ibid.,* p. 80 ff.
17. Deut. 25:5–10. Westermark, *History of Human Marriage,* p. 510 ff.
18. Bek. 13a; Yed. 109a.
19. Freehof, *Reform Jewish Practice,* p. 99 ff.
20. See Freehof, *Reform Jewish Practice* 2 vols. for a convenient and accurate digest of the various attitudes.
21. Gen. 37:34.
22. Prov. 20:27.
23. Abrahams, *Companion,* p. xxxix–xl.
24. Singer, p. 37, 75, 77, 86, 321.

XIX. HOLY DAYS (INTRODUCTORY)

1. Exod. 31:16–17.
2. Ezek. 20:12.
3. Deut. 16:11.
4. Ps. 95:1; 100:2.
5. Tanna di-be Elijahu, p. 144.
6. Bezah 15b.
7. Mid. Ps. on Ps. 24:3.

XX. THE SABBATH

1. Exod. 20:8–11.
2. Deut. 5:12–15.
3. A famous hymn of the synagogue is *L'cho Dodi*—"Come, beloved, the bride to meet, the Princess Sabbath let us greet,"—composed by Solomon Alkabets of Safed, in the 16th century. See Idelsohn, *Jewish Liturgy,* p. 129.
4. *Ibid.,* Ch. 11.
5. Ps. 104:15.
6. Gen. R. XVII; Ber. 57b.
7. Bezah 16a.
8. Mekilta to Exod. 13:14, ed. Lauterbach, III, p. 199.
9. Exod. 35:3.
10. Maimonides, *Yad,* III:3.
11. Idelsohn, *Jewish Liturgy,* Appendix IV.

XXI. DAYS OF AWE

1. Hosea 14:2.
2. Lev. 23:24; Num. 10:10; 28:11; 29:11.
3. Ed. Adler, pp. 146–7.
4. *Ibid.,* p. 152.
5. Zech. 14:9.
6. Maimonides, *Hilchoth Teshubah.* For fuller explanation of

the significance of the shofar see Adler, *Service for the New Year,* pp. 126–7, and Note V, p. 265. For Reform version see U.P.B., II, pp. 75–81.

7. Micah 7:19. For *Tashlich,* and also *Kaporoth,* see Schauss, *The Jewish Festivals,* p. 160 ff.
8. Lev. 16:29–34; 23:26–32.
9. Ps. 145:18.
10. U.P.B., II, pp. 116–17. For the more traditional version see Adler, pp. 26–8.
11. 58:3–8.

12. Num. 30:3.
13. Yoma VIII.
14. *Ibid.;* Sanh. 106b.
15. Yoma VIII. For further study see the following: art. *Kol Nidre* in J.E. and in U.J.E.; Idelsohn, *Jewish Liturgy,* pp. 225–8; Adler, *Services for the Day of Atonement,* pp. 77–8; Bloch, *Israel and the Nations,* pp. 272–82; Hertz, *Pentateuch and Haftorahs,* pp. 730–31.
16. Ezek. 18:31.
17. Ps. 51:19.

XXII. THE THREE FESTIVALS

1. Exod. 23:14; Lev. 23:17; Deut. 16:16–17.
2. Bik. 3:28.
3. Ps. 121:1–2.
4. Ps. 122:1–4.
5. Ps. 30:1.
6. Deut. 16:14.
7. Lev. 23:5–6.
8. Exod. 12:39. See *Union Haggadah,* p. 125 ff.
9. Amos 3:1–2.
10. Lev. 19:33–34.
11. Ps. 114.

12. See Schauss, *The Jewish Festivals,* pp. 38–85.
13. Lev. 23:15–16. See Hertz, *Pentateuch and Haftorahs* to these verses.
14. Lev. 23:9.
15. Ps. 24:1.
16. I Chr. 29:14.
17. Deut. 16:9–12.
18. Yalkut to Is. 58:7.
19. Exod. 19:8.
20. Lev. 23:39–43.
21. Translation by I. Zangwill.

XXIII. FASTS AND MINOR FESTIVALS

1. Schauss, *The Jewish Festivals,* Ch. XI.
2. *Ibid.,* Chapters XXXV–XXXVIII; Abrahams, *Jewish Life in Middle Ages,* Ch. XIV.
3. Cornill, *History of the People of Israel,* pp. 178–9.

4. I. Macc. 2–3.
5. *Ibid.,* 3:58–60.
6. See Bentwich, *Hellenism.*
7. Zech. 4:6.
8. Moore, *Judaism,* II, pp. 49–50.

SUPPLEMENT

1. Mtt. 10:5–6; John 4:22; Mtt. 15:24; 7:6.
2. Montefiore, *Synoptic Gospels* to verse.
3. Klausner, *Jesus,* p. 237.
4. Mtt. 17:18.
5. Johnson in *Interpreter's Bible* to above verses.
6. Montefiore, *Synoptic Gospels* to above verses.

7. Klausner, *Jesus,* p. 259.
8. *Ibid.,* p. 248.
9. Mtt. 3:16; Mk. 1:10.
10. *Out of My Life and Thought,* p. 53. See his *The Quest for the Historic Jesus.*
11. *Synoptic Gospels,* p. 34–5.
12. *Ibid.*
13. Mk. 12:17.
14. Lk. 6:20–23.

15. Mtt. 5:21, etc.
16. Friedlander, *Jewish Sources of the Sermon on the Mount*, p. 262.
17. Johnson, *Interpreter's Bible* to Mtt. 5:21–6.
18. Hag. 2:1; 13a.
19. Mtt. 12:27.
20. Mk. 2:1–12.
21. *Jesus*, p. 376.

SELECTED ENGLISH BIBLIOGRAPHY

Shorter studies, embodied in larger
works, are not included in this bibliography; they may be found in the Notes

Abrahams, Israel, *A Companion to the Authorised Daily Prayer
Book*, London, Eyre and Spottiswoode, 1922.
——, *Jewish Life in the Middle Ages*, ed. Roth, London, E. Gold-
ston, 1932; *Studies in Pharisaism and the Gospels*, 2 volumes;
Cambridge, 1917.
Bamberger, Bernard J., *Proselytism In the Talmudic Period*, Cin-
cinnati, H.U.C. Press, 1939.
Baeck, Leo, *Essence of Judaism*, N.Y., Macmillan Co., 1936.
Baron, Salo Wittmayer, *A Social and Religious History of the Jews*,
3 volumes, N.Y., Columbia University Press, 1937.
Bentwich, Norman, *Hellenism*, Philadelphia, Jewish Publication
Society, 1919.
——, *Solomon Schechter*, Philadelphia, Jewish Publication Society,
1940.
Bible—*The Holy Scriptures*, Philadelphia, Jewish Publication So-
ciety, 1917.
Bloch, Joseph S., *Israel and the Nations*, Berlin, 1927.
Braude, William Gordon, *Jewish Proselytism*, In the first five cen-
turies of the Common era, Brown University Studies, volume
VI.
Buber, Martin, *Tales of the Hasidim: The Early Masters*, N.Y.,
1947. Schoken Books.
——, *The Later Masters*, N.Y., 1948.
Central Conference of American Rabbis, 46 annual volumes.
Cohen, A., *Everyman's Talmud*, N.Y., E. P. Dutton & Co., 1932.
Cohon, B. D., *The Prophets: Their Personalities and Teachings*,
N.Y., Scribner's, 1939.
Cohon, Samuel S., *What We Jews Believe*, Cincinnati, Union of
American Hebrew Congregations, 1931. (Reform)
——, *Judaism A Way of Life*, Cincinnati, U.A.H.C., 1948.

Cornill, Carl H., *History of the People of Israel*, Chicago, Open Court, 1917.

Danby, Herbert, *Mishnah*, Oxford, Clarendon Press, 1933.

Dinin, Samuel, *Judaism in a Changing Civilization*, N.Y., Teachers College, Columbia University, 1933. (Reconstructionist)

Eisenstein, Ira, *What We Mean By Religion*, N.Y., Behrman's Jewish Book House, 1938. (Reconstructionist)

Epstein, Louis M., *The Jewish Marriage Contract*, N.Y., Jewish Theological Seminary of America, 1927.

——, *Marriage Laws in Bible and Talmud*, Cambridge, Harvard University Press, 1942.

Festival Services and Services for the New Year and Day of Atonement, ed. Adler, Zangwill, Davis, N.Y., Hebrew Publishing Co., 1927. (Orthodox)

Finkelstein, Louis, *Tradition in the Making*, Centennial Volume, N.Y., Jewish Theological Seminary of America, 1939.

Fishberg, Maurice, *The Jews: A Study of Race and Environment*, N.Y., Charles Scribner's Sons, 1911.

Freehof, Solomon B., *Reform Jewish Practice*, 2 volumes, Cincinnati Hebrew Union College Press, 1944.

——, *The Responsa Literature*, Philadelphia, Jewish Publication, 1954.

Friedlander, Gerald, *The Jewish Sources of the Sermon on the Mount*, London, 1911.

Friedlander, M., *The Jewish Religion*, London, Shapiro, Vallentine and Co., 1935. (Orthodox)

Gaster, Theodore H., *Festivals of the Jewish Year*, N.Y., Wm. Sloane Associates, 1953.

Ginzberg, Louis, *Legends of the Jews*, 7 volumes, Philadelphia, Jewish Publication Society, 1938.

——, *Students, Scholars and Saints*, Philadelphia, Jewish Publication Society, 1928.

Goldin, Hyman E., *The Rabbi's Guide: A Manual of Jewish Religious Rituals, Ceremonials and Customs*, N.Y., Hebrew Publication Co., 1939. (Orthodox)

——, *The Treasury of Jewish Holidays*, N.Y., Twayne Publishers, 1953.

Greenstone, Julius H., *Jewish Feasts and Fasts*, N.Y., Bloch, 1947.

Habib, Jacob Ibn, *En Ya'akob*, tr. Goldin, N.Y., Hebrew Publishing Co., 1916.

The Haggadah, with English translation, Introduction and Notes by Cecil Roth, London, Soncino, 1934; (Orthodox) *Union Haggadah*, C.C.A.R. (Reform) *New Haggadah*, ed. Kaplan *et al.* Behrmans, N.Y., 1941. (Reconstructionist)

Heschel, Abraham J., *Man Is Not Alone*, Jewish Publication Society, 1953.

Hertz, Joseph H., *Pentateuch and Haftorahs*, London, Soncino Press, 1938.

———, *The Authorised Daily Prayer Book*, London, Soncino Press, 1948. (Orthodox)

Herzog, Isaac, *The Main Institutions of Jewish Law*, London, Soncino Press, 1936.

Hirsch, Samson Raphael, *The Nineteen Letters of Ben Uziel*, tr. Drachman, N.Y., Funk and Wagnalls Co., 1899.

Hooton, Ernest Albert, *Twilight of Man*, N.Y., G. P. Putnam's Sons, 1939.

———, *Up From the Ape*, N.Y., Macmillan, 1931.

Husic, Isaac, *A History of Jewish Philosophy*, Philadelphia, Jewish Publication Society, 1930.

Idelsohn, Abraham Z., *The Ceremonies of Judaism*, Cincinnati, The National Federation of Temple Brotherhoods, 1930.

———, *Jewish Liturgy in Its Historic Development*, N.Y., Henry Holt & Co., 1932.

Jewish Library, ed. Leo Jung, N.Y., Bloch Publishing Co., 1943.

Kaplan, Mordecai M., *Judaism as a Civilization*, N.Y., Macmillan, 1934. (Reconstructionist)

———, *Judaism in Transition*, N.Y., Covici-Friede, 1936. (Reconstructionist)

Kertzer, Morris N. *What is a Jew?*, N.Y., World Pub. Co. 1953. (Reform)

———, *The Future of the American Jew*, N.Y., Macmillan. (Reconstructionist)

Klausner, Joseph, *Jesus of Nazareth*, N.Y., Macmillan, 1926; *From Jesus to Paul*, tr. Stinespring, N.Y., Macmillan, 1943.

Kohler, Kaufmann, *Jewish Theology*, N.Y., Macmillan, 1918. (Reform)

———, *Origin of Synagogue and Church*, N.Y., Macmillan, 1929.

———, *Studies, Addresses and Personal Papers*, N.Y., Bloch Publishing Co., 1931. (Reform)

Lauterbach, Jacob Z., *Rabbinic Essays*, Cincinnati, H.U.C. Press, 1951. (Reform)

Levin, S. I., and Boyden, Edward A., *The Kosher Code of the Orthodox Jew*, University of Minnesota Press, 1940.

Levin, Raphael H., *Holy Mountain*, Portland, Oregon, Binfords & Mort, 1953. (Reform)

Levinthal, Israel H., *Judaism: An Analysis and an Interpretation*, N.Y., Funk & Wagnalls Co., 1935.

Liptzin, Solomon, *Germany's Stepchildren*, Phila. J.P.S., 1944.

Maimonides (Moses ben Maimon), *Eight Chapters*, ed. Gorfinkle, N.Y., Columbia University Press, 1912.

——, *Yad ha-hazakah* or *Mishneh Torah*, ed. Hyamson, N.Y., Bloch Publishing Co., 1937; *Guide for the Perplexed*, tr. Friedlander, London, 1928.

Margolis, M. L. and Marx A., *A History of the Jewish People*, Jewish Publication Society, 1927.

Mattuck, Israel, *Jewish Ethics*, London, Hutchinson Library, 1953.

May, Max B., *Isaac M. Wise*, Cincinnati, 1906.

Midrash Rabbah, 10 volumes, London, Soncino Press, 1940.

Montefiore, C. L., and Loewe, H., *Rabbinic Anthology*, London, Macmillan, 1938; *Synoptic Gospels*, 2 volumes, London, Macmillan, 1927; *Rabbinic Literature and Gospel Teaching*, N.Y., Macmillan, 1930.

Moore, George Foot, *Judaism in the First Centuries of the Christian Era*, 3 volumes, Cambridge, Harvard University Press, 1927.

Mordecai M. Kaplan, an Evaluation, ed. Eisenstein and Kohn, N.Y., Jewish Reconstructionist Foundation, 1954.

Newman, Louis I., *Hasidic Anthology*, N.Y., Charles Scribner's Sons, 1934.

Parkes, James, *End of an Exile*.

——, *Israel, the Jews and the Gentile World*, London, Vallentine, Mitchell & Co., 1954.

——, *Judaism & Christianity*, Chicago, U. of C. Press, 1948.

——, *The Conflict of the Church and the Synagogue*, 1934.

Philipson, David, *The Reform Movement in Judaism*, N.Y., Macmillan Co., 1931.

Philipson, David and Grossman, Louis, *Selected Writings of Isaac Mayer Wise*, Alumni Association, Hebrew Union College, Cincinnati, 1900.

Prayer Books, Singer, *Authorized Daily Prayer Book*, London, 1935 (Orthodox); *Union Prayer Book*, 2 volumes, C.C.A.R. (Reform); *High Holy Day Prayer Book*, ed. Silverman, Hartford, 1951 (Conservative); *Sabbath and Festival Prayer Book*, *Rabbinical Assembly of America* (Conservative), N.Y., 1946; *Sabbath Prayer Book*, Jewish Reconstructionist Foundation, N.Y., 1945.

Proceedings of the Rabbinical Assembly of America, N.Y., Jewish Theological Seminary of America.

Rabbi's Manual, Cincinnati, Central Conference of American Rabbis, 1928. (Reform)

Raisin, Jacob S., *Gentile Reactions to Jewish Ideals, with Special Reference to Proselytes*, N.Y., Philosophical Library, 1953.

Roth, Cecil, *A Short History of the Jewish People*, London, East and West Library, 1953. (See bibliography)

Schauss, Hayyim, *The Jewish Festivals*, Cincinnati, Union of American Hebrew Congregations, 1938.

——, *Lifetime of a Jew: Throughout the Ages of Jewish History*, Cincinnati, Union of American Hebrew Congregations, 1950.

Schechter, Solomon, *Seminary Addresses*, Cincinnati, 1915.

——, *Studies in Judaism*, Series I, II, III, Philadelphia, Jewish Publication Society, 1896–1924. (Conservative)

——, *Aspects of Jewish Theology*, Macmillan, N.Y., 1923.

Shulan Aruk (Joseph Caro), tr. Goldin, *Code of Jewish Law*, 4 volumes, N.Y., Hebrew Publishing Co., 1927.

Silver, A. H., *Messianic Speculations in Ancient Israel*, New York, Macmillan, 1927.

Silver, Maxwell, *The Way to God*, N.Y., Philosophical Library, 1950.

Solis-Cohen, Solomon, *Sabato Morais: Teacher and Leader*, Philadelphia, Jewish Publication Society, 1940.

Talmud, Babylonian, English tr., Soncino Press, London, 1932.

Vainstein, Yaakov, *The Cycle of the Jewish Year:* A study of the Festivals and of Selections from Jewish Liturgy, Jerusalem, 1954. (Orthodox)

Waxman, Meyer, *A History of Jewish Literature*, 4 volumes, N.Y., Bloch, 1953.

Wise, Isaac Mayer, *Reminiscences*, ed. Philipson, Cincinnati, 1901.

INDEX

Abrahams, Israel, 128, 226
Adon Olam, 63, 140
Agada, 5f
Agunah, 163
Akiba, 24, 63, 105, 161, 196
Albo, 8, 84
Amos, 111, 191
Amram, 130
Angelology, 35
Anthropomorphism, 35, 61
Antiochus, 203-5
Apocrypha, 5
Aristotle, 107
Ark, 152
Arnold, Matthew, 101
Asceticism, 95
Ashkenazic, 129f
Assyria, 9
Augustine (Saint), 15
Autopsy, 163-4

Babylon, 13; influence, culture, 9
Bar Mitzvah, 36, 153, 157, 174
Bible, 3f, 93, et passim
Body and soul, 93
Burial and disinterment, 163-4

Caro, Joseph, 7, 26
Catholic Israel, 46, 51
Celibacy, 95, 107
Central Conference of American Rabbis, 1937, Columbus, Ohio, "Guiding Principles," 37f, 47, 130
Ceremonies, 35
Charity, 114f
Chazars, 80
"Chosen People," 35, 105
"Christ-killer," 226
Christian culture, 8; influence, 9; theologians, 84
Christianity, Jewish influence on, 129

Cicero, 15
Circumcision, 36, 136
Coleridge, S. T., 138
Confirmation, 36, 157
Conscience, 96
Conservatism, 18-9, 43f; questions facing, 211f
Conversion, 81
Copernicus, 31
Covenant with God, 89-90
Cremation, 164
Crescas, 8, 84
Crusaders, 195
Customs and ceremonies, 140f

Darwin, 31
David, 8, 74
Days of Awe, 177-8, 183, 186
Diaspora, 82f
Dietary laws, 149-51
Divorce, 162-3
Dogma, 25-6

Ecclesiastes, 99, 120
Ecclesiasticus, 203
Eighteen Blessings, 136
Elijah Gaon, 151-2
Emancipation, 84-5
Emerson, R. W., 138
Enlightenment, 41, 43
Erusin, 159
Esrog, 198
Essenes, 95
Ethical monotheism, 62-3, 69-70
Ethics, 101f
European culture, 18
Euthanasia, 105
Exegesis, 7
Ezekiel, 79-80, 108, 214
Ezra, 80-1, 127, 128

247

Fasts, 201
Festivals, Three, 188f
Finkelstein, L., 48
Firstborn, redemption of, 156-7
Frankel, Z., 44-5, 50
Freedom of will, 96-7
French liberalism, 36; Revolution, 18, 88
Friendship, 118-9

Gabirol, ibn, 9, 84
Gaonim, 129-30
Geiger, A., 32f
Gemara, 4
Germany, 36; apostacy, 29; baptisms, 19; emancipation, 41
Gershon ben Judah, abolishes polygamy, 158
Gersonides, 8
Get, 162
God, imitation of, 102; kingdom of, 3, 102; names of, 59-61; rabbinic definition, 65-7; 57f et passim
Golden Mean, 108
Golden Rule, 106
Greek culture, 8; influence, 9

Haftarah, 153
Haggadah, 5-7; for Passover, 130-1, 193-4
Halakah, 5f, 23, 32, 48
Halizah, 162
Hallel, 189-90
Hanukah, 202
Hasidim, 69
Head covering, 151-2; in Mohammedanism, 152
"Hebrew," 76
Hebrew, in worship, 35, 45; language, 83
Hebrew Union College, 37
Hellenic theologians, 84
Hellenism, 202f
Hillel, 106
Holidays, 103, 169f
Holiness Code, 103
Holmes, O. W., 143
Hoshana Rabba, 199

Hukat-Hagoim, 27
Huppah, 159

Ibn Ezra, 63
Immortality, 97f
Isaiah, 67-8, 86-7, 88, 111, 142, 184
Israel, peoplehood, race, nation, 79f
Israel, State of, 50n, 77, 85; Israeli and Israelis, 77, 85
"Israelite," 76

Jacobson, I., 30-1
Jeremiah, 89, 112
Jerusalem, 84
Jesus, rejected by Jews, 215f
"Jew," 76
Jewish home, 146-7
Jewish Theological Seminary, 48-9
Job, 58, 120-2
Josephus, 5
Josiah, Reformation of, 191
Judah Halevi, 8, 64, 69, 84
Judah ha-Nasi, 4
Judas Maccabaeus, 205
Justice, 110f

Kabbalah, 7; Kabbalists, 69
Kaddish, 139-40, 164-5
Kalir, 9
Kawwanah, 141
Ketubah, 160-2
Kinot, 131
Kiddush, 171, 175
Klausner, J., on Jesus, 225, 226
K'neset concept, 78, 81
Kohler, K., 42
Kol Nidre, 185-6
Koran, 93
Kosher laws, 149-51

Lag B'Omer, 195-6
Labor, 116-7
Law, study of, 16
Levinthal, I. H., president of Rabbinical Assembly, 48
Levirate marriage, 162
Levites, 13
Love, 117-8
Lulav, 198

Maccabees, 80, 82, 202
Machzor, 8, 130
Maimonides, 8, 21-2, 25-6, 39f, 84, 107, 140; on almsgiving, 116; on Sabbath, 175
Marriage, 157f
Matzot, 193
Mendelssohn, 8, 31
Messiah, not Jesus, 220-1
Mezuzah, 147
Micah, 111
Midrash, 5f
Minhag, 9n
Minyan, 155
Mishnah, 4f
Mitzwot, 23f; 613 commands, 23
Mohammedan culture, 8; influence, 9; theologians, 84
Montefiore, Claude G., on Gospels, 221, 226
Moore, George F., 14
Moses, 20-2, 40, 49, 72, et passim; and Jesus, 222-3
Mourning rites, 163f
Mystics, 68-9

Naming child, 156
Nationalism, 50-1
Nebuchadnezzar, 13; Jeremiah's letter to, 89
Nissuin, 159

Omer, 195
Oral Law, 20f, 73
Orthodoxy, 4, 7, 18-9, 20f, 41; questions facing, 208f

Palestine, 40, 50, 82, 83-4
Paschal lamb, 192
Passover, 190f
Peace, 113-4
Perpetual light, 154
Persian influence, 9
Pentateuch, 3, 49, 71f
Pharisaism, 123, 174, 224
Pharisees, 75, 98
Philadelphia, Reform statement in, 1869, 37

Philo, 5, 8, 84
Pilgrim feasts, 188f
Pittsburgh "Platform," 37
Piyyutim, 8, 130
Polygamy, 158
Prayer, 133f; language of, 35
Prayerbook, 35f; 127f
Proverbs, 107, 122, 175
Psalms, 24, 53, 60, 69, 74, 78, 90, 111, 127, 132, 134, 138, 165, 189
Pseudepigrapha, 5
Purim, 201-2

Rabbinical Assembly of America, 213; committee on law, 50
Reform, 4, 18-9, 29f; questions facing, 210-1
Renaissance, 18
Response, 8
Revelation, 22
Roman culture, 8; influence, 9
Rosh Hashanah, 177f
Ruth, 197

Saadia, 8, 84
Sabbath, 27, 35-6, 45, 103, 147, 173f
Sabbath of Repentance, 177
Sadducees, 15
Scrolls of Law, 152-3
Schechter, S., 46-7, 51
Seder, 193-4
Selihot, 131
Sephardic, 129f
Shabuot (Pentecost), 82, 195f
Shechina, 155
Shivah, 164
Sh'ma, 63, 117, 128
Shofar, 178, 181
Shulhan Aruk, 7, 26, 49, 159
Siddur, 8
Sidrot, 153
Simchas Torah, 199
Simeon ben Gamaliel, 109-10, 112, 113
Social ideals, 109f
Suicide, 105
Sukkot (Tabernacles), 197f
Synagogue, 13f

Talmud, 4f, 71, 84, 93
Tefillin, 148-9
Tehinot, 131
Temple, 13, 15
Ten Commandments, 66, 103, 122, 128, 140, 173, 191, 197
Ten Days of Penitence, 177
Thirteen Principles, 25, 39f, 140
Torah, 3, 5f, 20f, 71f, 93, et passim
Tradition, authority of, 45-6
Truth, 109-10
Tzizit, 148

Union Hymnal, 132
Union of American Hebrew Congregations, 37
Union Prayer Book, 130, 132, 139

"Wandering Jew," 88
Wise, I. M., 36f
Wissenschaft des Judentum, 32
Women, status of, 36
Written Law, 20f

Yahrzeit, 165
Yetzer, 95
Yigdal, 140
Yizkor, 166
Yom Kippur, 177f
Yomim Noraim, 177f

Zangwill, I., 28
Zedakah, 114
Zemirot, 132
Zion, 13, 85

296
C67